English for BUSINESS LIFE

IAN BADGER   PETE MENZIES

VALERIE LAMBERT

Trainer's Manual

…ediate

Acknowledgements

We would like to thank our business 'students' from organisations including UPM-Kymmene, Metso Paper, BEMIS, Vattenfall, the International Maritime Organisation, GE Finance, ABN Amro (Investment Bank), Dresdner Kleinwort (UK), Panasonic Europe, Nokia and Marketing Akademie Hamburg for providing the inspiration and feedback that underpins *English For Business Life*.

Text © Ian Badger and Pete Menzies 2007

Illustrations, layout and editorial arrangement
© Marshall Cavendish Ltd 2007

First published 2007 by Marshall Cavendish Education

Marshall Cavendish Education is a member of
the Times Publishing Group

All rights reserved; no part of this publication may be reproduced, stored in a retrieval system, transmitted in any form, or by any means, electronic, mechanical, photocopying, recording, or otherwise, without the prior written permission of the publishers.

Marshall Cavendish Education
119 Wardour Street
London W1F OUW

ISBN: 978-0-462-00769-4

Designed by Hart McLeod, Cambridge
Printed and bound by Times Offset (M) Sdn. Bhd. Malaysia

Contents

		Contents chart	4
		Introduction	9
UNIT 1		Business travel	13
UNIT 2		Representing your company	17
UNIT 3		Following up	21
UNIT 4		Dealing with change	25
UNIT 5		Culture and values	29
UNIT 6		Environmental issues	33
UNIT 7		Recruitment and training	37
UNIT 8		Staff relations	41
UNIT 9		Retirement and redundancy	45
UNIT 10		Conferences and exhibitions	49
UNIT 11		Networking	53
UNIT 12		Security abroad	57
UNIT 13		Salaries, incentives and rewards	61
UNIT 14		Personal and company finances	66
UNIT 15		Managing credit	71
UNIT 16		Time management	75
UNIT 17		Delivering quality	79
UNIT 18		Working practices	84
UNIT 19		Advertising and promotion	88
UNIT 20		Offers and orders	92
UNIT 21		Customer care	96
UNIT 22		Home and family	101
UNIT 23		Work / life balance	105
UNIT 24		Getting away	110
UNIT 25		Politics and business	114
UNIT 26		Taxation	118
UNIT 27		Legal matters	122
UNIT 28		Planning	126
UNIT 29		Work in progress	131
UNIT 30		Feedback and review	136
		Progress checks	140
		Progress checks: answers	148
		Glossary of business-related terms	149
		Grammar / language index	152

Contents chart

UNIT	EXPRESSIONS	LANGUAGE CHECK	PRACTICE
1 Business travel	Why don't you come and see what we are doing? How do I get to the site? We've moved the meeting to the afternoon. The best beaches are only a few kilometres away.	Countability: *some / any / none much / many / a lot of (a) few / little all / whole* Vocabulary: *rural, urban, industrial, temperature (20°C = 68°F), set up, pick up, come up*	Setting up a visit Confirming a visit in writing Listening to travel advice
2 Representing your company	I'd like to welcome you to Van Breda. The organisation consists of three divisions. This is what we are working on at the moment. Mel, this is Donna Ng. She's with the group from Shanghai.	Articles: (*a, the, –*) Present tenses: Simple (*work / works*) and Continuous (*is / are working*) Vocabulary: *slippery, sharp, wet, mission, aim, objective, show round, look round, run through*	Showing someone round A web page presenting the company Writing a letter introducing your company
3 Following up	How are you getting on? How is it going? I managed to get hold of the figures you wanted. Generally, I think it was well worth going. I'm just calling to thank you for organising such an interesting programme.	More on present tenses Simple: *I wonder why …, I gather …* Continuous: *It's always going wrong.* Present Passive: *The system is being changed.* Giving feedback: *really, quite, rather,* etc. Vocabulary: *visit, trip, programme, problem, issue, hassle, making progress, going well, follow up, find out, get back to*	Following up on a project Thanking by email Reporting back
4 Dealing with change	Three years ago, we were taken over by BSK. We now process orders centrally. All the transactions that used to be handled by my team are now handled by the global team based in Frankfurt. There's more pressure than there used to be.	Past tenses, Active and Passive Past time markers: *a year later, the previous year used to, be used to, get used to* Vocabulary: *reorganisation, restructuring, business unit, division, department, go bankrupt, go into liquidation, take over, close down, cut back*	Explaining operational changes to a customer Talking about changes during your working life Talking about your company history
5 Culture and values	It was a traditional / progressive company. The workforce was skilled but unmotivated. Working practices have been changing. The management attach a lot of importance to loyalty.	Past tenses, of continuous forms Opposites of adjectives: *friendly / unfriendly, honest / dishonest* Vocabulary: *mission, aim, strategy, enterprising, innovative, progressive, bureaucratic, cautious, critical, look after, try out, fit in*	Writing for advice on working practices and values Discussing corporate culture A questionnaire on values at work
6 Environmental issues	What impact are green issues having on your business? How are the new regulations affecting you? In our view the environmental costs are too high. We believe that conservation is the key.	Terms used in discussion: *In my view …, I take your point …* Adverbs used in phrases: *environmentally friendly, extremely dangerous* Vocabulary: *pollution, spillage, waste, global warming, green issues, bottle bank, recycling plant, clean up, get rid of, use up*	An article on nuclear processing Answering a complaint from the public Case study: The Body Shop

UNIT	EXPRESSIONS	LANGUAGE CHECK	PRACTICE
7 Recruitment and training	We get most of our applications through job-search sites. What kind of person are you looking for? Have you filled in your personal development plan? I'd like to go on a documentation course.	Relative clauses, defining and non-defining Prepositions in relative clauses Vocabulary: *resume, bio, CV, background, history, record, university, college, institute, short list, turn down, fill in*	Talking about training experiences Filling in a personal development planner A job application letter
8 Staff relations	There are good relations between management and staff. The workforce feel they have a stake in the company. Relations have deteriorated since the job cuts. I'm afraid we can't meet your demands in full.	Terms for making and countering demands Linking ideas: *Not being in a union – I can't get a job.* Vocabulary: *strike, stoppage, dispute, job cut, compulsory redundancy, pay freeze, pay, reward, benefit, work out, work on, work under (pressure)*	Management / union issues Simple negotiations Assessing your manager Assessing employee satisfaction (questionnaire)
9 Retirement and redundancy	I am very sorry to hear that you are leaving. I'm looking forward to having some free time. I would like to wish you a very happy retirement. Good luck for the future. Keep in touch.	Verb + gerund / infinitive: *miss working, plan to retire* Preposition + verb: *after retiring, before being made redundant* Expressions of regret: *I'm sorry to hear, it must have been a shock* Vocabulary: *unemployed, out-of-work, redundant, retired, pension, lump sum, golden handshake, early retirement, voluntary redundancy, lay off, let someone go, break news*	Discussing retirement / early retirement Recounting news of redundancy A letter of regret / sympathy
10 Conferences and exhibitions	I'll be in Prague next week for the exhibition. It starts on Monday. I'll leave a pass for you at the information desk. The session on Internet selling is about to start.	Future tenses: *will (I'll see you tomorrow.)* *going to (It's going to rain.)* Present Continuous: *I'm leaving at 6.00pm.* Simple Present: *It finishes on Friday.* *due to: It's due to start in five minutes.* Vocabulary: *conference, exhibition, trade fair, lecture, seminar, workshop, speaker, exhibitor, visitor, meet up, try out, take out*	Responding to a conference mailout Working on an exhibition stand Coordinating a visit
11 Networking	Mary Jones suggested I contact you. I was wondering if I could come and see you. It's a good idea to send an email before you call. It's John Smith; we met in Manheim.	Expressing intentions: *I intend to call Maria.* Etiquette advice: *It's best not to talk too much.* *be supposed / meant to: I was meant to send some samples.* Vocabulary: *network, socialise, circulate, work colleague, professional contact, business associate, custom, convention, guideline, keep in contact with, follow up with*	Corporate hospitality packages Writing an invitation to a client Networking tips and practice
12 Security abroad	I have to report a theft. My car's been towed away. There's something wrong with the air conditioning. It won't be working again till after lunch.	Future Continuous tense: *How will you be paying?* Future Perfect tense: *We will have left by then.* Order of adjectives: *a brown leather wallet* Vocabulary: *switch, plug, bulb, basin, tap, drain, pipe, fused, faulty, broken, dead, blocked, cracked, leaking, jammed*	A difficult trip to Torreon (Mexico) Safety guidelines for San Diego (USA) Dealing with travel hassles

UNIT	EXPRESSIONS	LANGUAGE CHECK	PRACTICE
13 Salaries, incentives and rewards	What I earn depends on my sales figures. My total package is worth about 90 grand. Directors get a free car; it's a perk that goes with the job. The Board have agreed to an increase of 5%.	Modal verbs, present forms: *would, could, should*, etc. Expressing likelihood: *bound to, likely to* Rates and charges: *time and a half, flat-rate fee* Symbols and numbers: +, -, =, 10K, 7½ Vocabulary: *reward, benefit, perk, salary, wage, pay rise, raise, increase, put in for, turn down, think over*	A letter about executive rewards Benefit packages (listening realia) A pay review
14 Personal and company finances	Altogether, our running costs amount to $1.7 million. Sales are up from $9.8 million to $10.7 million. We made a profit of $2.2 million on sales of $20.7 million. I had to sell my shares in Unicorn to pay off a debt.	Modal verbs, past forms: *would have, would have been* Spelling rules: *i* before *e*, except after *c* Use of hyphens: *day-to-day expenses* Vocabulary: *add* Financial terms: *add up to, cut back on, go up / down*	Talking about financial performance Talking about expenditure and assets A news item about Caffè Nero Writing a request for a salary increase An article about the sale of a company
15 Managing credit	I'm calling about our invoice number AK-40 7/AZ. It was passed for payment ten days ago. My card's just been declined. What's going on? How can I protect myself from ID theft?	Advising and suggesting: *I think / don't think you should …* Modal verbs (criticism / regret): *You ought to have …* Conditional sentences without *if*: *otherwise, or else* Vocabulary: *credit limit, credit record, credit status, due, overdue, due date, look into, sort out, pay off*	Handling credit card and mobile phone problems Querying an invoice Writing a message about late payment An article about ID theft
16 Time management	In this job, you have to be able to work under pressure. It is important to delegate and prioritise. The course showed us how to establish priorities. They gave us tips on running meetings.	More on conditionals without *if*: *or, or else, otherwise* *wish / if only*: *I wish I could …* Reflexive pronouns: *yourself, themselves* Latin expressions: *vice versa* Vocabulary: *planning, prioritising, delegating, workload, paperwork, backlog, problem solving, fire fighting, keep on top of, build up, get through*	Reviewing time management skills Time management questionnaire Organising to go on a training course Tips on running meetings
17 Delivering quality	What we sell is quality and service. It would improve our performance … if we had better procedures for logging faults. We encourage best practice in all areas. The secret is to listen to what your clients say.	More on conditionals (2nd / 3rd conditionals) Alternative sentence structures *prevent* vs. *avoid* Vocabulary: *high / low quality, well / poorly made, very / not very good, really first class, user-friendly, value for money, be above / below / up to standard*	Talking about quality performance Handling compliments and complaints Writing a letter of apology A customer care questionnaire
18 Working practices	Our management style is very informal. We are very customer focused. We have to comply with the regulator's requirements. The main changes have been in the area of technology. There is more competition – the pace is faster.	More on conditionals: *should they, were they to*, etc. Expressions of frequency: *three times a year, very seldom*, etc. Accord, indicating parallels: *X does and so does Y* Terms relating to compliance: *comply with, enforce*, etc. Vocabulary: *flexitime, job sharing, equal opportunities, requirements, guidelines, procedures, industrial / staff relations, do spot checks, give a good / bad impression*	Talking about dress and behaviour codes Interview with an employee relations manager Article on managing paperwork Questionnaire on company culture

UNIT	EXPRESSIONS	LANGUAGE CHECK	PRACTICE
19 Advertising and promotion	The service is promoted over the Internet. We depend a lot on personal recommendation. Do you have a leaflet or something? The price list is printed on the back. We should try a campaign based on radio ads.	Passive verb forms: present, future, past Omissions in clauses: *being the client* vs. *as we are the client*, etc. Vocabulary: *advertising agency / campaign / slogan, focus group, market survey, sponsored link, brochure, leaflet, flyer, junk mail, nuisance calls, spam, highlight, target, put across*	Talking about your advertising Promoting a company / a product Preparing promotional literature An article on spam and nuisance calls
20 Offers and orders	The unit weighs 2½ kilos. I'm calling to place an order. We had to put our prices up. We ought to have been informed. Some customers order on-line (in order) to cut costs.	More on passives: continuous, infinitive, *-ing* forms Giving reasons: *because, in order to, so that*, etc. Measurements: dimensions, volume, capacity, etc. Vocabulary: *retail, retailer, wholesale, wholesaler, quantity / trade discount, take someone up on an offer, put prices up / down, place an order*	Taking / placing / confirming an order Product enquires – written and by phone Querying an invoice Dealing with late deliveries
21 Customer care	It sounds as if the machine is overheating. Do you have a service contract? Call out time is supposed to be two hours. This isn't the result of normal wear and tear. We're very unhappy about the way we're being treated.	Impressions: *seem / look / sound, as if / though*, etc. Cause and effect: *be caused by, the result of*, etc. Complaining: *complain about, be unhappy about*, etc. Vocabulary: *care, concern, support, guarantee, warranty, protection plan, neglect, misuse, wear and tear, refund, replacement, credit note, put customers first, take it back, look into it*	Practice in giving and receiving customer care Managers talk about service they receive Writing a letter of complaint Case practice: returning goods to a shop
22 Home and family	In this picture you can see the house where we live. That's my son; he doesn't look like me at all. We're about 15 minutes from the centre of town. The alarm usually goes off just before 6 o'clock. I drop the children off at school on the way to the station.	Similarities and differences: *similar to, the opposite of*, etc. *each / every / all* Possessive *'s*: *a friend of my sister's, her parents' house*, etc. Vocabulary: *single, engaged, divorced, mother / father-in-law, half brother / sister, a top-floor apartment, a terraced house, grow up, bring up, move in / out*	Taking about your home and family Listening to people talking about family photos Writing a request for time off A feature on couples in business together
23 Work / life balance	I find it difficult to balance work and domestic commitments. I'm very keen on golf; it's fun and it helps me unwind. I take exercise on a regular basis. I'd much rather eat out than entertain at home. It's far more relaxing and a lot less hassle.	More on comparisons: *far more / less interesting than* Preference: *prefer, would rather, rather than* Agreement: *agree with, accept, in agreement with* Alternative adverb forms: *regularly* vs. *on a regular basis* Non-verbal communication: *Ah, Hey, Oh* Vocabulary: *get together, meet up, come round, take up, give up, be keen on*	Talking about leisure time Interview with a publishing director A questionnaire on work / life balance Article and discussion on taking exercise
24 Getting away	I want to get away for a few days, preferably somewhere warm. The climate is good, although it can be chilly at night. It's best to go before the high season. I have to get back to my office. If you want to travel tomorrow, you'll have to upgrade to business class.	Contrasting ideas: *although, even so, all the same* Giving (holiday) advice: *Remember that …, I'd advise you to …* Short form questions: *Where to? How long for?* *whatever, whoever, whenever* Vocabulary: *travel agent, local rep, stand-by passenger, package holiday, high / off season, fully booked, on stand-by, get away, head for, check in / out*	Organising a holiday People talking about their holidays Sending a greetings message back to colleagues A feature on mini-breaks in New York

UNIT	EXPRESSIONS	LANGUAGE CHECK	PRACTICE
25 Politics and business	The government is a coalition of the left and centre. It is difficult to predict who will win the next election. However, the right have a good chance. They announced a new trade agreement on the news. The evidence against privatisation is very clear.	Verbs of reporting: *say, announce, warn,* etc. Contrasts and alternatives: *however, whereas,* etc. Vocabulary: *local / state / federal government, balance of payments, imports, exports, vote for / against, hold a referendum*	Talking about government policies Discussing political / economic issues Considering election possibilities Writing a political / economic briefing on an area
26 Taxation	How much did we pay in tax last year? Companies are taxed at a rate of 25%. They announced they would cut the rate to 15%. As far as I know, you can reclaim the tax. Our accountant promised she'd file the return the next day.	Reported speech: *asked us if, announced that* Reported speech timeframes: *following day, previous year,* etc. Terms used to qualify statements: *as far as I know, I'm not an expert but,* etc. Vocabulary: *income tax, corporation tax, sales tax, tax liability, tax allowance, tax assessment tax exempt, tax refund, tax free, go in tax, go up / down, fill in a return*	Talking about personal and company tax Dealing with tax queries – examples from a specialist site Tax case studies – reading and listening 'Death and taxes' – an article
27 Legal matters	Our lawyers warned us it wouldn't be worth going to court. Their finance director was convicted of fraud. Why weren't we notified? I thought it was required by law. This document is a mess. We need to add another bullet point.	More on reported speech: advice, commands, questions Making reference: *concerning, with regard to,* etc. Terms related to text layout: *underlined, in brackets,* etc. Vocabulary: *laws, legislation, regulations, a case, a trial, a legal decision, a judge, a jury, a verdict, to go to court, to sue for, to settle out of court*	Talking about legal matters Listening – a journalist talking about medical liability Summarising legal advice Case study – a document on customers' rights
28 Planning	The scheme was planned in three phases. My role is to liaise with the other participants. To start with, I need to make an action plan. There are a number of factors to be taken into account. At the moment we are on schedule.	Indicating sequence: *to start with, in the second stage,* etc. Terms related to structuring ideas / arguments: *for one thing, in addition to that* Gender-free reference: *he or she, they* Tag questions: *You do, don't you?* Vocabulary: *schedule, timetable, deadline, phase, stage, milestone, feasibility study, contingency plan, on target, on schedule, on track, take into account, put forward / back*	Talking about plans and commitments Listening to a project update Writing an outline plan Reading about a major project and assessing it
29 Work in progress	I need an update on the state of play. The project has fallen behind schedule. Do we have a contingency plan? This table shows ... / The dotted line indicates ... Before I summarise the key points, are there any questions?	Reporting on the state of play: *go according to plan, on / behind schedule* Terms used in presentations Referring to graphs / tables: *This table shows ..., As you can see from the dotted line ...* Vocabulary: *update, progress check, overview, contingency plan, alternative, plan B, improvement, increase, rise, deduction, decrease, fall, be held up, be let down, chase up*	Giving project updates, discussing progress Listening to reports by project managers Writing a project update Reviewing a company's performance Presenting conclusions
30 Feedback and review	What's your overall assessment? Bearing in mind the circumstances, I thought we did really well. I'm disappointed I didn't meet my targets. To sum up, I'd say you did a good job.	More on giving opinions: *am positive, consider, guess* Terms used in evaluating: *really outstanding, quite disappointing* Summarising: *My overall view ..., On the whole ...* Indicating context: *Bearing in mind ..., Considering ...* Vocabulary: *assessment, evaluation, feedback, aim, target, objective, meet targets, put into practice, make progress*	Performance review (self and others) Work style questionnaire Discussing next steps

Introduction

English for Business Life is a four-level course designed for people who need English for their everyday work.
English for Business Life is:
- a course written by authors with a wide experience of teaching English for business in a range of international contexts, countries and cultures
- a course that respects the modern need for flexibility; learners can follow fast, standard or comprehensive tracks through the materials
- a course that follows a progressive and comprehensive grammar syllabus, with the stress on the effective use of grammar for clear communication
- a course that satisfies the requirements of the Common European Framework, BEC and equivalent global testing authorities
- a course that supports the learner in a highly connected modern world.

The Upper Intermediate level of the course consists of:
- a Course Book with detachable Answer Key and Business Grammar Guide
- Course Book listening exercises on CD
- a Self-study Guide packaged with an accompanying audio CD
- a Trainer's Manual.

Learners can follow fast, standard and comprehensive tracks through the material – 45 to 90 hours of work:
- fast track – 45 hours
- standard track – 60 hours
- comprehensive track – 90 hours.

Summary of components

Course Book

The Course Book consists of:
- 30 units
- support materials where necessary
- a Glossary of business-related terms
- a Grammar / language index
- audioscripts of all listening activities
- Business Grammar Guide and Answer Key in separate booklets.

Two audio CDs are available as a separate component.

Self-study Guide

The Self-study Guide consists of:
- 30 parallel units
- material that can be used in support of the Course Book or as a self-standing resource
- two audio CDs containing recordings of core language, and extra listening exercises
- reinforcement / consolidation exercises
- a Grammar / language reference section
- a Glossary of business-related terms.

Trainer's Manual

The Trainer's Manual consists of:
- notes on exercises and ideas for consolidation / extension work
- a Glossary of business-related terms
- notes on business practice
- answers and audioscripts for Course Book exercises
- Progress Checks.

Business English exams / testing equivalence

Levels	Common European Framework Level	ALTE	BEC	London Chamber of Commerce (EFB)
Upper Intermediate	C1 – C2	4	Higher	Level 3
Intermediate	B2 – C1	3	Vantage	Level 2
Pre-Intermediate	B1 – B2	2	Preliminary	Level 1
Elementary	A2 – B1			Preliminary / Level 1

Useful websites

For more on the European Framework visit www.alte.org
For BEC visit www.cambridgeesol.org/exams/bec.htm
For the Business Language Testing Service visit www.bulats.org
For the London Chamber of Commerce Exams visit www.lccieb.org.uk
For the TOEIC American exams for working people visit www.ets.org/toeic

A range of training situations

English for Business Life presents the language that is essential for doing business in English; it has strong global relevance. Groups that will benefit from using the materials include:
- business schools and colleges
- language schools which offer English for business courses
- company training courses and study programmes
- vocational adult education classes
- schools and colleges which aim to equip their students with the language skills they will need in their working lives.

Upper Intermediate level

The Upper Intermediate level of ***English for Business Life*** is for learners who have studied English for perhaps four to six or seven years at school and / or college. They will probably be able to use the language with a good degree of fluency and will be able to manage in most situations where they need English.

At this level, learners will probably feel that they need to improve the appropriateness and structural accuracy of the language they use – especially in written formats. They will also need to develop their knowledge and use of everyday business idiomatic language. This book focuses on helping learners to develop these key areas of language.

Content

The materials cover everyday business speaking, listening, reading and writing skills, through a range of guided and free exercises. The aim is to find out what learners can do in English within a given theme, then help them to develop their skills.

There are 30 units, each covering a different topic area; each unit consists of five sections designed to cover a range of everyday business speaking, listening, reading and writing skills. The Trainer's Manual contains notes for each of the exercises, and ideas for consolidation and extension work.

Each unit begins with a Core Practice section, which consists of four short listenings. These encapsulate the target language of the unit and expose learners to different types of English, in line with the fact that English is used as an international language of communication between speakers of many nationalities. Each listening is followed by a speaking activity designed to practise the key language and personalise the topic where appropriate.

The second activity is the Language Check section. This consists of ten multiple-choice questions designed to develop accurate use of the main language points and vocabulary covered in the unit. There are general guidelines at the beginning of the Language Check notes in the Trainer's Manual and also detailed notes for the individual questions with cross-references to the Business Grammar Guide.

There are three further activities related to the theme of the unit. Most units contain further listening exercises and a range of activities (e.g. Case study, Writing, Feature) designed to develop speaking, writing and reading skills in a business context.

At the end of the Course Book there is a Glossary of business-related language. The Business Grammar Guide and an Answer Key appear in a separate booklet.

In addition to the Glossary, there are clear explanations of business vocabulary and terminology throughout the book. These are designed to make it easier for teachers to:
- discuss business concepts
- prepare lessons
- explain vocabulary items.

There are five photocopiable Progress Checks and answers at the end of the Trainer's Manual:
- page 140 – Units 1 – 6
- page 141 – Units 7 – 12
- page 143 – Units 13 – 18
- page 144 – Units 19 – 24
- page 146 – Units 25 – 30.

Flexibility

There are different possible tracks through the materials.

Fast track: 45 hours (approximately 1½ hours per unit) involving, for example:
- introductory discussion on each theme linked to the Preparation suggestions at the start of each unit
- Core Practice – listening and speaking (activity 1 in each unit)
- Language Check – language analysis and review (activity 2)
- Reading and Writing (usually activities 3 and 4)
- Progress Checks (multiple-choice tests, pages 140 – 147 in the Trainer's Manual).

Standard track: 60 hours (approximately 2 hours per unit) involving, for example:
- introductory discussion on each theme linked to the Preparation suggestions at the start of each unit
- Core Practice – listening and speaking (activity 1 in each unit)
- Language Check – language analysis and review (activity 2)
- Reading and Writing (usually activities 3 and 4)
- Further Practice – activity 5
- Language Notes (final page of each unit)
- Selected exercises from the related unit in the Self-study Guide
- Progress Checks (multiple-choice tests, pages 140 – 147 in the Trainer's Manual).

Comprehensive track: 90 hours (approximately 3 hours per unit) involving, for example:
- introductory discussion on each theme linked to the Preparation suggestions at the start of each unit
- Core Practice – listening and speaking (activity 1 in each unit)
- Language Check – language analysis and review (activity 2)
- Reading and Writing (usually activities 3 and 4)
- Further Practice – activity 5 in each unit
- Selected use of the 'Further step' suggestions in the Trainer's Manual
- Language Notes (final page of each unit)
- Detailed study of related Self-study Guide materials
- Progress Checks (multiple-choice tests, pages 140 – 147 in the Trainer's Manual).

Teaching English for business

It takes a long time to become a competent language teacher, and a long time to have the skills to work in business. Teachers with language skills and qualifications need to learn about how business operates on a day-to-day basis in order to understand the needs of business learners. Without such knowledge they will find it difficult to monitor the communication that takes place in the classroom.

On the other hand, trainers with business knowledge are not automatically qualified to become teachers of English to speakers of other languages.

In most cases, learners will have far more experience and expertise than their trainers in doing business; but learners will also have far more confidence in a trainer who is interested in learning about the business world than one who is not.

The *English for Business Life* Trainer's Manual contains guidance on how to exploit the material and has suggestions for further practice. However, it is not intended to be a basic guide to teaching English as a foreign language. For the less experienced teacher, we recommend *The Practice of English Language Teaching* (by Jeremy Harmer) for a sound introduction to general English language teaching theory and practice. Other useful publications on teaching business English include the following.
- Sylvie Donna, *Teach Business English*, Cambridge University Press.
- M. Ellis and C. M. Johnson, *Teaching Business English*, Oxford University Press.
- Evan Frendo, *How to teach business English*, Longman.

Trainers who are not familiar with areas of specific business terminology used in the Course Book and Self-study Guide should refer to the unit notes throughout the Trainer's Manual and to the Glossary of business-related terms on pages 149 – 151. (This glossary also appears in the Course Book on pages 158 – 160 and again in the Self-study Guide on pages 117 – 119.)

English for Business Life provides learners with the essential language they need to do business in English, but no one course can meet the industry-specific needs of individual learners.

As teachers of business English, it is vital to help learners to acquire the specific language they require by researching company websites and other sites of interest. Newspapers, magazines and in-house newsletters are all a valuable source of information and teaching material. If possible, make video recordings of discussions, meetings, telephone calls, etc. Such recordings can be made in the offices of your learners' associated companies, or of customers, suppliers, agents and so on. These can be used in class and, if possible, made available for your learners' private use.

Help your learners to develop the self-study habit

Rival work commitments can often mean that the attendance of business learners in long-term language teaching programmes is irregular. Learners often have to miss classes because of work commitments, and consequently progress can be slow. They should therefore be encouraged to use the Self-study Guide which accompanies the Course Book at this level for further practice to increase their rate of progress. Some ideas we recommend that you discuss with your learners include the following.

Some study tips

- Make time for your English studies. Approach them with the same level of commitment that you would any other project in your work or spare time.
- Find the study pattern that works best for you. In our view 'little and often' is more effective than occasional long sessions.
- Keep an organised study file. Make sure that the language that is most relevant to your needs is clearly highlighted.
- Ensure that you relate the language presented in the course back to your area of business or study. If there are terms you need which are not included in the material, consult your trainer, English-speaking colleagues and friends, and make thorough notes.
- Make use of the English-speaking media – web pages (including company websites), radio, TV, professional journals, magazines and newspapers to follow up your business and leisure interests in English.
- Make use of monolingual and bilingual dictionaries. A number of dictionaries are available online, and the 'synonym' and 'thesaurus' keys on your computer are always useful.
- Use the Self-study Guide which accompanies this Course Book (approximately 30 to 60 hours of study).

Study themes in *English for Business Life*

Upper Intermediate level

- Business travel
- Following up
- Dealing with change
- Culture and values
- Conferences and exhibitions
- Networking
- Delivering quality
- Work / life balance
- Feedback and review

Other levels

Elementary level

- You and your job
- Your company
- Brief exchanges
- Arrangements
- Telephoning
- Business hospitality
- Business trips
- Your working environment
- Enquiring and booking

Pre-Intermediate level

- You and your company
- Meeting people
- Time off
- The workplace
- Numbers and figures
- Business travel
- The product
- Arrangements
- Business entertaining
- Sales and selling
- Requesting / supplying information

Intermediate level

- Contacts
- Companies
- Personnel
- Products and services
- Entertaining
- Meetings
- Travel
- Money and finance
- Presentations

The authors

IAN BADGER has extensive experience of developing courses and systems of language training for business, and is a regular speaker at international conferences. He is a partner in Business and Medical English Services (BMES), and a director of English4 Ltd (www.english4.com). He is series editor of *English for Work*, and his publications include *Everyday Business English*, *Everyday Business Writing* and *Business English Phrases*.

PETE MENZIES is an associate of Pod (Professional and Organisational Development) and founder of Commnet, a dedicated training agency specialising in written communication and email management. Awards for his published work include the Duke of Edinburgh ESU Prize and the Gold Medal at the Leipzig Industrial Fair.

UNIT 1 Business travel

PREPARATION

- There are three possible tracks through the unit: fast (about 1½ hours), standard (about 2 hours) and comprehensive (about 3 hours). For more information on the different tracks, see the notes in the Introduction on pages 10 and 11.
- For details of the aims of the unit, look at the Contents box on this page, the Language Notes at the end of the Course Book unit and the Useful Phrases below. There are answers and audioscripts on pages 15 and 16 of this book.
- If available to you, you can use the Self-study Guide as a source of supplementary exercises on the key themes of the unit.
- If you have taught the unit before, check the notes you made at the time.

USEFUL PHRASES

We'd be pleased to organise a programme for you.
How's the 12th? Would the 19th suit you better?
I really don't mind. Both dates are OK by me.
Let's make it the 19th then.

There aren't many people here in July; it's holiday time.
Why don't you come in June?
Are there any rooms available in June?
Yes, a few.   Yes, but very few.   No, none.

Where are you in relation to the town centre?
The easiest way is to catch the express bus.
In the arrivals hall, follow the signs to the bus station.
On arrival in (Amsterdam), take a taxi to (your hotel).

How do I get to the site?
We'll send a car to pick you up.
There are directions on our website – I'll send you a link.

We're only 15 minutes from the mountains.
The best beaches in the country are just a few kilometres away.
It rains all the time in September.
The temperature at that time of year is over 30 degrees.
You must remember to bring your skiing gear.
Don't forget to bring plenty of warm clothing.

I'm afraid something has come up.
Can we reschedule the meeting for the following week?
Provisionally, let's arrange it for the 27th.
If that doesn't work, we'll have to set up a video conference.

LEAD IN (SUGGESTIONS)

- Refer to the Preparation section at the start of the unit in the Course Book (page 13). Check whether learners have brought to the class documents relating to business travel (invitations, timetables, alterations). These can be used as a resource through the lesson.
- Check also whether they have looked at the Useful Phrases on page 16 in the Course Book (copied above). Comments from learners may indicate which areas of the target language they need to focus on and the level of interest in the topic.
- Consider leading into the subject by eliciting accounts from the group of trips they have made in the past or plan to make in the future. Be prepared to talk about an example of your own.

Contents

Expressions
Why don't you come and see what we are doing?
How do I get to the site?
We've moved the meeting to the afternoon.
The best beaches are only a few kilometres away.

Language check
Countability: *some / any / none*
much / many / a lot of
(a) few / little
all / whole
Vocabulary: *rural, urban, industrial, temperature*
(20°C = 68°F), *set up, pick up, come up*

Practice
Setting up a visit
Confirming a visit in writing
Listening to travel advice

1 CORE PRACTICE

Listening and speaking

- This exercise provides an opportunity to practise a range of situations relating to business travel.
- The exercise is in two parts – listening and speaking. The listening activity (part i) provides learners with ideas and models for the speaking activity (part ii).
- Ask learners to identify the verbal clues they used when answering the comprehension questions in part i.
- In part ii, encourage learners to adapt the scenarios to their needs. If appropriate, they should introduce the documents they have brought to the class.
- Question a: The first speaker has a non-standard accent.
- Question b: The first speaker has a US accent. Note *minus five* = minus five degrees centigrade. 0° centigrade (freezing point) = 32° Fahrenheit. The Fahrenheit scale is used in the USA.
- Question c: Both speakers have non-standard accents. Note that *(re)schedule* is pronounced in the American way. Check that learners understand *come up* = happened (unexpectedly); *set up* = arranged; *provisionally* = for the time being / could possibly change.
- Question d: The second speaker has a US accent. Note *a block* = a series of buildings forming a square with buildings on all sides.
- **Further step:** Ask learners individually or in pairs to prepare a further question for each dialogue.

Business travel 13

2 LANGUAGE CHECK

- This section provides opportunities to review the language needs of the group and to practise as necessary.
- As you go through the multiple-choice questions, point out the Language Notes at the end of each Course Book unit, and the related notes in the Business Grammar Guide (see the booklet that accompanies the Course Book).
- Point out the Glossary on pages 158 – 160 of the Course Book.
- The multiple-choice questions give a starting point. Ensure that the related language points are explored and revised as necessary. The Specific Points section below gives you further detailed guidance.
- For each question consider the following options.
  - Identify the answer.
  - Explore why the other options are wrong.
  - Ask learners to prepare examples that relate to their working needs, e.g.:
    Question 1: *There is some money in the budget for gifts but not much.*
    Amended version: *There is some money available for entertaining foreign visitors but not very much.*
- **Further step:** Ask learners to put the examples in the questions into exchanges. What might the line before be? What could the next line be?

SPECIFIC POINTS

Questions 1 to 7: Countability and quantifiers
(BGG 10.1, 10.2, 10.3)

- Q1: Note that *some* needs to be stressed here to emphasise that it is a limited quantity. Note that *a bit of* (and less commonly *a little*) could also be used before *money*; *lots of* must be followed by a noun or pronoun.
- Q2: *any* is used in yes / no questions when we are not sure if the answer is going to be yes. *some* indicates we expect a positive answer; *some* is also commonly used in offers and requests, e.g. *Could you send me some samples?* Check learners can use short answers with adverbial modifiers (e.g. *very, really, absolutely*).
  Yes, quite a lot.
  No, not very much / many.
  No, really very few / little.
  No, absolutely none.
- Q3: Point out we use *an amount of* + uncountable noun (e.g. *an amount of money*) and *a number of* + countable noun (e.g. *a number of customers*). If appropriate, bring in *a volume of*, *a quantity of* and quantifiers like *a batch of*, *a case of*, *a range of*, *a list of*, etc. Note *a quantity of* can be used with a countable or uncountable noun (e.g. *a quantity of books*, *a quantity of water*).

- Q4: Note *some / a few / few* can all be used with plural nouns but with *only* or *just* we use *a few*. With uncountable nouns we use only *a bit (of) / a little*, e.g.:
  – *How much Sellotape do you need?*
  – *Just a bit.*
- Q5 and 6: *no, none, not any*. Note *none* is a pronoun (so it is not followed by a noun). *none of* is used with a noun or pronoun. *no* can be used instead of *not any* with a plural or uncountable noun. When *not any* in used, *not* is attached to the verb element (*We do**n't** have any* …). Check learners know that *any / not any* cannot stand alone as a short answer; *none* is used instead, e.g.:
  – *How much time will you have in Damascus?*
  – *None. / I won't have any.*
  It is not possible to use *Not any* or *Any* here.
- Q7: *all the* and *the whole* (BGG 10.3). With uncountable nouns we use *all the* (e.g. *all the money / water / food*). Point out that *the whole money / water / food* is not possible. *the whole* is only used with singular countable nouns (e.g. *the whole sum of money / bottle of water / box of food*). Before *the* + noun, we used *some of*, not just *some* (e.g. *some of the time*).

Questions 8 and 9: Verb phrases

- Review the verbs listed in the Language Notes. See also BGG 8 for more on phrasal verbs.
- Q8: Elicit *postpone* for *put off* and *cancel* for *call off*.
- Q9: Review word order with phrasal verbs. Elicit *get / fetch / collect* for *pick up*.

Question 10: Vocabulary to describe location

- Go through the items listed. Provide extra vocabulary as required (see the Vocabulary section in the Language Notes).
- Discuss the difference in meaning between <u>in</u> the north of and (<u>to the</u>) north of, e.g. *in the north of Beijing* means in the northern part of Beijing; (*to the*) *north of Beijing* is outside Beijing. Often the latter is preceded by a distance, as in the example.

3 LISTENING

Travel tips

- In this authentic recording, Speaker 1 is a secondary school teacher from France and Speaker 2 is a newspaper columnist from South Africa.
- Note *fund management* (referred to by Speaker 2) = dealing with the investment sums of money on behalf of clients.
- If your learners have been to India or the USA, ask if they have had the same kind of experiences as the speakers. What aspects of their own countries would they expect visitors to find unusual?
- **Further step:** Learners can give each other similar briefings on places which they know, using the categories mentioned in the table on page 14 of the Course Book as prompts.

4 WRITING

Confirming a visit

- Discuss the business situation indicated by the email in the question. Who is Felix Bezst? What does he want? (He is an external supplier. He is hoping to build a relationship with a potential customer to make a sale.)
- Discuss how formal the email is. (It's semi-formal in style.)
- Elicit other semi-formal ways of closing an email, e.g.:
  (Kind) regards
  (With) best wishes.
- Note that the use of the Present Continuous with *look forward to* has a less formal, more personal feel than the use of the Present Simple.
- Point out the use of *I attach* (Present Simple) for email attachments. This parallels the use of *I enclose* for letters. The following forms are also used:
  Attached is / are …
  … is / are attached.
- Point out the use of the preposition *at* for web addresses.
- There is a possible response in the Answer Key.
- Encourage learners to demonstrate best practice in their business writing. Where possible they should apply the acronym KISS – Keep It Short and Simple.
- **Further step:** Consider asking learners to prepare and perform the phone conversation referred to in the question.

5 FEATURE

Setting up a visit

- You may want to gloss the text with your learners, asking them to compare the situation in Norway with that in their own countries with reference to transport, food and drink, weather / temperature, etc.
- There is a possible draft in the Answer Key.
- **Further step:** Ask learners to write similar notes on their own country / region for a visitor. Where possible, they should refer to the realia documents they have brought to the lesson.

REVIEW

- Go through the Language Notes and Useful Phrases in the Course Book, if you have not already done so.
- Check that the items listed under Vocabulary in the Language Notes in the Course Book have been covered.
- Encourage learners to note down the terms they found particularly useful – especially the ones they need in their working lives.
- Make a note of this language for your future reference.
- Encourage learners to practise new language outside the classroom – to bring it into their communication.

Answers

1 Core practice
a i [T]   b i [U]   c i [T]
d i [U]

2 Language check
1 b   2 c   3 a   4 b   5 c
6 a   7 c   8 c   9 a   10 b

3 Listening

Travel information mentioned ✓ not mentioned ✗	car hire	public transport	telephone system	accommodation	food	restaurants	night life	the people	hospitality	gifts	conventions	dress / clothing	climate	landscape	currency	prices / cost of living	tipping	doing business	regulations	other
Speaker 1 Country / area **India**	✗	✓	✗	✓	✗	✗	✗	✓	✓	✗	✗	✗	✗	✗	✗	✓	✗	✗	✗	✗
Speaker 2 Country / area **Phoenix USA**	✓	✗	✗	✓	✓	✗	✓	✗	✓	✗	✓	✓	✗	✗	✗	✗	✗	✗	✗	✗

4 Writing
(*possible answer*)

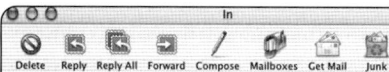

Subject: Visit 11 March

Dear Felix Bezst
To confirm our phone conversation, I recommend you take the express bus from the airport into town – the journey takes about two hours. In the Arrivals Hall follow the signs to where the buses stop; ask for the one to the city centre. Generally, we recommend the Garret Hotel to visitors. You can reach their bookings at www.garrethotel.com/santigo/bookings. The express bus stops right outside.
I will pick you up in the morning at 8 o'clock and take you to the plant.
I have asked one or two members of my team and our Logistics Manager, Anatol Sebesi, to meet you.
We are very much looking forward to seeing you and Peter Holst here at Nootex.
Regards
Sonya Digell
Purchasing Manager

5 Feature
(*possible answer*)

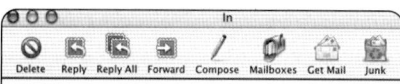

Trip to Norway

Dear Ms Ruban

I understand you are visiting the new Norwegian plant in February. I have been asked to send you some background information on the country. I attach a country profile that covers many of the points you raise. I would stress that the weather will be cold at that time of year compared with Durban, and that you should bring plenty of warm clothing. As you will see the guide is fairly general – if you have more detailed questions, please contact me again.

With best wishes

Audioscripts

1 Core practice
a – Come and see for yourself what we're doing here. I think you'd find it interesting.
– Yes, I'd like to. But my diary is pretty full till July.
– There aren't many people here then – it's holiday time. Why don't you fly down in June? I can show you round and introduce you to some of our people. What about the week of the 12th?
– Er, no, I'm afraid I'm busy that week.
– Well how about the 19th? That's the following week.
– That's Tuesday, isn't it?
– Yes, or Wednesday would be OK, if that suits you better.
– Er, can we make it Tuesday?
– Sure. Just let me know what time you are arriving and I'll pick you up from the airport.
b – Remember to bring your skiing gear; we're only 30 minutes from the mountains.
– I didn't realise you were near mountains.
– Yes, we're in an agricultural area between the mountains and the sea. It's good for farming – the countryside round here is quite flat and we get plenty of rain.
– So is it going to be cold?
– In the mountains, it's about minus five at this time of the year.
c – We've had to change your hotel arrangements.
– That's OK, but I'm afraid something has come up, and I'm not going to be able to make the 17th.
– But it's all set up.
– I know, I'm really sorry but there's not a lot I can do. I'd like to put the trip off till the 28th. Do you think that would be possible?
– I'm sure it's possible, but they won't like it.
– Well, let's reschedule for the 28th provisionally.
– And if that doesn't work for them, we'll have to set up a telephone conference.
d – How do I get to you?
– The easiest way is by public transport – take the express bus. They leave from outside the arrival hall in Terminal 1, about every 12 minutes. It's a direct service to Central Square. Where are you staying?
– It's a place called the Shereema Lodge.
– The stop is right outside.
– OK. And where are your offices in relation to that?
– Pen Avenue South is about two blocks from Central Square. I'll send you a link to our map for visitors.

3 Listening
Speaker 1
You know, there are often delays with long journeys, and when you arrive in India everything closes very early, so therefore you know it's always a bit of a worry if you arrive after eight o'clock in the evening for instance. And then one thing that er you know, anybody going to India should remember – is that … people appear very, very helpful. In fact they are all very, very keen to … you know, offer you accommodation and so on, but one has to, you know, kind of discriminate about that, because … you know, people just could take you anywhere, so one has to be very careful. But … you know, hotels are definitely wonderful in India and … you know it is very cheap for us, so it is lovely to actually … indulge and … go to a, you know, kind of little palace really.

Speaker 2
Last year I went to Phoenix in Arizona … er … to the Phoenican Resort Hotel er to attend a convention. And the convention was of people in the fund management business in America and their wives. And the Phoenician Resort Hotel is quite far from the airport but you don't need to hire a car because the convention people provide a lift for you from the airport er to the hotel. Dress is very informal in that sort of place. Umm, shorts and a shirt or jeans and T-shirt are there. But in the evening and … when there are formal dinners, then of course a suit and tie is a good idea.

16 UNIT 1

UNIT 2 Representing your company

PREPARATION

- It is possible to complete this unit at different speeds, in more or less detail. The fast track takes about 1½ hours, the standard track about 2 hours and the comprehensive track about 3 hours. For more information on the three options, see the notes in the Introduction on pages 10 and 11.
- For details of the aims of the unit, look at the Contents box on this page, the Language Notes at the end of the Course Book unit and the Useful Phrases below.
- If available to you, you can use the exercises in the Self-study Guide as extra practice.
- If you have taught this unit before, review the notes you made at the time.

USEFUL PHRASES

I'd like to welcome you to Van Breda and to thank you for coming.
I'm glad you could all make it.

While we are waiting, I'll run through the timetable.
There are a couple of changes to the programme.
The first presentation starts at 10.00.
Jan our MD is joining us later.

Come and meet Dick.
The best person to talk to is Mel.
Have you been introduced?
I'm sorry – I thought you knew each other.
John, this is Meg Kato, head of training at TLK.

We are part of the Levit group of companies.
We are mainly a sales organisation.
The organisation consists of three divisions.
We're in the process of reorganising our manufacturing division.

I'd like to show you round the factory.
Please follow me up the stairs.
I'm afraid this area is closed to visitors.
Mind out! The floor is slippery.

This is what we are working on at the moment.
We're installing a new system which will make it possible for us to turn orders round in four hours.
Is everything clear so far?

LEAD IN (SUGGESTIONS)

- Check how learners have prepared for the lesson – see the Preparation section at the start of the unit in the Course Book (page 17). Have they looked at Useful Phrases on page 20 in the Course Book (copied above)? Comments from group members may indicate which areas of the target language they need to focus on, and the level of interest in the topic.
- You might lead into the subject by asking participants to 'represent' their organisation (or one they know) – as if they were speaking on behalf of their company in a meeting. This would involve briefly stating what the company does, putting it in a positive light, and a brief comment (if relevant) on their role in the company. Alternatively, they might discuss the image on page 17 – the message from Honda presented on a banana.

Contents

Expressions
I'd like to welcome you to Van Breda.
The organisation consists of three divisions.
This is what we are working on at the moment.
Mel, this is Donna Ng. She's with the group from Shanghai.

Language check
Articles: (*a*, *the*, –)
Present tenses: Simple
(*work / works*) and Continuous (*is / are working*)
Vocabulary: *slippery*, *sharp*, *wet*, *mission*, *aim*, *objective*, *show round*, *look round*, *run through*

Practice
Showing someone round
A web page presenting the company
Writing a letter introducing your company

---

1 CORE PRACTICE

Listening and speaking

- This exercise provides an opportunity to practise a range of situations related to representing your company.
- The exercise is in two parts – listening and speaking. The listening activity (part i) provides learners with ideas and models for the speaking activity (part ii).
- Ask learners to identify the verbal clues they use when answering the comprehension questions in part i.
- In part ii, encourage learners to adapt the scenarios to their needs. Where possible, they should introduce the documents and realia they have brought to class.
- Question a: *Swansea* is a coastal city in South Wales. Explain that *state-of-the-art* = as advanced as possible; *strategic services* = support services such as IT, Security and Property Management; *the tie-up with* = (here) the merger with.
- Question b: The speaker has a US accent. Point out that *teething problems* = early stage problems; *up and running* = functioning; *turn orders round* = complete them.
- Question c: Mel d'Abo has an Australian accent.
- Question d: *R&D* = research and development.
- **Further step:** When learners have completed their individual practice in part ii, ask them to prepare and perform it to the rest of the class.

2 LANGUAGE CHECK

- The multiple-choice questions link to the Language Notes at the end of the Course Book unit (page 20) and the related notes in the

Business Grammar Guide (see the booklet that accompanies the Course Book).
- The multiple-choice questions enable you to treat the language programme flexibly. Points that are known can be handled briefly. Points that require more remedial attention can be explored in more detail. The Specific Points section below gives you further guidance for the questions.
- For each question consider the following options.
  - Identify the answer.
  - Explore why the other options are wrong.
  - Ask learners to prepare examples that relate to their working needs, e.g.:
    Question 1: *We're meeting for lunch at the Marriot Hotel on June 27th.*
    Amended version: *I'm meeting my boss for coffee in the lounge on the fifth floor tomorrow at 8.30.*
- **Further step:** Ask learners to work individually or in pairs to prepare extra multiple-choice questions for the class, using the Language Notes and the related notes in the Business Grammar Guide for reference.

SPECIFIC POINTS

Questions 1 to 3: Use of articles *a, the, –* (BGG 9.1, 9.2, 9.3)
- Q1: Note that even though we usually use an article with singular countable nouns, we do not generally use one with names of meals after *have* and after prepositions (e.g. *have lunch, at dinner*).
- Point out that, in spoken British English, *the* goes before the day rather than the month (e.g. *July the eleventh / the eleventh of July*). In American English, *the* is often omitted in the spoken language when the day follows the month (e.g. *July eleventh / eleven*). *the* is not usually used in the written language, except when only the day is used (e.g. *We're meeting on the eleventh*).
- Q2: *the* can be used with countable singular and plural nouns and uncountable nouns, but it makes the meaning both specific and definite. The first example is both specific and definite in meaning (both the speaker and listener know which frames are being referred to), so *the* is necessary. The second example is specific but indefinite in meaning. *fibreglass* is uncountable, so no article is needed. An easy explanation is that we don't use articles after *X is made of ....*
- Q3: Both nouns are countable, so an article is required. In the first example, *the* is used (rather than *a*) because there is only one European representative. In the second, *the* is used because both the speaker and listener know which board is being referred to.
- As further practice, ask learners in pairs to go through one of the documents they have brought to the lesson and check the use of articles. Mark examples they are not sure about and discuss them with the class.

Questions 4 to 6: Use of the Present Simple and the Present Continuous tenses (BGG 1.1)
- Q4: Elicit the correct preposition after *concentrate*. (It is *on*.)
- Q5: Encourage learners to correct the wrong answers (i.e. *is divided into, is made up of*). Also point out the verb *comprise* (no preposition needed).
- Q6: Note that *is being replaced* is the continuous form of the Present Passive.

Questions 7 and 8: More uses of the Present Simple and the Present Continuous – with future meaning and with adverbs
- Q7: Notice that adverbs do not usually stand directly after the main verb – except when *be* is used as a main verb (e.g. *runs normally our catalogue sales* is OK if the order is changed to *normally runs our catalogue sales* – see BGG 14.3). Explain that *catalogue sales* = sales via a catalogue that is mailed to buyers.
- Q8: Review the use of present tenses for the future (BGG 2.1). Note that the Present Simple tends to be used more with verbs like *start, finish, open, close, arrive, leave* when talking about scheduled events or timetables.

Question 9: Verb phrases
- Note *take* could also be used here.
- Point out also *Would you like to look / see / go round the factory?*

Question 10: Warnings
- Go through the examples listed in the Language Notes.
- Check particular needs in the class, e.g. *sharp, poisonous, uneven* (*the floor / surface is uneven*).

3 LISTENING

A tour of the company

- Van Breda Footwear is a fictitious company. The audioscript is adapted from a real recording.
- When learners have completed the activity, work intensively on the recording, checking for precise comprehension of words and phrases.
- Note that *round-up session* = a final meeting to conclude something (note also *to round something up*); *gauges* = devices for measuring the size or amount of something.
- You could also check comprehension of *responsible to* someone vs. *responsible for* something.
- **Further practice:** Working in pairs, ask learners to prepare further questions for the rest of the class, e.g. *Where is the company's head office?*

4 WRITING

An introduction

- Prepare for the exercise by going through the Useful Language listed alongside the activity (page 18 of Course Book).

- Ask learners to make use of the ideas and language they prepared before the class so they can 'represent' their organisation.
- There is a sample draft in the Answer Key.
- The exercise can be given for homework.
- **Further step:** Ask learners, in turn, to read aloud what they write. Do their letters sound OK? Is the writing style natural and direct? Remind learners of the key criteria for good business writing – it should be clear, brief and easy to read. Finally, ask them to evaluate each others' work.

5 FEATURE

Company purpose / mission

- In pairs, ask learners to discuss their experience of Honda and list the key features of the brand as they perceive it.
- Ask pairs to discuss their findings with the rest of the class and build up a class view. List the main features of the class view.
- In pairs, ask learners to go through the text on Honda (page 19 of Course Book) and complete the activity.
- There is some overlap, but for general business purposes *values* = the norms and ideas that are important to the business; *mission* = the concrete objective, the thing(s) that need to be done to realise the dream. Note the singular form *value* can also be used to mean something that makes a product more appealing to a customer, as in the example in the text (*creation of new value*) and the phrase *added value*.
- In this text *consolidated* refers to sales and employees of Honda in Japan; *unconsolidated* (*non-consolidated*) = the worldwide total.
- Summarise the Honda mission as expressed in the article.
- As a class, discuss whether the image put forward by Honda fits the views held individually by those in the class.
- **Further step:** Ask learners to look through the realia documents they have brought to class and prepare a summary statement about their organisation (or one they know).

REVIEW

- Go through the Language Notes and Useful Phrases in the Course Book, if you have not already done so.
- Encourage learners to list terms they found particularly useful – especially those they need in their work.
- Make a note of this language for future reference.
- Encourage learners to use the new language they have learnt outside the classroom, e.g. they might aim to use key points in a presentation, report or email.

Answers

1 Core practice
a i [U]   b i [F]   c i [F]   d i [T]

2 Language check
1 a   2 a   3 b   4 a   5 a
6 a   7 b   8 a   9 c   10 c

3 Listening
Extract 1: 9.15
Extract 2: 9.30
Extract 3: 10.30
Extract 4: 11.15
Extract 5: just before 12.00 midday

4 Writing
(*possible answer*)
Dear …

Mr Jim Toaro of SGK Associates has suggested that I contact you. I am planning a visit to South East Asia in July and I would welcome the opportunity to meet you or a representative of your company.

As you may know, we are part of Vible Group. We specialise in developing and manufacturing environmentally friendly insecticides for domestic animals that can be used safely in the home.

We are very interested in the possibility of working with a Malaysian company, possibly in a joint venture capacity. We feel that there are potentially several areas of common interest between your company and ourselves.

I enclose a copy of our annual report and a selection of our current brochures. Please do not hesitate to contact me if you need further information.

I look forward to hearing from you.

5 Feature
(*possible answers*)
a To build and sell the Honda brand.
c It's a mix of global and localized – suggesting that the company focuses effectively in both areas.
d It sounds like an exaggeration; it is probable that Honda's chief competitors can match Honda in most fields.
e The use of 'z' in place of 's' in *realizing* and *glocalized*.
f
- Honda has been motivated / inspired by dreams.
- We are making the dream real.
- We're always more developed / advanced than other companies.
- Producing / developing technologies.
- We have accepted the challenge.

Audioscripts

1 Core practice

a We're a medium-size manufacturing company – we're part of the Melox group, which has its head office in Toulouse. We're based here in South Wales – our main plant is in Swansea, where we produce a range of state-of-the-art domestic cookers. The organisation consists of three divisions: production, marketing and strategic services (which includes finance). Since the tie-up with Melox, export sales have more than doubled. At present we operate a two-shift system, but we are planning to introduce a third shift from the beginning of next month.

b This is what we're working on at the moment. It's an automated sorting and packing machine, linked to our computer database. We're having one or two teething problems, but when the system is up and running, it'll make it possible for us to turn orders round in four hours.

c – Look, come and meet our building manager, Mel d'Abo, he's responsible for project planning. He's the best person to answer your query. He's just over here.
    Mel, this is Donna Ng; she's with the management group from Shanghai.
   – Hello, welcome to Sydney.
   – Thank you. Pleased to meet you.
   – Donna has a question for you.

d – Have we lost anyone?
   – No, I think we're all here.
   – OK, please follow me. We go down these stairs and through the swing doors.
   – Is there any chance of seeing the new high-speed processor you mentioned?
   – No, I'm afraid not – it's still being trialled by our R&D people. And the R&D area is closed to visitors.
   – Oh, that's a pity.
   – I can show you an older model which we're in the process of modifying. It's just along here on the left.
     This is it. Mind your clothes, the paint might be wet.

3 Listening

Extract 1
– Well, good morning. I'd like to welcome you to Van Breda Footware, and to thank you for coming. Did anyone get lost?
– No, I think we're all here.
– OK, we have an interesting programme for you today. First of all we'll go up to our boardroom. I've organised some coffee for us, and during the course of coffee I'll introduce you to some of the guys who run the place. Our Managing Director is joining us. The first presentation starts at 10.00. Then we can have a look round the plant and show you what we're working on.

Extract 2
– First of all then, while we're waiting for coffee, can I introduce you to Jan Ruse, who is our MD.
– Hello and welcome. It's good to see you all here. I'll be joining you for the round-up session, so if you have any questions specifically for me, you can catch me then – OK? I hope you enjoy your tour.
– Thanks, Jan. Jan is responsible to our head office in Brazil for the running of this site and the whole of our European operation.

Extract 3
– Aah, there's a slight change of plan – there's a fire inspection in the plant this morning, so we're going to look round the showroom first. Are we all here?
– Yes, I think so.
– Right ... as you can see, this is where our samples are on display. As you know, we make a whole range of leather shoes and we specialise in all-weather footwear. You can see some samples on those racks over there.

Extract 4
This is the new XL20. Can everyone see? It heat-welds the uppers to the soles. It's a state-of-the-art machine, which more or less runs itself. The only trouble is, it's very sensitive. We're having a few teething problems with it, because it keeps stopping. Can you see these gauges down here? Mind your heads. If the reading goes into the red, the whole machine shuts down.

Extract 5
– Excuse me, the boardroom is along here, through the swing doors.
– Oh ...
– Mind the step! In fact we're a little early; we're not meeting Jan for another 10 minutes. Anybody need the toilet? It's on the left here. OK, where were we? Oh yes – you had a question ...
– Yes, I was wondering how many people you employ.
– Do you mean on this site or in the whole company?

UNIT 3 Following up

PREPARATION

- There are three possible tracks through the unit: fast (about 1½ hours), standard (about 2 hours) and comprehensive (about 3 hours). For more information on the different tracks, see the notes in the Introduction on pages 10 and 11.
- For details of the aims of the unit, look at the Contents box on this page, the Language Notes at the end of the Course Book unit and the Useful Phrases below. There are answers and audioscripts on pages 23 and 24 of this book.
- If available to you, you can use the Self-study Guide as a source of supplementary exercises on the key themes of the unit.
- If you have taught the unit before, check the notes you made at the time.

USEFUL PHRASES

How are you progressing with the X50 project?
How you getting on? How is it going?
I managed to get hold of the figures you wanted.
I understand you don't need the brochures.

I'm just following up on the samples you were going to send me.
Have you been able to send them yet?
As far I know, Guido is finding out about it.
Could you ask him to let me know what's happening?

You asked me to find out about the timetable.
The system is being upgraded.
They keep changing it.
It is always going wrong.
I'm afraid I am having problems getting the details.

I thought everything went pretty well.
I have to say, I was a bit disappointed.
I felt the presentations were rather boring.
I thought the organisation was absolutely first class.

I'm pretty sure I left some papers behind.
They were in a green folder, marked 'Liaison'.
Nothing has been handed in.
I'll let you know if anything turns up.

I'm just calling to thank you for organising such an interesting visit.
You're very welcome – it was a pleasure.
We're glad you could make it.
We are looking forward to seeing you again soon.

LEAD IN (SUGGESTIONS)

- Refer to the Preparation section at the start of the unit in the Course Book (page 21). Check whether learners have brought a 'thank you' message and a progress report relating to a trip or meeting to the class. These can be used as resources throughout the lesson.
- Check also whether they have looked at the Useful Phrases on page 24 in the Course Book (copied above). Comments from the class may indicate which areas of the target language they need to focus on.
- You might lead into the subject by discussing specific examples of follow-up they are involved in. Be prepared to give an example of your own.

Contents

Expressions
How are you getting on? How is it going?
I managed to get hold of the figures you wanted.
Generally, I think it was well worth going.
I'm just calling to thank you for organising such an interesting programme.

Language check
More on present tenses
Simple: *I wonder why ..., I gather ...*
Continuous: *It's always going wrong.*
Present Passive: *The system is being changed.*
Giving feedback: *really, quite, rather,* etc.
Vocabulary: *visit, trip, programme, problem, issue, hassle, making progress, going well, follow up, find out, get back to*

Practice
Following up on a project
Thanking by email
Reporting back

1 CORE PRACTICE

Listening and speaking

- This exercise provides an opportunity to practise a range of situations relating to following up.
- The exercise is in two parts – listening and speaking. The listening activity (part i) provides learners with ideas and models for the speaking activity (part ii).
- In part ii, encourage learners to adapt the scenarios to their needs. Where relevant, they should introduce the realia documents they have brought to the class.
- Question a: The speaker has a non-standard UK accent. Point out that *get hold of* = obtain; *let me know the state of play* = let me know what's happening.
- Question b: The second speaker has a US accent. Following the model in the recording, you might ask the group to practise dealing with incoming calls that interrupt a meeting. Note that *getting back to me* = calling me back.
- Question c: The second speaker has an Irish accent. Point out that *handed it in* = found and given to the people in charge.
- Question d: The second speaker has a non-standard accent. The caller might be on the sales side or a development partner in a joint project of some kind. She works for a different company.
- **Further step:** In pairs, ask learners to playread the dialogues to the rest of the group – see the audioscript on page 24 of this manual and page 141 of the Course Book.

Following up 21

2 LANGUAGE CHECK

- As you go through the multiple-choice questions, point out the Language Notes at the end of the Course Book unit (page 24), and the related notes in the Business Grammar Guide (see booklet that accompanies the Course Book).
- The multiple-choice questions are a starting point. Ensure that the related language points are explored and revised as necessary. The Specific Points section below gives you further detailed guidance.
- For each question consider the following options.
  - Identify the answer.
  - Explore why the other options are wrong.
  - Ask learners to prepare examples that relate to their working needs, e.g.:
    Question 1: *I wonder if you could help me?*
    Amended version: *I wonder if you could fax it through to me?*
- **Further step:** Reinforce vocabulary used in a simple word game. Using the Vocabulary section in the Language Notes as a starting point, class members work in teams. Team 1 chooses a word or phrase related to the themes of the unit; Team 2 scores a point by using it correctly in an example. Team 2 then chooses a word or phrase for Team 1 and so on.

SPECIFIC POINTS

Questions 1 to 7: Present tenses, active and passive (BGG 1.1, 4)

- Q1: *I wonder + if you could / if you'd mind* have the effect of making a request less direct (and therefore more polite). *I was wondering* can be used in the same way (but not *I am wondering*). *I wonder* can also be used with an indirect question, e.g. *I wonder when they will get back to us?*
- Q2 and 7: Verbs not normally used in the continuous form. Point out that when *have* is a state verb (used like 'possess'), it cannot have a continuous form. Elicit other examples of *have* as an action verb (e.g. *have a meal, have difficulty, have a good time, have a shower*), which can have a continuous form.
- Q3: The present passive. Point out the simple, continuous and infinitive forms – see the Language Notes.
- Q5 and 6: Expressing persistence and / or repetition. These special uses of *keep + -ing* and *always + Present Continuous* often suggest that the situation is annoying.
- Q7: Point out that *think* to give an opinion is used in the Present Simple. Elicit other verbs like *believe* (e.g. *know, want, prefer, realise, include, seem*) which are not normally used in the continuous form. Also elicit other verbs like *think* (e.g. *hope, see, expect*) which can be used in both present tenses and discuss whether the choice of tense affects the meaning (see BGG 1.1).

Questions 8 and 9: Giving feedback – the use of *really, quite, rather* to change the strength of adjectives (BGG 14.4)

- Notice that *slightly* (Q8) and *rather* (Q9) tend to be used with negative ideas, e.g. *I thought the presentation was rather / slightly long.*
- Q9: *quite* is the only word given in the possible answers that can combine with *not*. *not quite* is only used with non-gradable words such as *good enough* (where the meaning is absolute and cannot vary in degree). It indicates only a small difference (e.g. *That's not quite right* = It's almost right; *I don't quite understand* = I almost understand).

Question 10: Vocabulary and verb phrases

- Go though the Vocabulary section on page 24 of the Course Book. Note that a *set-back* = something that stops progress; *hassles* = irritating problems; *follow up* = take further action (point out the use of *on*).
- Note these other expressions with *get*: *I haven't got round to doing it yet* = I haven't done a job that I know needs doing; *Get onto* (*the suppliers and tell them it's urgent*) = contact; *How are you getting on with the project?* = How are you progressing with the project / how is it going?

3 APPLICATION

Following up on a project

- This exercise has four stages: agreeing the project details; summarising the details in an email; phoning for an update and dealing with slippage; writing an email summarising the points agreed in the call. Note *slippage* = falling behind schedule.
- It might be an idea to pre-teach the following forms to indicate who is responsible for follow-up action: *We agreed to* + verb for decisions reached; *X will* + verb or *X* + infinitive with *to* (e.g. *Jim will contact / to contact the London office*).
- Ensure learners bring into the exercise (where possible) the background realia they brought to class.
- The different stages of the exercise can be undertaken more or less thoroughly, depending on time available and relevance to the class.
- There are sample emails in the answers.

4 WRITING

A 'thank you' message

- An evaluation of the letter shown in the exercise (page 22 of Course Book) is given in the Answer Key. Points include the fact that it is too long and too wordy. Point out that in modern emails the focus tends to be on speed and simplicity. This means clear headings and simple language, e.g. *I am in your debt for the kind hospitality extended to our group* becomes *Thanks for all your kind hospitality*.
- There is a sample redraft of the letter in the answers (see page 24).

- Note *tapas* are small savoury snacks often served in Spanish bars to accompany drinks.
- **Further step:** Ask learners, in pairs, to review one of the documents they have brought to class, using the criteria discussed in the activity. Can the standard of readability be raised? If so, how?

5 CASE STUDY
Mismanagement of company funds

1
- Learners read the report.
- Peter Baska is the finance director of Yukon Tours, a holiday travel company with a branch office in Vancouver. There have been problems with the management of the local bank account, and Peter Baska had to review the situation.
- After visiting Vancouver and reviewing management of the account, Peter Baska sent a report to Donna Yang, CEO (Chief Executive Officer) of Yukon Tours. It is now a month since the report was circulated.
- Ask learners to read the report and, in pairs, prepare the questions that in their view need to be answered at this point.
- Gloss as necessary: *Cheques are drawn* = cheques are written; *The latter cheques* = the last cheques mentioned; *reviewing* = looking at (in order to give an opinion); *verify* = make sure they are correct / justified; *withdrawals* = when money is taken out of an account; *the whereabouts* = the location; *petty cash* = a small amount of money for everyday items.

2
- Learners listen to Peter Baska giving an update on the situation to Donna Yang and decide if the questions they prepared have been answered.
- Point out that *transactions* = payments, withdrawals, etc.; *up and running* = working; *misconduct* = unacceptable or immoral behaviour (by someone in a position of authority); *mismanagement* = poor management.
- Possible questions and answers:

Did Ray Felli supply the missing information by 21 February as required?
[✓] No, but he supplied it after some reminders.

What have you decided about Ray Felli? Is he guilty of misconduct?
[✓] Peter Baska is now satisfied with the information he has received. He feels this is mismanagement, not misconduct.

Are regular payments like salaries now being paid on the 15th of each month?
[½] Not yet, but from the beginning of next month they will be made at a regular time each month. They don't mention the date.

Has the new petty cash system been set up?
[✓] Yes, it is now up and running.

Has the part-time accountant been kept on?
[✓] Yes, but an external auditor is conducting a month-end review.

Are funds still being paid into Ray Felli's personal account?
[✓] No; this has improved the situation a lot.

Has a petty cash book been introduced for small day-to-day expenses?
[✗] Not mentioned.

What has happened about the review of local staff?
[✗] Not mentioned.

Has the missing US$7,000 been found?
[✗] Not mentioned.

- **Further step:** Learners review the situation and decide what further follow-up, if any, they would recommend.

REVIEW
- Go through the Language Notes and Useful Phrases in the Course Book, if you have not already done so.
- Make a note of the language that your learners found particularly useful for
- Encourage learners to practise new language outside the classroom and to bring it into their communication.

Answers

1 Core practice
a i [T]   b i [T]
c i [U]   d i [U]

2 Language check
1 a   2 b
3 b   4 a
5 a   6 c
7 b   8 b
9 a   10 c

3 Application
(*possible answers*)

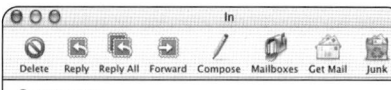

Summary
Subject box: Project meeting
Hello
Thanks to you all for your time and input. It was a useful meeting.
We agreed to break the project down into five main stages, as follows – completion dates in brackets:
- Customer research (4 April)
- Liaison and planning (11 April)
- Preparation (11 May)
- Testing and training (7 June)
- Delivery (10 July).

We will each take responsibility for leading the stage our team is responsible for:
- Eve – Customer Research
- Hans – Liaison & Planning
- Jackie – Preparation
- Rathan – Testing and training
- Rathan – Delivery.

Finally, we agreed to meet to monitor progress on Friday mornings – if necessary this would be a conference call.
Regards

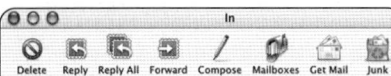

Project delays

Hi

Thanks for agreeing at short notice to the telephone conference this morning. We agreed to deal with the current slippage as follows.
- Eve will check with target users that the simplified specification we are proposing still meets their needs.
- Jackie's team will work with Hans's people to support the liaison and planning work, and prevent further slippage.
- Rathan will negotiate with the various stakeholders over the revised completion dates. These are:
  - Liaison & Planning (2 April)
  - Preparation (2 June)
  - Testing and training (3 July)
  - Delivery (4 August).
- Rathan will also work out the budget implications and ensure that the increase is covered by the contingency fund.

Good luck – please get back to me if you have queries.

Regards

4 Writing

(possible answers)

Opinion of the letter
- It has no heading – this would normally stand between the greeting (Dear Tom) and the first paragraph.
- It has no date.
- There are no job titles – standard practice requires Sr Milagros to add his position under his name at the end of the letter, and to give T. Sven's job title at the beginning.
- It is too long and too wordy – the tone is quite pompous.

Email version

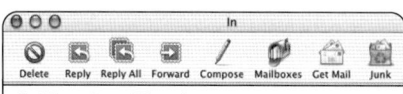

Subject box: Thanks

Dear Tom

Thanks again for all your kind hospitality. We enjoyed the visit very much indeed. Please thank Simo and Jan for my skiing lesson.

As I think you know, Mr Smithson was very impressed by your operation. We are all looking forward to working with you.

When the trials are complete and we get the go-ahead, you must visit us in Madrid. A tour of our tapas bars will be a good way of celebrating the start of our business relationship!

Kind regards

5 Case study

1 *(possible questions)*
- Did Ray Felli supply the missing information by the 21 February?
- What have you decided about Ray Felli? Is he guilty of misconduct?
- Are regular payments such as salaries, now being paid on the 15th of each month?
- Has the new petty cash system been set up?
- Has the part-time accountant been kept on?
- Are funds still being paid into Ray Felli's personal account?
- What has happened about the review of local staff?
- Has the missing US$7,000 been found?

Audioscripts

1 Core practice

a   This is a message for Jan Somensky from Ron Lomax. I'm just following up on our meeting. Have you been able to get hold of those samples yet? As far as I know, we haven't received anything at this end. Umm … do you know how soon we can expect them? Anyway, I'd be grateful if you could call me and let me know the state of play. Thanks.

b   – I managed to get hold of the figures you wanted.
– Oh, thanks for getting back to me.
– That's OK, but I'm calling because we're having problems with the samples. But I understand you don't need them now.
– Er, look, I'm in a meeting right now – can I call you back in about 10 minutes?
– Yes, of course. Could you call my landline? My mobile keeps switching to silent – there's something wrong with it.

c   – I'm calling to find out if I left some papers behind. They were in a green folder marked 'Liaison'.
– Er, I didn't see anything. Do you know where you left it?
– I'm pretty sure I put it down in the reception area.
– I'll call them and check whether anyone has handed it in.
– I'm sorry to bother you with this.
– That's OK. People are always leaving things behind. I'll contact you as soon as we find it.

d   – I'm just calling to thank you for organising such an interesting visit for us.
– I'm glad you could come.
– Thanks a lot for showing us round. It was very interesting.
– I hope you found it useful.
– Oh, we did. And next time you must visit us.
– We'd like to, very much.

– Just let me know when you want to come, and I'll organise it. We're looking forward to taking our relationship with your company to the next stage.

5 Case study

DY = Donna Yang
PB = Peter Baska

DY: How are you progressing with the Ray Felli business? Did he meet the deadline?
PB: The information relating to his bank account? You remember he was asked to account for the movement of company funds into and out of his personal account.
DY: Yes, by the 21st of February.
PB: Well, we didn't get the information on the date requested, but after a few reminders we did finally get it. Our position now is that we're satisfied with the information we've received, and we're going ahead more or less as recommended in my report. They're setting up the new procedures which will standardise most of the regular money transactions. From the beginning of next month regular cheques will be paid at a regular time each month. The new petty cash system for irregular cash payments is already up and running. Er … we've reviewed the situation of the part-time accountant and we've decided to retain his services, but to bring in someone from one of the international accounting firms to do a month-end review.
DY: You decided not to find someone else.
PB: No. The matter of any missing money has also been reviewed and our view again is that this is not misconduct, but mismanagement. Plus the decision not to pay any further funds into Ray Felli's personal account has helped the situation a lot.

24   UNIT 3

UNIT 4 Dealing with change

PREPARATION

- There are three possible tracks through the unit: fast (about 1½ hours), standard (about 2 hours) and comprehensive (about 3 hours). For more information on the different tracks, see the notes in the Introduction on pages 10 and 11.
- For the aims of the unit, see the Contents box opposite, the Language Notes at the end of the Course Book unit and the Useful Phrases below. Answers and audioscripts are on pages 27 and 28.
- If you have taught the unit before, check the notes you made at the Review stage.

USEFUL PHRASES

The company was founded 20 years ago.
In the early days we were based in Seattle.
Three years ago we were taken over by BSK.
Recently, we switched to local suppliers.
In the last year or so, we've been doing a lot of business in APAC.

John became head of my business unit.
It was an internal appointment.
The CEO retired three months ago.
A woman called Dena Stroe took over from him.
She used to work in Compliance.
In the new structure, I have a reporting line to John and a dotted line to Dena.

We now process orders centrally.
We no longer handle the work locally.
The work was outsourced to BLK.
I am no longer involved on a day-to-day basis.

Magda is now in charge.
You should send your queries to her.
But do feel free to contact me if there are problems.

All the transactions that used to be handled by my team are now handled by the global team based in Frankfurt.
There should be no difference in the day-to-day running of your account.

What are the main changes?
What difference has reorganisation made?
We have to do the same job with fewer resources.
There's more pressure than there used to be.

LEAD IN (SUGGESTIONS)

- Refer to the Preparation section at the start of the unit in the Course Book (page 25). Check whether learners have brought to class documents relating to a change programme they have been involved in (e.g. a cost-cutting programme).
- Check whether learners have looked at the Useful Phrases on page 28 in the Course Book (copied above).
- You might lead into the subject by eliciting from learners accounts of changes they are, or have been, involved in. Be prepared to contribute a story of your own.

Contents

Expressions
Three years ago, we were taken over by BSK.
We now process orders centrally.
All the transactions that used to be handled by my team are now handled by the global team based in Frankfurt.
There's more pressure than there used to be.

Language check
Past tenses, Active and Passive
Past time markers: *a year later, the previous year*
used to, be used to, get used to
Vocabulary: *reorganisation, restructuring, business unit, division, department, go bankrupt, go into liquidation, take over, close down, cut back*

Practice
Explaining operational changes to a customer
Talking about changes during your working life
Talking about your company history

1 CORE PRACTICE

Listening and speaking

- This exercise provides an opportunity to practise a range of situations relating to change.
- The exercise is in two parts – listening and speaking. The listening activity (part i) provides learners with ideas and models for the speaking activity (part ii).
- In part ii, encourage learners to adapt the scenarios to their needs. Where possible they should introduce the case realia they have brought to class.
- Question a: Point out that *bought in* = purchased externally / not developed in-house; *prior to* = before; *spec (specification)* = a detailed description of how something should be done or made.
- Question b: Explain that job titles can vary: *group financial controller* = CFO (chief financial officer) = finance director.
- Question c: *margins* = profit margins (see Glossary); *cut back on* = reduced expenditure on; *R&D (R and D)* = Research and Development.
- Question d: The first speaker has a non-standard UK accent. The second speaker has an Italian accent. *Back / middle office* (see Glossary).
- **Further step:** When learners have completed their individual practice in part ii, ask them to prepare and perform it to the rest of the class.

2 LANGUAGE CHECK

- As you go through the multiple-choice questions with the class, point out the Language Notes at the end of the Course Book unit (page 28), and the related notes in the

Business Grammar Guide (see the booklet that accompanies the Course Book).
- The Specific Points section below gives you further detailed guidance.
- When working on vocabulary questions, introduce special terms that class members need. Point out the Glossary on pages 158 – 160 of the Course Book.
- For each question consider the following options.
  - Identify the answer.
  - Explore why the other options are wrong.
  - Ask learners to prepare examples that relate to their working needs, e.g.:
    Question 1: *By the following year, the new CEO had been appointed.*
    Amended version: *By the end of October, we had already reached our sales target for the whole year.*
- **Further step:** In pairs or groups, ask learners to prepare a dialogue using all ten examples in the multiple-choice questions.

SPECIFIC POINTS

Questions 1 to 5: Past tenses (active and passive); see also questions 7 and 8
- Q1: Present Perfect, Past Simple, Past Perfect – active and passive (see BGG 1.2, 1.5). To illustrate the concept of the Past Perfect, you could write the following sentence (or a similar example) on the board: *By the time I joined the department, our help desk had been moved to India.* Draw a time line showing the main time focus of the sentence as the Past Simple verb (*I joined*), then the event described by the Past Perfect verb (*had been appointed*) as happening before. Note the main time focus could be a *by* + time phrase (as in the example) instead of a Past Simple verb.
- Q2: Point out *this July* is a past time marker (*this* because the year has not yet finished). Compare with *last July* (= the previous year). In order to clarify why the Past Simple is the correct tense, you could ask learners to transform the sentence into a positive sentence (*She started her new job in July*). The use of *not ... till / until* emphasises the fact that she didn't start the job before July.
- Q3: Review uses of the Present Perfect (BGG 1.2). Here the trigger is *so far this week* (= unfinished / unspecified time period).
- Q4: Past Continuous, Past Simple, *used to* (BGG 1.4, 1.5, 1.6). Point out that *used to* cannot be used when a length of time is given. The Past Continuous + a following *when* clause is used when a shorter event happens in the middle of a longer background event (e.g. *I was having a meeting with our agent when you phoned*). This is not the situation in the example.
- Q5: *used to*, Past Simple, Present Perfect. Elicit why *used to* has to be used here (= to emphasise the contrast between a past and current situation – *but now* is the trigger).

Question 6: Past time markers
- Note *To begin with* and *Originally* could be used here. *First (of all)* could not be used because what follows is not a sequence of events. *Initially*, etc. imply that the original situation subsequently changed (here the implication is that the product range is now wider).

Questions 7 and 8: Past tenses (active and passive)
- Q7: Past Perfect + *before* + Past Simple. Note the Past Simple could be used instead of the Past Perfect in front of a *before* clause (e.g. *She'd left / she left before we got there*). With *already* the Past Perfect is more natural, as it emphasises the completion of the previous event. See also notes for Q1.
- Q8: Tense usage with *after* clauses. Note the Past Perfect tends to be used (instead of the Past Simple) in an *after* clause when the subject of the two clauses is the same and when the event in the *after* clause is more of an intentional action, e.g. *After the company had launched its new IP70 range, it announced the opening of a new factory in Poland.*

Question 9: Vocabulary related to change
- Review the examples in the Vocabulary section of the Language Notes. Note *rationalistion* (also *rationalization*) = to make a company more efficient and profitable (e.g. by reducing staff numbers, combining parts of the company). Try to elicit synonyms or near synonyms for the verb phrases (e.g. *cut back on* = reduce; *take over* = acquire / buy; *set up* = establish; *go out of business* = close down / cease trading).

Question 10: *used to, be / get used to*
- Ensure learners don't confuse the meaning of these verb forms. Point out that *be / get used to* = be / become familiar with / accustomed to. Note that *get* must be used in this example, as the sentence involves change / action. Check learners know that if a verb follows *be / get used to*, the *-ing* form is used. It might also be worth pointing out that *used to* + verb is used for a past situation, not a present habitual situation (e.g. *In our country we use to drink coffee in the mornings* is a typical mistake).

3 LISTENING

Changes during working life

1
- Mark Jarvis talks about changes in his working life since he started work at British Aerospace 22 years ago.
  - Ask learners to make notes as they listen, then list the changes Mark Jarvis refers to.
  - Gloss specialised vocabulary: *PDA* (see Glossary); *direct dial* = a call which does not have to go via an operator / switchboard; *a typing pool* = a group of typists who copy letters using typewriters. Note *a latte* is an Italian-style milky coffee.

- Ask learners to identify the fundamental changes in Mark Jarvis's working life (= greater mobility and connectivity).

2
- Learners make a similar statement about changes in their own working lives. The statements might be written or spoken. Encourage learners to incorporate the information they have brought to class.
- Some useful language:
  When I first started, we used to …
  Now we just …
  We don't have to … anymore.
  Now we have much more …
  Things move more quickly now.
  The pace is faster.
- **Further step:** Ask learners to discuss changes in their working lives and to create an overview. What are the main themes? Which changes are for the better? Which do they find difficult?

4 WRITING

Liaising with customers

1
- Learners prepare a message explaining upcoming change(s) to a key customer (internal or external).
- Go through the points that might be covered in a letter of this kind, as listed in the activity (see page 26 of the Course Book).
- There is a draft of a possible message in the answers.

2
- Learners practise following up on a message of this kind by calling the customer.
- Working in pairs, learners practise the call. Ask them to think of specific customers and to anticipate their reactions. What questions will they ask? How can they reassure the customer? Check that they have the language they need, e.g.:
  The new arrangement will provide you with a 24-hour service.
  If there are any problems, you can always call me direct.
- **Further step:** Ask one of the pairs to demonstrate their scenario to the rest of the class.

5 CASE STUDY

IBM

- Go through the article glossing as necessary.
- Explain that *clones* = copies; *eroded profits* = reduced profits over a period of time; *racked up ($15bn)* = built up (a large sum); *cumulative losses* = losses added to previous losses over a period of time; *platform(s)* = a computer's operating system (e.g. a Windows platform, the Macintosh platform); *eminently positioned* = in a very good position (better than their competitors); *the only viable alternative* = the only other choice that was possible to achieve; *considered the idea of … anathema* = very strongly disliked the idea; *embraced* = included / took into account; *consolidated its dispersed software competence* = made its varied software more unified; *cross platform* = able to be used on different operating systems.
- Encourage discussion of the main themes.
- Ask learners to identify the key lessons relating to change for IBM and for themselves, and to present them as a statement to the rest of the group. There are some possible conclusions in the Answer Key that learners can use as a guide.
- **Further step:** There are many quotations about change. Elicit favourite quotes from the class, e.g. *I don't mind change as long as I don't have to do anything different.*

REVIEW

- Go through the Language Notes and Useful Phrases in the Course Book, if you have not already done so.
- Check that items listed under Vocabulary in the Language Notes in the Course Book have been covered.
- Encourage learners to note down the terms they found particularly useful – especially the ones they need in their working lives.
- Make a note of this language for your own future reference.

Answers

1 Core practice
a i [F]   b i [T] / [U]   c i [F]   d i [F]

2 Language check
1 c   2 c   3 a   4 b   5 b
6 c   7 c   8 b   9 a   10 a

3 Listening
1 (*possible answers*)
- There was no direct dial out.
- To make an outside call, he had to ask the operator to connect him.
- He didn't have a computer on his desk.
- He wrote letters by hand and gave them to the typing pool to type.
- There were very few photocopiers.
- You needed authorisation to use the photocopier.
- When he was travelling on business, nobody could contact him.

Dealing with change   27

4 Writing

The content of the email will depend on a number of factors, including your relationship with the customer, the service you offer and the cultural context. This answer assumes two global companies and a change from local to global / regional provision.

(*possible answers*)

Dear …

Current changes

I am writing in connection with proposed changes to the management of your account. As you may have heard, we plan in future to process orders centrally. This is part of our continuing drive to offer the best service possible to valued customers like yourselves.

In the new structure, the Asian Sales and Service team, under Romi Chouhan, will be responsible for meeting your needs. Centralising resources in this way will give you a number of benefits, including better order tracking and faster response times. Ms Chouhan will be in touch with you in the next few days to explain the improvements in more detail. Her contact details are …

From the 1st September my team will no longer be involved on a day-to-day basis. If you have any concerns or queries, please do not hesitate to contact me.

On a personal note may I say how much I have enjoyed working with you, and on behalf of my company may I say how much we are looking forward to building our business relationship in the future.

With best regards

5 Case study

(*possible answers*)

The lessons

IBM was able to bounce back because it stayed together, rather than breaking up into pieces. In this way, it retained options and the ability to add value in new ways. Becoming a successful integrator, for instance, was only possible because it possessed knowledge of software, networking and hardware.

Moreover, Gerstner shifted IBM's focus from products to the entire value chain. His non-IBM background helped to bring objectivity to the situation. It enabled him to see beyond the company to wider changes in the industry.

Finally, IBM's turnaround was due to Gerstner's leadership ability, an attribute often underemphasised in hi-tech industries. He combined a great ability to lead people with powerful strategic insight.

Adapted from *Business Life* magazine

Audioscripts

1 Core practice

a – I started work on the new catalogue in February. The work went well and I finished the job in about five and a half weeks. Then, at the beginning of May, I had to revise it all because the marketing director wanted to include a range of products we'd just bought in. But he said the Board didn't want the production timetable delayed in any way. At first I didn't think it would be possible, but once I'd entered all the new data, I found that the job wasn't as difficult as I'd expected. The team helped a lot.
 – Did you meet the deadline?
 – Yes, but just prior to the delivery they tried to change the spec again.

b – There have been some changes in the last few months. As you know, a new managing director has just been appointed. He became MD three weeks ago.
 – Was he an internal appointment?
 – In a way. He was from within the group, although I'd never met him. He'd been running our Spanish subsidiary.
 – Who did he take over from?
 – Beatrice Guyon, the previous MD; she's been promoted to the main board. She's now group financial controller.

c Our factory in Scotland has just been closed down. We used to make our industrial filters there, but recently production has been switched to China. Nowadays, margins are so tight that we can't afford to manufacture locally. In the last year, we've been forced to cut prices twice. These days, the European end of the operation concentrates on planning and marketing – that's all. Head Office has even cut back on R&D.

d – What difference will the reorganisation make?
 – We used to process orders locally, but now the back and middle office functions are moving to Milan, orders are going to be processed centrally.
 – So, the transactions you used to handle here are moving?
 – Yes, to the global customer care team.
 – How will it affect the service for people like me?
 – There should be no difference in the day-to-day running of your account. But if you have any problems you can always call me.

3 Listening

Mark Jarvis works in aircraft manufacturing

I woke this morning and turned on my PDA to check my overnight emails, which I then replied to in the taxi to Heathrow Terminal 1. Next, I checked in and settled into the departure lounge, where, with a hot latté, I connected to the Internet and downloaded my corporate mail with attachments. How different from when I started work at British Aerospace 22 years ago. I had a desk with a telephone and a filing tray. What did I do every day? Imagine coming to the office and sitting down at your desk with only a phone and not even direct dial – to place an outside call, you had to ask the operator to connect you. If I needed a letter typed, I had to write it and give it to the typing pool. They would type it with carbon copies that I would proofread and correct. There was one photocopier for 3,000 people that you needed authorisation to use! If you travelled overseas, for example to Nepal, you would be gone for two weeks and nobody could phone you – and you couldn't phone them.

(Adapted from *Business Life* magazine; the words of Mark Jarvis are spoken by an actor.)

UNIT 5 Culture and values

PREPARATION

- It is possible to complete this unit at different speeds, in more or less detail. The fast track takes about 1½ hours, the standard track about 2 hours, and the comprehensive track about 3 hours. For more information on the three options, see the notes in the Introduction on pages 10 and 11.
- For details of the aims of the unit, look at the Contents box on this page, the Language Notes at the end of the Course Book unit and the Useful Phrases below.
- If available to you, you can use the exercises in the Self-study Guide as extra practice.
- If you have taught this unit before, review the notes you made at the time.

USEFUL PHRASES

I used to work for a company in the UK.
It was a very traditional organisation.
The culture was very old-fashioned.
They weren't interested in innovation.

The workforce was skilled but unmotivated.
Junior staff were very badly treated.
Staff turnover was high.
The main aim was to avoid risk.

I've been working here for three months.
When I first started, it all seemed a bit strange.
I had never worked for a Japanese company before.
Previously, I had been working with manual systems.

When I first started, the department was much bigger.
We used to check the machines by hand.
The technology involved has changed completely.
The equipment had to be upgraded.

We've been learning new skills.
The company has been investing a fortune in training.
Our working practices are changing.
It is a very competitive environment.

The atmosphere is extremely businesslike.
We work together as a team.
There are good bonus and incentive schemes.
The management attach a lot of importance to loyalty.
We're all highly motivated.

LEAD IN (SUGGESTIONS)

- Check how learners have prepared for the lesson – see the Preparation section at the start of the unit in the Course Book (page 29). Have they looked at the Useful Phrases on page 32 in the Course Book (copied above)?
- Check whether learners have brought brochures and / or web pages relating to their company's culture, values, direction, the mission, etc. If you can use these resources in the lesson, it will make the relevance of the content more obvious.
- You might lead into the lesson by asking participants to talk about the culture and values of their organisations – making use of the work they have prepared. Have your own contribution ready.

Contents

Expressions
It was a traditional / progressive company.
The workforce was skilled but unmotivated.
Working practices have been changing.
The management attach a lot of importance to loyalty.

Language check
Past tenses, of continuous forms
Opposites of adjectives:
friendly / unfriendly,
honest / dishonest
Vocabulary: *mission, aim, strategy, enterprising, innovative, progressive, bureaucratic, cautious, critical, look after, try out, fit in*

Practice
Writing for advice on working practices and values
Discussing corporate culture
A questionnaire on values at work

1 CORE PRACTICE

Listening and speaking

- The exercise is in two parts – listening and speaking. The listening activity (part i) provides learners with ideas and models for the speaking activity (part ii).
- Ask learners to identify the verbal clues they used when answering the comprehension questions in part i.
- In part ii, encourage learners to adapt the scenarios to their needs. Where possible, they should introduce the documents they have brought to class.
- Question a: The speaker has a non-standard UK accent. Indicate that *middle of the road* = average; *your face didn't fit* = you did not belong; *get on* = progress.
- Question b: The second speaker has a non-standard accent. Explain that *premium (prices)* = higher than usual; *walked out* = left; *I didn't fit in* = I wasn't accepted.
- Question c: Point out that *cutting-edge* = technically very advanced; *sunshine industries* = companies in high-tech sectors; *attach ... importance to* = consider to be important.
- Question d: Explain that *joint venture* = project where two or more companies join together; *put up with* = tolerate.
- **Further step:** When learners have completed their individual practice in part ii, ask them to prepare and perform it to the rest of the class. Video the sketches and use the recordings to analyse wider communication factors such as body language.

2 LANGUAGE CHECK

- The multiple-choice questions enable you to treat the language programme flexibly. Points that are known can be handled briefly. Points that require more remedial attention can be explored in more detail. The Specific Points section below gives you further detailed guidance.
- When working on vocabulary questions, point out the Vocabulary notes in the Language Reference at the end of the unit in the Course Book and the Glossary on pages 158 – 160. Introduce, as necessary, any special terms that learners need.
- For each question consider the following options.
  - Identify the answer.
  - Explore why the other options are wrong.
  - Ask learners to prepare examples that relate to their working needs, e.g.:
    Question 1: *The new management were trying to introduce a more enterprising culture, but it wasn't working.*
    Amended version: *We were trying to break into new markets but we weren't having much success.*
- **Further step:** Working in pairs, invite learners to prepare statements about company culture, their own or another, using as many of the terms listed in the Vocabulary section as possible, e.g.:
  I work in an enterprising environment. It's an innovative company. The manager I report to is very supportive. In my previous job the culture was very bureaucratic and traditional, which I found demotivating. Staff turnover was high and there was a lot of absenteeism.

SPECIFIC POINTS

Questions 1 to 6: Past tense – Simple and Continuous (BGG 1.2, 1.3, 1.4 1.5)

- Q1: Ensure learners understand the meaning of *work* here (= be successful). The Past Continuous must be used to agree with the tense in the first clause. A time line might be useful to illustrate a period of time continuing in the past but not up to the present (BGG 1.4). Note also the use of a plural verb after *management*. This is quite common after a singular noun which refers to a group of people (e.g. *company, government, police*). Explain that *enterprising* = imaginative and willing to undertake new (often risky) projects.
- Q2: The correct choice of tense here (Present Perfect Continuous) indicates an activity happening over a period of time until the present (BGG 1.3).
- Q3: Note the Past Perfect Simple (not Continuous) must be used here as the verb refers to a single completed action (BGG 1.3). To practise this sequence of tenses, you could ask learners to complete the following:

  We got there early but … (all the best tables had been reserved).
  I rang you yesterday morning but … (you had already left the office).

- Q4: Ask learners to try to make similar sentences with *so* to practise the Past Perfect Continuous, e.g.:
  I had been living in the UK for two years so I was used to driving on the left.
  She had been driving for four hours so she was very tired.
  Alternatively, you could just write the *so* clause on the board and ask learners to suggest (verbally or in writing) a suitable beginning.
- Q5: Time expressions. Elicit tenses (and example sentences) that could be used with *recently* and *for several months now*, e.g.:
  I saw him recently. / I haven't heard from her recently.
  (Note the use of the Past Simple for a specific event in the recent past.)
  She's been off work for several months now. / We've been having problems for several months now.

Questions 6 to 8: The opposite of adjectives using prefixes (BGG 13.2)

- To practise, go round the class. One person provides an adjective (e.g. *efficient, normal, overpaid*). He / she invites another member of the class to give the opposite (e.g. *inefficient, abnormal, underpaid*). This could also be played as a team game. You could include words where the opposite is a completely different word (e.g. *sharp / blunt; modern / old-fashioned*).

Questions 9 and 10: Vocabulary and verb phrases

- Review the examples in the Vocabulary section of the Language Notes. Elicit / provide synonyms where possible. Explain that *staff turnover* = the number of people who leave an organisation and are replaced; *head count* = the number of people employed.

3 WRITING

Panasonic's values

1
- Explain the background to the information on the bookmark (see page 30 of the Course Book).
  - The Panasonic Basic Business Philosophy is an expression of a company's culture. It states the core values and the actions that arise from those values.
  - The Basic Management Objective (i.e. the mission) is to live the values through the actions.
- Ask learners to work in pairs to rewrite the Values and Actions as fuller statements. Gloss as necessary: *autonomous management* = having the power to make their own decisions and work independently; *co-existence and mutual prosperity*

= being able to live together (peacefully) and create wealth for everyone. Point out that the main task is to supply a verb that can be used with the noun phrase, as in the example in the Course Book. To make the task easier, you could supply a range of verbs on the board (e.g. *demonstrate, practise, make, show, use, put, support, encourage, strive for, foster*). This is a good exercise in collocation.

2
- Here learners might work in groups of three or four to prepare a list of their top ten values.
- Encourage learners to use the documents they have brought to class for reference.

4 LISTENING

Working abroad

1
- The recording is based on a real interview but the details are fictitious.
- The interviewer has a Dutch accent.
- Questions for further discussion arising from the recording include the following.
  - What are the manager's attitudes to the local Dutch community?
  - How important is it to learn the language if you want to integrate into another culture?

2
- Lead into the email-writing activity by asking those learners who have lived and / or worked in another country to say something about their experiences. What problems would your learners foresee if they were to move to another country or another region of their own country?
- There are some Useful Phrases on page 133 of the Course Book and a sample message in the answers.

5 QUESTIONNAIRE

Courtesy at work

1
- Gloss the language of the questionnaire and discuss the issues which generate the most interest. Explain that *a blunder* = a mistake; *(an) upheaval* = a big / sudden change (causing or involving a lot of difficulty).
- Depending on the composition of your class, you may need to adapt the quiz. If your learners do not work for a company, ask them to answer from a hypothetical point of view.
- As you work out the quiz scores, ask your learners whether they agree with the scoring system and the interpretation given. How would they vary it?
- **Further step:** Elicit other questions which your learners feel could be included in a questionnaire of this nature, e.g.:

Whose job would it be to make the coffee?
How would you deal with an employee who came to work in inappropriate clothes?

2
- This is the stage of the lesson where learners can discuss the specific cultures of their own and other companies. Refer to the box on page 31 of the Course Book and focus on the categories that interest your class members.
- **Further step:** Extend the discussion to cover learners' observations on courtesy in other countries. Are there any noticeable differences? Are they ever surprised by the way people behave?

REVIEW

- Go through the Language Notes and Useful Phrases in the Course Book, if you have not already done so.
- Check that the items listed under Vocabulary in the Language Notes in the Course Book have been covered.
- Encourage learners to note down the terms they found useful – especially the ones they need in their work.
- Make a note of this language for your own future reference.

Answers

1 Core practice
a i [F]   b i [U]   c i [T]   d i [F]

2 Language check
1 b   2 c   3 a   4 a   5 c
6 a   7 b   8 b   9 a   10 c

3 Writing
(*possible answers*)
Values
- Seek to make a contribution to society.
- Practise fairness and honesty.
- Foster cooperation and team spirit.
- Make continuing efforts for improvement.
- Demonstrate courtesy and humility in your working relationships.
- Demonstrate adaptability wherever possible.
- Show gratitude wherever it is justified.

Actions
- Put the customer first in all your dealings.
- Use profit as a measure of your contribution and the contribution of others.
- Strive for successful co-existence and mutual prosperity.
- Support good management based on the collective wisdom of colleagues and co-workers.
- Encourage fair competition.
- Always put people before products.

4 Listening

(*possible answers*)

1 a She's enjoyed her stay so far; people have been very kind.
   b Everyone's been friendly and helpful, and she's been welcomed by the group.
   c Her main role is to be the contact person between the new company in Holland and the head office in Manchester.
   d Some of the people there refuse to speak anything but Dutch.
   e The head office is in Britain. This is the first Hub Textiles factory in Holland.
   f No, there don't seem to be any drawbacks.

2

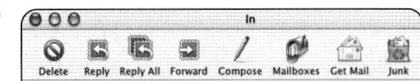

Dear Mr Unas
I am writing in connection with my move to Malaysia.
As you know, I am due to start work on 27 June. Before then, I need to organise:
- accommodation for my family – there are four of us
- schools for a daughter of 11 and a son of 7
- a car.

I would be grateful for any information you can send me. Could you let me have the contact details of the people I should speak to, please?
I would also welcome any general advice you may have on matters such as weather conditions, dress codes and tipping.
Finally, can you recommend a good Malay phrase book?
Many thanks.
Regards

Audioscripts

1 Core practice

a We use to be a middle-of-the road company; the workforce was skilled but fairly unmotivated – it was the kind of place where if your face didn't fit you couldn't get on. The management were living in the past. Then, 18 months ago, we were taken over, and we got a new managing director – an American. And the change was dramatic. She introduced new technology – we all had to learn new skills.

b – We used to produce high quality products that sold at premium prices, at the top end of the market. Many of the processes were still done by hand. I wanted to mechanise some of the operations, but the bosses weren't interested. They were only concerned about one thing – the exclusivity of their products. And they weren't concerned about modern ideas of staff relations.
   – How were the workers motivated?
   – Erm, they used to pay well. They weren't bad employers; the management style was just very old fashioned.
   – What about staff turnover?
   – It was quite low. Some people couldn't stand the atmosphere and walked out, but unemployment in the area was over 17%.
   – How long were you there?
   – Only six months; I didn't fit in.

c The people I work for are very willing to try out new ideas. It's a young company – we're involved in a lot of cutting-edge technology and we're working in an expanding market. It's one of the so-called 'sunshine industries'. So my work is changing all the time. Change is the norm. It's like a constant learning and retraining process. The atmosphere is extremely businesslike, but it isn't at all formal. We work together in teams – whoever has the right mix of skills becomes responsible for the job. The management attach a lot of importance to motivation – they expect you to think for yourself.

d I'd never worked with Japanese managers before – this is a joint venture with a Japanese company. Previously I'd been working with manual systems, and here all the equipment is state of the art – we use all the most up-to-date methods. About 80% of the operation is automated. It took me a little time to get used to it. But everyone here is very supportive. The company is very well run. Everyone in the company from the top to the bottom knows the importance of quality and customer service – the management won't put up with low-quality work.

4 Listening

– People in the factory have been very kind to me. I've really enjoyed my stay here so far.
– You have not found it difficult to get on with people, and to do your job here?
– Not at all. No. Everyone's been very friendly and helpful. I've been really welcomed into the group, so to speak. And when I have tried to learn Dutch they are all very helpful. I've been having lessons here, and I attended some intensive training courses before I came.
– So you have learnt quite a lot.
– I really don't know if it's quite a lot, but I try to manage. There are some people who refuse to speak anything but Dutch, and I have to be able to say something and to understand something in the factory.
– How are you getting on in your job here? What is your job exactly?
– Well, this is the first factory for Hub Textiles in Holland, and that's why everything is new, not only for me but for the whole organisation. I suppose that my main role is to be the contact person between the new company here and our head office in Manchester. I need to find out a lot more about this market, the area, how customers behave here, and how the factory needs to operate in the market. To report this information back to the UK is possibly my most important job.

32 UNIT 5

UNIT 6 Environmental issues

PREPARATION

- There are three possible tracks through the unit: fast (about 1¹/₂ hours), standard (about 2 hours) and comprehensive (about 3 hours). For more information on the different tracks, see the notes in the Introduction on pages 10 and 11.
- For details of the aims of the unit, look at the Contents box on this page, the Language Notes at the end of the Course Book unit and the Useful Phrases below.
- If available to you, you can use the Self-study Guide as a source of supplementary exercises on the key themes of the unit.
- There is a Progress Test covering Units 1 to 6 on pages 140 – 141, which can be photocopied and circulated. The answers are on page 148. For best results, give learners time to prepare.

USEFUL PHRASES

What impact are green issues having on your business?
Customers are worried about the environmental impact of the products they buy.
People ask questions about our environmental practices.
Environmental performance is a competitive issue.

We are running out of landfill sites.
We now recycle our waste.
We used to throw it away.
The cost of waste disposal is so high that recycling is economically viable.

How are the new laws affecting you?
laws   regulations   guidelines
They are adding to our costs.
Something has to be done about pollution.
The level of air pollution is rising.
But in our view the cost of compliance is too high.

Alternative sources of energy are very important.
They say that existing supplies will run out in 20 years' time.
We can't rely on green technologies to fill the gap.
We believe that conservation is the key.

I don't accept that we have an energy problem.
There are many alternative sources.
How do you feel about nuclear energy?
What about the environmental costs?
We need a source of renewable energy.

LEAD IN (SUGGESTIONS)

- Refer to the Preparation section at the start of the unit in the Course Book (page 33). Check whether learners have come ready to speak about green strategies. Have they brought to class related documents? If so, these can be used as a resource throughout the lesson.
- Check also whether they have looked at the Useful Phrases on page 36 in the Course Book (copied above).
- Consider leading into the subject by eliciting comments on the topic from each member of the group. The comments may indicate which areas of the target language they need to focus on.

Contents

Expressions
What impact are green issues having on your business?
How are the new regulations affecting you?
In our view the environmental costs are too high.
We believe that conservation is the key.

Language check
Terms used in discussion: *In my view ..., I take your point ...*
Adverbs used in phrases: *environmentally friendly, extremely dangerous*
Vocabulary: *pollution, spillage, waste, global warming, green issues, bottle bank, recycling plant, clean up, get rid of, use up*

Practice
An article on nuclear processing
Answering a complaint from the public
Case study: The Body Shop

1 CORE PRACTICE

Listening and speaking

- This exercise provides an opportunity to practise a range of situations relating to environmental issues.
- The exercise is in two parts – listening and speaking. The listening activity (part i) provides learners with ideas and models for the speaking activity (part ii).
- Ask learners to identify the verbal clues they used when answering the comprehension questions in part i.
- In part ii, encourage learners to adapt the scenarios to their needs. Where possible they should introduce the realia documents they have brought to the class.
- Question a: Point out that *exhaust emissions* = waste gases from an engine (e.g. cars); *used up* = consumed / exhausted.
- Question b: The first speaker has a Scottish accent, the second a Latin-American accent. Explain that *take ... for granted* = to fail to appreciate the value.
- Question c: The first speaker has a US accent.
- Question d: The first speaker has a non-standard UK accent, the second a US accent. Tell learners that *running out of* = exhausting the supply; *landfill site(s)* = hole(s) in the ground where waste is dumped.
- **Further step**: If possible, video learners during part ii and analyse the recordings for wider communication factors. If relevant, draw attention to the fact that in different cultures body language may be interpreted in different ways.

Environmental issues 33

2 LANGUAGE CHECK

- The multiple-choice questions provide a starting point for the Language Check. Ensure that the related language points are explored and revised as necessary. The Specific Points section below gives you further detailed guidance.
- Adapt the points to learners' needs. Concentrate on areas where practice is needed.
- When working on vocabulary questions, introduce special terms not covered that the class need. Point out the Glossary on pages 158 – 160.
- For each question consider the following options.
  - Identify the answer.
  - Explore why the other options are wrong.
  - Ask learners to prepare examples that relate to their working needs, e.g.:
    Question 1: *Do you go along with the new guidelines?*
    Amended version: *Do you agree with the management proposals for reducing our paper waste?*
- **Further step:** Ask learners to summarise some of the opinions on the environment that have been expressed during the lesson.

SPECIFIC POINTS

Questions 1 and 2: Asking for and giving opinions (BGG 21.3)
- Q1: Ask learners to provide other ways of asking for opinions (both *yes / no* and *wh-* questions), then give a range of replies, e.g.:
  - *What do you think of the new legislation?*
  - *It's ridiculous / unworkable.*
  - *It's a great improvement / ... step forward.*
  - *Are you happy with the new recycling guidelines?*
  - *Not really. / I suppose so. / Not at all.*
- Q2: Elicit other ways of introducing an opinion, e.g.:
  In my opinion ...
  From my point of view ...
  The way I see it ...
  Encourage learners to voice their own opinions on the environment using one of these phrases. Ensure they stress *I / my*.

Question 3: *effect* and *affect*
- Elicit other uses of the noun *effect* and the verb *affect*:
  - *Will the new regulations have a big effect on your business?*
  - *They won't affect us at all.*

Question 4: Use of adverbs to modify meaning (BGG 14.4)
- Note *fairly* weakens the meaning of the adjective. Here *fairly* would be grammatically correct but the meaning would be wrong. *completely* and *extremely* both intensify the meaning of a following adjective. However, *completely* cannot be used here because it can only be used with an ungradable adjective (where the meaning is absolute and cannot vary in degree). *dangerous* is a gradable adjective.

Note some other combinations with *completely*: *completely destroyed; completely successful; completely different; completely sure.*

Question 5: Adverbs used with adjectives (BGG 14.4)
- Explain that *technically possible* = possible from a technical point of view.
- The adverbs *technically, environmentally, logically, financially, politically, economically* are commonly used in combination with adjectives, e.g.:
  It isn't very environmentally friendly.
  It would be economically disastrous.
  Ask learners to suggest some more combinations.

Question 6: *level / volume / number of* + countable / uncountable nouns
- Go through the examples in the Language Notes. Elicit which can be used with countable nouns only (= *number*), uncountable nouns only (= *level, degree, amount*) and both countable / uncountable (= *quantity, volume*).
- Give some nouns and ask learners to choose a suitable *amount / level* word, e.g.:
  traffic – the level / amount / volume of traffic
  unemployment – the level / amount of unemployment
  factories – the number of factories
  difficulty – the level / degree of difficulty.

Questions 7 to 9: Environmental vocabulary
- Refer to the Vocabulary section in the Language Notes.
- Point out that *alternative technologies* = technologies that use renewable resources (e.g. wind farms, solar panels); *sustainable* = not using up the world's natural resources; *organic* = not using chemicals to grow food or raise animals; *biodegradable* = breaks down naturally in the environment; *a bottle bank* = a large container into which you put bottles or glass for recycling; *an incineration plant* = a place where rubbish is burnt; *to phase out* = to remove in stages (over a period of time); *to decommission* = to take out of use.
- Q8: Note that *dumping* = leaving rubbish in a place where it should not be left.
- Q9: Point out that *spillages* = escapes of liquid (e.g. oil) from a container.

Question 10: Verb phrases
- Go through the verb phrases in the Language Notes. Ensure learners know that *run out* is followed by *of* with a following noun (e.g. *run out of oil*).
- Elicit the passive of *use up*, which could also be correct here. Explain that *to get rid of* = to remove or throw away (something unwanted).

3 READING

Radioactive waste

1. - After your learners have filled the gaps in the text, check their understanding of the words they did not use.

34 UNIT 6

- Elicit collocations based on the language in the box (e.g. *illegal emissions, energy conservation, compulsory recycling, landfill site*). Then invite your learners to relate the language back to their own experiences, e.g.:
  There has been a reduction in the number of landfill sites in this area.
  The surrounding lakes are badly polluted.

2
- Lead a discussion about nuclear power based on the questions listed on page 34 of the Course Book.
- Encourage learners to focus on cost effective sustainable options.
- If the point isn't made by the group, introduce the fact that nuclear power has a smaller carbon footprint (volume of carbon emissions) than many alternative forms of power.
- Ask participants to weigh up the long-term environmental costs of the nuclear option against the fact that in some ways it is more sustainable.

4 WRITING
A complaint from the public

- In this exercise learners work in pairs.
- Partner A has to reply to an environmental complaint using Partner B as a technical adviser.
- The text of the complaint is in the exercise. There is extra information for Partner B on page 133 of the Course Book about how to reply to a message of complaint.
- There is a sample reply to the complaint in the answers.
- For an easier task, ask learners to look at the sample reply first and link Partner B's notes to parts of the letter, identifying and noting down individual phrases where appropriate (e.g. apologise to the sender for any inconvenience or discomfort = *We very much regret any inconvenience or unpleasantness caused*). They could then write the letter from Partner B's notes, incorporating phrases they have remembered or noted down.
- **Further step:** Discuss with the group whether they agree with the advice given to Partner B on replying to a complaint. Some professionals advise against admitting liability, which means never apologising.

5 CASE STUDY
The Body Shop

1
- The speaker is the environmental audit manager from the Body Shop. The Body Shop is a franchise operation which has stores selling a range of goods, including toiletries and cosmetics, in many countries worldwide. The Body Shop was originally founded in 1976 by Anita and Gordon Roddick – their first shop was in Brighton – but in 2006 they sold the business to cosmetics giant L'Oreal.
- Lead in to the exercise by asking your learners if they have heard of the Body Shop chain.
  - What do they know about it?
  - Do they shop in the Body Shop or other shops that share a similar philosophy?
  - Do they make an effort to shop in so-called 'green' stores?
- Gloss specific vocabulary from the audioscript before playing the recording, e.g. *a set of benchmarks* (see Glossary); *dead against* (slang for *totally opposed to*); *secondary packaging* (a retailing term meaning the goods are pre-packaged for enhancement purposes).

2
- Ask learners to study the download from the Body Shop homepage and work out their own position on the green strategies advertised.
- Then ask them to establish a group position on each of the strategies.
- Encourage them to practise during the activity the terms used in discussion listed in the Language Notes.

REVIEW

- Go through the Language Notes and Useful Phrases in the Course Book, if you have not already done so.
- Check that the items listed under Vocabulary in the Language Notes in the Course Book have been covered.
- Make a note of the language your learners found particularly useful for future reference.
- Encourage learners to practise the new language they have learnt in their live communication. They might use Post-It notes to remind themselves.

Answers

1 Core practice
- a i They agree 'on the whole' that population control is the key issue – the second speaker does not agree completely.
- b i They are arguing about whether there is an energy problem.
- c i Because environmental performance is now a competitive issue.
- d i Yes, but he / she thinks there is too much.

2 Language check

| 1 c | 2 a | 3 a | 4 c | 5 a |
| 6 c | 7 c | 8 b | 9 b | 10 a |

Environmental issues 35

3 Reading
a waste b reprocessing
c disaster d recycle
e Environmentalists f leakages
g dump

The writer of this article is fair (see the last paragraph), but the overall tone is critical, as the following expressions / references demonstrate:
- environmentalists who fear another Chernobyl-like disaster
- the traffic is bound to increase
- Environmentalists point to the dangers involved
- the threat to the local environment
- a number of radiation leakages
- reprocessing is dirty, dangerous and uneconomic
- a nuclear dump.

4 Writing
(*possible answer*)

Dear …

Discharge Zone 26

Thank you for your message about a discharge from one of the chimneys on our Zone 26 site. We very much regret any inconvenience or unpleasantness caused by the yellow dust. Our Environmental Protection Team say the dust is a sulphur by-product – it is inert, non-corrosive and non-toxic unless ingested in large quantities.

The discharge was caused by a mistake in the application of a new cleaning process. A human error allowed an amount of yellow dust to escape into the atmosphere for about 11 minutes, when the error was spotted and corrected. Our environmental support team are now reviewing the situation and checking how this error can be prevented in future. I will contact you again when they report back to me.

In the mean time, they say the dust in question can be washed away with cold water. Most of it will disappear completely as soon as it rains. Any expense claims arising from the spillage should be sent to me at the address above. We will of course meet valid claims in full.

I would like to stress that we have an excellent environmental safety record, and to reassure you that we will do everything possible to ensure that an error like this does not happen in future. If you would like further information please contact me direct on the number given above.

Best wishes

5 Case study
1 The speaker refers to a and c.

Audioscripts

1 Core practice
a – As far as I'm concerned, the key issue is population control.
 – What about global warming?
 – I agree that exhaust emissions and so on are a big problem. But I think the central issue, the cause, is overpopulation. The earth's resources are being used up at an alarming rate. In my view, we have to ensure that we deal with the cause, not the effects.
 – I agree on the whole …

b – We tend to take energy supplies for granted. But the truth is that oil and natural gas supplies will only last a few decades.
 – I take your point, but I don't really go along with the idea that the world has an energy problem. We have enough coal to last hundreds of years – and there are many alternative sources of energy.
 – Look, I don't think we can rely on green technologies to supply all our energy needs.
 – OK, but what about nuclear power? We have enough uranium to last thousands of years.
 – And what about the environment costs?

c – Where do you stand on green issues?
 – As a company we believe it makes sound business sense to have environmentally friendly policies. New environmental regulations are coming in every year.
 – Specifically, how does the situation affect your company?
 – Well, we are moving over to an environmental procurement policy. This means that when we are awarding contracts to suppliers, we ask questions about their environmental practices. Environmental performance is now a competitive issue.

d – We manufacture soft drinks, which we sell in aluminium cans, and the new government legislation requires us to recycle 50% of the cans used. Basically, they're running out of landfill sites where they can bury rubbish.
 – How does the legislation affect you?
 – From our point of view, it's bad news. We're having to spend a lot more on collection. I suppose something has to be done about pollution, but my personal view is that the volume of environmental legislation is too high at the moment.

5 Case study
– Can you explain to me, what is an environmental audit?
– These days, environmental auditing is defined quite well in various textbooks and even now in European Law. An audit really is an opportunity to take stock of your environmental performance against a set of benchmarks or standards which are now universally accepted. But within … for example, the European Union Eco-management and Audit Regulation, the audit is only one part of an overall, comprehensive approach to minimising and managing your effects on the environment.
– Now could you tell me something about your packaging policy?
– The Body Shop has a quite radical approach to packaging which follows … best practice, we believe, and also the most forward thinking approaches that … come from a non-profit sector. And we have a very very strong commitment to minimising waste in the first instance, so anyone who walks into one of our stores will see that the … packaging we use is absolutely minimal. We are dead against having … secondary packaging just to make the products look good; we are absolutely against that. Er, but we go further, so once we have minimised, we are committed to … reusing packaging, so again we have a fairly unique system for refilling our packaging where customers can bring their bottles back to the stores and have them refilled … with a discount on the purchase price … for the item that they are buying.

UNIT 7 Recruitment and training

PREPARATION

- It is possible to complete this unit at different speeds, in more or less detail. The fast track takes about 1½ hours, the standard track about 2 hours and the comprehensive track about 3 hours. For more information on the three options, see the notes in the Introduction on pages 10 and 11.
- For details of the aims of the unit, look at the Contents box on this page, the Language Notes at the end of the Course Book unit and the Useful Phrases below.
- If available to you, you can use the exercises in the Self-study Guide as extra practice.
- If you have taught the unit before, review the notes you made at the time.

USEFUL PHRASES

I joined the company straight from school.
Most of my training has been on the job.
I qualified in chemical engineering at Berlin University.
I have a degree in Business Studies.

We get most of our people through job-search sites.
We get a large number of unsolicited applications.
We make very little use of recruitment agencies.
We also post vacancies on our website.

I'm ringing about your advert for a product manager.
Could you give me some further details?
What kind of person are you looking for?
Could you tell me something about yourself?

Have you filled in your PDP (personal development plan)?
You haven't put anything in the final column.
You need to decide your action steps.
How are you going to improve your performance?
Do you want me to go through the form with you?

I'd like to go on a documentation course.
Is there one you could recommend?
There's nothing advertised on the web page.
Can I go on the waiting list?

I was very happy with the course.
I was disappointed.
The course didn't really stretch us.
The course was very demanding.

LEAD IN (SUGGESTIONS)

- Check how learners have prepared for the lesson – see the Preparation section at the start of the unit in the Course Book (page 37). Have they looked at the Useful Phrases on page 40 in the Course Book (copied above)?
- Check whether they have brought to class a job advertisement, an application form and training information. These can be used as a resource later in the lesson.
- Consider leading into the subject by asking learners how they were recruited. Participants who are at college might talk about the college's admission strategies.

Contents

Expressions
We get most of our applications through job-search sites.
What kind of person are you looking for?
Have you filled in your personal development plan?
I'd like to go on a documentation course.

Language check
Relative clauses, defining and non-defining
Prepositions in relative clauses
Vocabulary: *resume, bio, CV, background, history, record, university, college, institute, short list, turn down, fill in*

Practice
Talking about training experiences
Filling in a personal development planner
A job application letter

1 CORE PRACTICE

Listening and speaking

- This exercise provides an opportunity to practise a range of situations relating to recruitment and training.
- The exercise is in two parts – listening and speaking. The listening activity (part i) provides learners with ideas and models for the speaking activity (part ii).
- In part ii, encourage learners to adapt the scenarios to their needs. Where possible they should introduce the documents they have brought to class.
- Question a: The first speaker has a Scottish accent. Explain that *small ads* = classified advertisements in newspapers or at the back of magazines; *head hunters* = people or companies that find senior staff and offer them jobs in other companies.
- Question b: The first speaker has a US accent.
- Question c: The speaker has an Indian accent. Explain that *took me on* = gave me a job; *day-release courses* = work-related courses which employees get time off work to attend.
- Question d: The first speaker has an Irish accent. Point out that a *portal* = an Internet site that provides links to useful information and other Internet sites.
- **Further step:** Ask learners to work individually or in pairs to prepare a further question for each dialogue.

2 LANGUAGE CHECK

- The multiple-choice questions link to the Language Notes at the end of the Course Book unit (page 40), and the related notes in the

Business Grammar Guide (see the booklet that accompanies the Course Book).
- The multiple-choice questions enable you to treat the language programme flexibly. Points that are known can be handled briefly. Points that require more remedial attention can be explored in more detail. The Specific Points section below gives you further in-depth guidance.
- When working on vocabulary questions, point out the Vocabulary notes in the Language Reference at the end of the unit in the Course Book, and the Glossary on pages 158 – 160. Introduce special terms that learners need, as necessary.
- Consider these options for each question.
  - Identify the answer.
  - Explore why the other options are wrong.
  - Ask learners to prepare examples that relate to their working needs, e.g.:
    Question 1: *I have spoken to everyone who is coming to the interview.*
    Amended version: *I was at school with the person who interviewed me.*
- **Further step:** Ask learners to put the examples in the questions into exchanges. What might the line before be? What could the next line be?

SPECIFIC POINTS

Questions 1 to 7: Relative clauses
- Talk through the examples in the Language Notes and the Business Grammar Guide (BGG 16.1). Ensure learners understand the differences between defining and non-defining relative clauses.
- Q1: Defining relative clauses – notice that no commas are needed before or after a defining relative clause. The relative pronoun *who* is the subject of the relative clause, so cannot be omitted. However, *who is* could be omitted here. This is because the relative pronoun can be omitted when followed by a form of *to be* + *-ing / -ed* verb, e.g.:
  I've spoken to everyone (who is / was) involved.
  The person (who is) dealing with this is off today.
- Q2: Possessive relative clauses – defining; see BGG 16.3 for further details. Explain that *the shortlist* = the list of candidates reduced from a longer list and from which the successful person will be chosen. Note also the verb *to shortlist / be shortlisted (for a job)*.
- Q3: Prepositions in non-defining relative clauses (BGG 16.2). Note that commas are needed before or after a non-defining relative clause. The clause adds new information; it is additional to the basic sentence. Note that *whom* and *which* (not *that*) are the only relative pronouns used after a preposition in a relative clause. Point out that just *where* (without *in*) could also be used here.
- Q4: Defining relative clauses. For some speakers, **b** and **c** might also be acceptable but **a** is the most natural and acceptable form, especially in the spoken language.

- Q5 and 6: Prepositions in defining relative clauses. These are both examples of informal style where the preposition is not at the beginning of the relative clause. The relative pronoun (*which / that* for a thing; *who / that* for a person) has been omitted. This is possible because in both questions the relative pronoun is the object of the verb in the relative clause (BGG 16.1, 16.2).
- Q6: Point out that a *CV* (*curriculum vitae*) is a summary of your personal details, education, work experience, etc. that you send to an employer when you apply for a job (US = *resumé*).
- Q7: Possessive relative clauses – non-defining (BGG 16.2). Notice the use of *of which* to refer to a noun which is a thing in the main clause (= *notebook*). Point out the word order (you cannot say *of which the contents* …). Some speakers might use *whose* for things as well as people in a defining relative clause (not possible in a non-defining relative clause).

Questions 8 to 10: Verb phrases
- Review the terms related to recruitment and training in the Vocabulary section of the Language Notes.
- Q8: Try to elicit *rejected* for *turned down*.
- Q9: There is no direct synonym for *get on*. Try to encourage learners to paraphrase, e.g.:
  The interview didn't go very well.
  I didn't do / manage very well.
  It would also be useful to practise the question form *How did you get on?* and responses.
- Q10: Point out that s*eeking* could be used for *looking for* but is a little formal. Check that learners can use the wrong options correctly.

3 LISTENING

Training

1
- The speakers are: (1) the English director of a market research company; (2) a Scottish Assistant Business Support Manager.
- Speaker 1: Point out that *on the job* (training) = provided or obtained while working; *strict training regimes* = systematic / fixed training programmes; *It's … been to do with* = it has involved.
- Speaker 2: *initial* (degree) = first; *I sat the … exams* = I took / did the …exams.
- The speakers' answers do not all fit neatly into the categories from *The Manager's Handbook* (see page 38 of the Course Book). Ask learners to summarise the main features of each speaker's training (or lack of it) and to give their impressions on the appropriacy of this training, e.g. Is it common for business support managers / accountants to have a degree in biochemistry, or for management trainers to have trained as secondary school teachers?

- Note that *The Manager's Handbook* (published by Ernst and Young), from which the table is adapted, is a useful reference book.

2
- Pre-experience learners can focus on specific aspects of their education and how this equips them for their working lives. All learners can talk about the courses which they would like to attend in the future.
- **Further step:** Ask learners to write a brief summary of their education and training to date as part of an application for a course.

4 WRITING
Application letter

- The aim here is to write an application letter.
- Go through the suggestions for writing such a letter set out in the exercise. Do learners agree with the four suggestions given in the box on page 38 of the Course Book? Is there anything missing that, in your view, would improve the application?
- Ask learners to go through the job advertisements they have brought to class. If possible, each learner should select one and write an application letter in response to that advertisement.
- Working individually or in pairs, learners then draft the letter.
- There is a sample letter in the answers. Ask learners to compare their work with the sample and modify if necessary.
- If you think your learners require further help with application letters, discuss other phrases which could be used, e.g.:

I am writing to apply for the position of ..., which I saw advertised in The Times */ on your website.*
I have considerable experience of (working with) ... / in the field of ... .

- The Internet is a good source of sample job application letters.
- **Further step:** If possible, ask someone from HR / Recruitment to review the letters.

5 APPLICATION
Personal development planning

- Have learners go through the five-step guide to using the personal development planner.
- Working in pairs, learners then go through the process and fill in the planner. A completed sample is given in the Support Materials on page 133 of the Course Book.
- **Further step:** Ask your manager or supervisor to review your planner and give feedback.

REVIEW

- Go through the Language Notes and Useful Phrases in the Course Book, if you have not already done so.
- Check that the items listed under Vocabulary in the Language Notes in the Course Book have been covered.
- Encourage learners to note down the terms they found useful – especially the ones they need in their work.
- Make a note of this language for your own future reference.
- Encourage learners to practise the new language they have learnt – to bring it into their communication.

Answers

1 Core practice
a i [F]   b i [T]   c i [U]   d i [U]

2 Language check
1 c   2 b   3 c   4 a   5 a
6 b   7 c   8 a   9 c   10 c

3 Listening
Acquiring skills and experience

	Speakers: 1	2
General business knowledge, e.g. health and safety trade affairs	☐	☐
Technical skills, basic knowledge needed to carry out specific tasks	☐	☐
Development of core skills through on-the-job training	✓	✓
Knowledge of related functions, e.g. finance and marketing	☐	✓
Business-related skills, e.g. communication, decisions-making, negotiating	✓	☐
People-related skills, e.g. leadership, motivation, team building, delegation	✓	☐

4 Writing
(possible answer)
Dear Sir / Madam
Service Manager Job Reference: MPSM-04
I enclose my completed application form, downloaded from your website, for the above position. I also enclose my CV.
I am extremely interested in this position. I qualified in electrical engineering from the University of Caracas three years ago, and have worked in the mobile phone business as a service engineer in Spain since then. As part of my continuing development, I took the KVD courses and recently passed my KVD Level 2 Diploma. I am now keen to move into a supervisory role.
I would very much appreciate the chance to meet you to answer any questions you might have about my qualifications and experience, and to find out more about the vacancy.
My contact details are as follows:
Mobile: ...
Email: ...
I look forward to meeting you.
Yours sincerely

Audioscripts

1 Core practice

a
- We normally use small ads in the local paper when we want to recruit operators, clerical staff, etc.
- What about managerial staff?
- Sometimes we advertise in the national press, but more often we post vacancies on the net – there are one or two specialised job-search sites we use. And for top positions we sometimes use head hunters.

b
- Is that the recruitment manager?
- Yes, it is.
- Hello, my name's Jeb Milhey. I'm calling about your advert for a Business Support Manager. The reference number is 27216. I sent you a couple of emails, but I don't think you got them.
- I'm sorry – let me check. Jeb Milhey – when did you send them?
- I sent the last one this morning.
- No, I didn't get it. If you give me your address, I'll send you the details and the application form – or you can get them from our website.

c I left school when I was 18 and started life as a trainee clerk in the bank. I actually just walked into the bank one day and asked if they had any vacancies. To my amazement, they took me on. I was sent on day-release courses and took various banking exams. By the time I was 30, I was manager of a local branch. Not long after that I was transferred to Head Office.

d
- I'm very keen to go on an export documentation course. Do you know of any? There have been so many changes recently that I'm very much out of date. Is the training department running anything at the moment? I've looked on the training portal and can't see anything.
- There's nothing at the moment, but we're thinking of doing something. We've had a lot of similar requests.

3 Listening

Speaker 1
I work in market research, in qualitative research. I've been doing it for about 12 years. The training I've had has been almost entirely on the job because I've worked in small companies which don't have strict training regimes. It's basically been to do with developing interviewing skills, developing the ability to listen to people as well as to talk to get the most out of people. Other training … has been to do with expressing myself verbally and in writing … and again that's been largely on the job with the help of people who have got more experience than I have.

Speaker 2
I'm an accountant and my job title is Assistant Business Support Manager, which basically involves producing month-end reports for both of the business managers and the US parent of the company. I have a degree in biochemistry – that was my initial degree – and after that I sat the Certified Institute of Management Accountancy exams while I was working. I've now been qualified for four years and I've been in my present job for four and a half years. Most of my training has been on-the-job training. I've done a few courses, but they were related to sitting and passing the accountancy exams.

UNIT 8 Staff relations

PREPARATION

- There are three possible tracks through the unit: fast (about 1½ hours), standard (about 2 hours) and comprehensive (about 3 hours). For more information on the different tracks, see the notes in the Introduction on pages 10 and 11.
- For details of the aims of the unit, look at the Contents box on this page, the Language Notes at the end of the Course Book unit and the Useful Phrases below. There are answers and audioscripts on page 44 of this book.
- There are supplementary exercises in the Self-study Guide.
- If you have taught this unit before, check the notes you made at the time.

USEFUL PHRASES

The firm encourages good relations between management and staff.
The workforce feel that they have a real stake in the company.
Many disputes are pay-related.
Compulsory redundancy has been a major issue.
There have been a number of stoppages.
In my view the bosses are out of touch.
The shop stewards have too much power.

There's a 'them and us' mentality.
Relations have deteriorated since the job cuts.
The atmosphere has improved since the new CEO took over.
We have a no-strike agreement.
Any disputes go to arbitration.

Have you had a chance to consider our proposals?
What's your reaction to our revised offer?
We feel the terms need to be improved.
We're doing what we can to meet your demands.

We will need to look at your proposals in detail.
I'm afraid we can't meet your demands in full.
We're prepared to meet you half way.
I'm afraid it's the best I can do.

Leave it with me ... I'll see what I can do.

LEAD IN (SUGGESTIONS)

- Refer to the Preparation section at the start of the unit in the Course Book (page 41). Check whether learners are prepared to talk about staff relations in their organisation. (Be aware, though, that this can be a sensitive area.) Have they brought related articles and reports to class? These can add variety and relevant context to the lesson.
- Check also whether they have looked at the Useful Phrases on page 44 in the Course Book (copied above).
- You might lead into the lesson by reviewing the articles and reports learners have brought to the class. Learners can introduce them, then answer questions from the rest of the group. Alternatively, you might discuss the picture on the first page of the unit (page 41). Why are group members standing in a line? Why are they smiling? Why are they clapping?

Contents

Expressions
There are good relations between management and staff.
The workforce feel they have a stake in the company.
Relations have deteriorated since the job cuts.
I'm afraid we can't meet your demands in full.

Language check
Terms for making and countering demands
Linking ideas: Not being in a union – *I can't get a job.*
Vocabulary: *strike, stoppage, dispute, job cut, compulsory redundancy, pay freeze, pay, reward, benefit, work out, work on, work under (pressure)*

Practice
Management / union issues
Simple negotiations
Assessing your manager
Assessing employee satisfaction (questionnaire)

1 CORE PRACTICE

Listening and speaking

- This exercise provides an opportunity to practise a range of situations relating to staff relations.
- The exercise is in two parts – listening and speaking. The listening activity (part i) provides learners with ideas and models for the speaking activity (part ii).
- Ask learners to identify the verbal clues they used when answering the comprehension questions in part i.
- In part ii, encourage learners to adapt the scenarios to their needs.
- Question a: Gloss as necessary. Explain that *a pay freeze* = a stop on all pay increases; *an overtime ban* = a stop on working more hours than usual for the job; *gone downhill* = got worse / deteriorated.
- Question b: Explain that *turned things round* = improved a bad situation; *'them and us'* = opposition between management and staff; *the Workers' Council* = an organisation in some EU countries that represents employees; *buy into* = accept a situation and become involved.
- Question c: The second speaker (the manager) has a US accent. Explain that *time off in lieu of overtime* = time off work instead of overtime payment.
- Question d: Tell learners that *an across-the-board increase* = an increase for all staff.
- **Further step:** Ask learners, in pairs, to playread the dialogues to the rest of the group – see the audioscript on page 44.

Staff relations 41

2 LANGUAGE CHECK

- As you go through the multiple-choice questions with the class, point out the Language Notes at the end of the Course Book unit (page 44) and the related notes in the Business Grammar Guide (see the booklet that accompanies the Course Book). There are cross-references from the notes to the BGG.
- The multiple-choice questions provide a starting point for the Language Check. Ensure that the related language points are explored and revised as necessary. The Specific Points section below gives you further detailed guidance.
- Adapt the points to learners' needs. Concentrate on areas where practice is needed.
- When working on vocabulary questions, introduce special terms not covered that participants need. Point out the Glossary on pages 158 – 160.
- For each question consider the following options.
  - Identify the answer.
  - Explore why the other options are wrong.
  - Ask learners to prepare examples that relate to their working needs, e.g.:
    Question 1: *We are looking for a 10% increase.*
    Amended version: *My people are looking for 2.5% backdated to August.*
- **Further step:** Ask learners, working individually or in pairs, to prepare extra questions using the Language Notes on page 44 and the related notes in the BGG for reference. This might be undertaken in teams as a quiz.

SPECIFIC POINTS

Questions 1 to 4: Making and countering demands
- Go through the examples in the Language Notes. Practise proposing, accepting and rejecting financial terms.
- Q1: Ask learners to paraphrase *We are looking for …* (= We are hoping to get / achieve …). Note *a 10% increase* can also be expressed as *an increase of 10%*.
- Q2: Ask learners to make more examples using *be willing / prepared to ….* e.g.:
  Would you be prepared to extend the warranty?
  We'd be willing to reduce the price by 2%.
  We wouldn't be prepared to accept your offer on those terms.
- Q3: Ensure learners know how to use prepositions with percentages, e.g.:
  We've already lowered the price by 5%.
  Our market share has fallen to 7%.
  That's a reduction of 10%.

Questions 5 and 6: Giving reasons using *as / because / since* or an *-ing* clause
- Review ways of linking two ideas in one sentence – see the examples in the Language Notes, and BGG 6.4 and 18.1.
- Q5: Note all three forms are grammatically correct but only **b** gives the correct meaning.
- Q6: Ask learners to transform this sentence using *as* (= *As we are a non-unionised company …*).

Questions 7 to 10: Vocabulary related to working conditions
- Review and practise the examples in the Vocabulary section on page 44. Explain that *fringe benefits* (also *perks*) = extra rewards in your job which are not pay (e.g. free health insurance); *a binding agreement* = one that cannot legally be broken; *a sympathy strike* = a strike in support of other workers who are on strike (note also *to come out in sympathy*); *to work itself out* = to resolve itself.
- Q7: See Glossary for a definition of *shop steward*.
- Q8: Explain that *workforce* is a useful word that refers to a group of people who work in a factory, company, industry, etc. It is often used to refer to *the workers*, as opposed to *the management* (as in the example). It can also be used in a more general sense to refer to the working population of a country, e.g. *Many mothers leave the workforce due to lack of childcare facilities*.
- Q9: See the Glossary for a definition of *arbitration*.
- Q10: Verb phrases with *work*. Go through the verbs listed in the notes. Check that learners understand them and can use them. Note that *to work to a timetable / schedule* = to follow; *to work to a (tight) deadline* = to have a deadline (which might be difficult to meet).

3 LISTENING

Getting on with your boss

- Ask learners, in pairs, to review the do's and don'ts of getting along with a boss (see page 42 of the Course Book). Gloss the language as necessary. Explain that *behind his / her back* = not directly to them but to other people; *find fault with* = criticise.
- Check whether learners agree with the do's and don'ts list. Are there any they would add?
- Listen to the recording of two young employees talking about their relationships with their managers. The second speaker has a US accent. Point out that *fumbling in the dark* = working in an uncertain way; *taken the initiative* = done something without being told to do it.
- Working in pairs, ask learners to identify how the do's and don'ts apply to what the speakers say in the recording – which points did they refer to?
- **Further step:** Ask learners to prepare a statement about their relations with their manager and deliver it to the rest of the class. Pre-experience learners might talk about an authority figure in their lives, e.g. a tutor.

42 UNIT 8

4 WRITING
Manager review

- As a whole class, go through the article entitled 'How to spot the boss from hell'. Gloss vocabulary as necessary. Note that *sickies* (UK slang) = days employees take off work because they claim to be ill; *quick-fix solutions* = quick answers to problems which may not really solve them; *over-commit the team* = give the team too many jobs; *face up to* = recognise and take action.
- Ask class members whether they think the article covers the key points about bad bosses. Is there anything they would add?
- Agree with the class what an informal review of a manager might include, e.g. strengths, weaknesses and areas for improvement.
- There is a sample review in the answers. You might want to circulate it as a guide.
- Ask learners to think through their review in pairs, but to write it on their own.
- **Further step**: In pairs, groups or as a whole class, learners discuss how the bosses they have described in writing affect staff relations. Encourage learners to use vocabulary from the Language Notes.

5 QUESTIONNAIRE
Job satisfaction

1
- Here learners complete a questionnaire which shows job satisfaction. The questionnaire was designed by John Nicholson, a business consultant.
- Elicit views on the questionnaire and the interpretation on page 133 of the Course Book.
- Lead into the exercise by checking how your learners feel about such questionnaires. Do they consider them to be useful or a waste of time?
- Ask learners if they would expect very different answers to the questions from people from other cultures.

2
- This is a three-part exercise. Part **c** offers an opportunity for vocabulary development. Check learners' knowledge of vocabulary related to the terms given. Note the following: *lay offs* (see Glossary); *contract staff* (see Glossary); *maternity leave* = time off work which a woman is legally entitled to before and after the birth of a baby (check that *paternity / parental leave* are also known); *pension plan* = a financial fund that employees and / or employers pay into that allows the employee to receive money when they retire; *industrial unrest* = protest activities such as strikes and work to rule by the workforce; *pickets* (see Glossary); *arbitration* (see Glossary); *productivity agreements* = benefits (e.g. wage increases) related to the rate of output per worker; *flexible working / flexitime* (see Glossary).
- Other terms that might be useful in this exercise: *downsizing* (see Glossary); *rationalisation* = to make a company or way of working more effective by stopping or combining some of the activities or parts of the company; *outsourcing* (see Glossary).

REVIEW

- Go through the Language Notes and Useful Phrases in the Course Book, if you have not already done so.
- Check that the items listed under Vocabulary in the Language Notes in the Course Book have been covered. Encourage learners to note down the terms they found particularly useful – especially the ones they need in their working lives.
- Make a note of this language for your own future reference.
- Remind learners that practice is the key to progress. One way to practise more effectively is to link the practice to regular reviews, e.g. learners might spend five minutes every morning assessing their progress the day before and thinking about opportunities for practice during the day ahead.

Answers

1 Core practice
a i [F] b i [U] c i [T] d i [T]

2 Language check
1 c   2 b   3 c   4 c   5 b
6 c   7 a   8 a   9 c   10 b

3 Listening

Speaker 1
Do believe in yourself. If *you* don't, who will?

Speaker 2
Don't wait for a bad situation to get better. It won't, so act now.
Don't be scared of confronting your boss with your problems. Honesty is always the best policy.

4 Writing
(*possible answer*)
Review of my manager's performance (confidential)

- Most of the time my boss is generally cheerful and positive. This creates a good atmosphere and helps us all work together and feel good about our jobs.
- In this mood he has reasonable expectations of what the team can do. This motivates us because it gives us a chance of succeeding.
- But when he is under a lot of pressure he changes. He becomes unreasonable and demanding. He expects us to support him by working long hours. He forgets that we have families, that we have a life away from work.
- At these times he delegates tough tasks, but doesn't take the time to explain properly what he wants, because he is too busy and too stressed. Morale drops.
- He needs a coach – someone to help him to manage in a more consistent way.

Audioscripts

1 Core practice
a Things aren't so good at the moment. There was a pay freeze last year, then an overtime ban. As you can imagine, the atmosphere in the plant deteriorated badly. It is very unfortunate because we used to have an excellent working relationship here. We were famous for it. If you ask me, the place has gone downhill.
b – How is it at Tenco these days?
   – Things are going well. We had a new production manager who started at the beginning of the year and he's really turned things round. There's no more of that 'them' and 'us' nonsense. It's mainly because of him that the Workers' Council is now making a real contribution. He makes sure they really understand the business plan, and buy into the business objectives.
c – Can I have a word?
   – Sure? What's the problem?
   – I need a couple of days off next week. I hope that's OK.
   – We're pretty busy at the moment.
   – Yes, I know, but I think Nina can handle it.
   – Which days are we talking about?
   – Wednesday and Thursday.
   – Is this holiday or what?
   – No, I'm owed five days – time off in lieu of overtime.
   – Yes, OK … that's fine by me – but make sure everything is covered!
d – What we're looking for is an across-the-board increase of 5% on current pay levels. We'd also like to see a review of the company health-care plan. The current plan does not really cover our present needs.
   – Yes, I agree with your point about the health plan, but obviously we will need to look at all your proposals in detail.

3 Listening

Speaker 1 (a 23 year-old TV researcher)
The best thing I ever did was to ask my boss for weekly update meetings. I'd been fumbling in the dark for so long that I finally decided to confront him and ask for these sessions when I could check that everything was OK and that there wasn't anything else he needed. After all, I'm not a mind reader. It took courage to ask him, but I believed that I had to do it. In the end he was really pleased that I'd taken the initiative.

Speaker 2 (a 21 year-old personal assistant)
My boss was a cool and withdrawn person, and I found it difficult to break the ice. She never praised me and I never asked her how she thought I was doing. I thought that she wasn't very happy with my performance. When a chance for promotion came up, I didn't apply for the job and someone else was brought in. I later found out that my boss was surprised that I hadn't gone for the job as she thought that I was ready for it. You can imagine how frustrated I felt.
(Note: the words of the TV Researcher and the Personal Assistant are spoken by actors.)

UNIT 9 Retirement and redundancy

PREPARATION

- It is possible to complete this unit at different speeds, in more or less detail. The fast track takes about 1½ hours, the standard track about 2 hours and the comprehensive track about 3 hours. For more information on the three options, see the notes in the Introduction on pages 10 and 11.
- For details of the aims of the unit, look at the Contents box on this page, the Language Notes at the end of the Course Book unit and the Useful Phrases below.
- If available to you, use the exercises in the Self-study Guide as extra practice.
- If you have taught this unit before, review the notes you made at the time.

USEFUL PHRASES

We have never had any redundancies in our company.
We have never made anyone redundant.
We had to lay people off in the summer.
It was a great shock for everyone.

I am very sorry to hear that you are leaving.
I was terribly sorry to hear that you have lost your job.
I hope that you find something soon.
It must have been a shock.

The company operates its own pension scheme.
I have opted out of the scheme.
I'll get a state pension when I retire.
How much do you contribute?

I'm planning to retire in three years' time.
I'm looking forward to having some free time.
I don't like working on my own.
I try not to think about retiring.
Are you interested in working part time?

It is possible to take early retirement in our company.
They have reduced numbers by a system of 'natural wastage'.
Do you lose your pension entitlement if you leave early?

I would like to wish you a happy retirement.
Good luck for the future.
All the best. Keep in touch!
Come and see us.

LEAD IN (SUGGESTIONS)

- Check how learners have prepared for the lesson – see the Preparation section at the start of the unit in the Course Book (page 45). Have they looked at the Useful Phrases on page 48 in the Course Book (copied above)?
- Check whether they have brought to class a message of sympathy and the reply. These can be used as resources later in the lesson.
- Consider leading into the subject by eliciting stories from the group of retirement and / or redundancy. As the discussion develops, you can monitor the language needs of learners and the level of interest.

Contents

Expressions
I am very sorry to hear that you are leaving.
I'm looking forward to having some free time.
I would like to wish you a very happy retirement.
Good luck for the future.
Keep in touch.

Language check
Verb + gerund / infinitive: *miss working, plan to retire*
Preposition + verb: *after retiring, before being made redundant*
Expressions of regret: *I'm sorry to hear, it must have been a shock*
Vocabulary: *unemployed, out-of-work, redundant, retired, pension, lump sum, golden handshake, early retirement, voluntary redundancy, lay off, let someone go, break news*

Practice
Discussing retirement / early retirement
Recounting news of redundancy
A letter of regret / sympathy

1 CORE PRACTICE

Listening and speaking

- This exercise provides an opportunity to practise a range of situations relating to retirement and redundancy.
- The exercise is in two parts – listening and speaking. The listening activity (part i) prepares learners for the speaking activity (part ii).
- As you work through the comprehension questions in part i, ask learners to explain how they have arrived at their answers.
- In part ii, encourage learners to adapt the scenarios to their needs. If appropriate, they should introduce the realia they have brought to the class.
- Question a: Note that *laid off one of the machine crews* = dismissed them (until more work is available); *things are picking up* = things are improving. Note also that the second speaker has a US accent.
- Question b: It is possible that Paul is retiring because he has been made redundant. But the speaker sounds as if he is a manager, speaking officially, so it is likely that Paul is simply retiring. If he had been made redundant, the situation would be more awkward and the manger would probably wish him well in a more private way.
- Question c: The first speaker has a French accent. Point out that *taking early retirement* = stopping work before the normal retirement age, usually with some financial incentive from the company (it is also a way for companies to

Retirement and redundancy 45

reduce employee numbers); *pension entitlement* = the pension an employee is legally entitled to; *I opted out* = I chose not to participate.
- Question d: Note the use of *if anything* in *We were expecting this plant to expand, if anything*. Here, *if anything* = if anything was going to happen.
- **Further step:** Lead a discussion in which learners talk about cultural differences they have observed in the area of retirement and redundancy, and the impact of these differences on the workplace.

2 LANGUAGE CHECK

- The multiple-choice questions link to the Language Notes at the end of the Course Book unit (page 48) and the related notes in the Business Grammar Guide (see the booklet that accompanies the Course Book).
- The multiple-choice questions enable you to treat the language programme flexibly. Points that are known can be handled briefly. Points that require more remedial attention can be explored in more detail. The Specific Points section below gives you in-depth guidance for the questions.
- When working on vocabulary questions, point out the Vocabulary notes in the Language Reference at the end of the unit in the Course Book, and the Glossary on pages 158 – 160. Introduce special terms that learners need, as necessary.
- For each question consider the following options.
  - Identify the answer.
  - Explore why the other options are wrong.
  - Ask learners to prepare examples that relate to their working needs, e.g.:
    Question 1: *I can't get used to not going to work any more.*
    Amended version: *We had to get used to living on much less money.*
- **Further step:** Each learner prepares an example of a verb + verb construction that he or she sometimes gets wrong, and offers it to the class. Class members then say if the example is correct or not.

SPECIFIC POINTS

Questions 1 to 5: Verb + infinitive or *-ing*
- Check the examples in the Language Notes. Point out that some verbs can be followed by either the infinitive or the *-ing* form, sometimes with a difference in meaning, e.g. *remember, try* (BGG 6.5).
- Q1: Verb + preposition + *-ing* (BGG 6.3, 6.4). Note that the *-ing* form is used after a verb + preposition(s) combination. Elicit other examples (e.g. *be opposed to doing something; be in favour of doing something*). Point out the use of *not* + *-ing*, e.g. *I am fed up with not working*. Elicit examples from participants.
- Q3: Verb + infinitive (BGG 6.1, 6.2). Point out that *to* in *look forward to* is a preposition and is therefore followed by an *-ing* verb.
- Q4: *after* + *-ing*. Elicit *After I had left* (or *I left*) … as an alternative. Note *after* + *-ing* is used when the subject of the two clauses is the same. This structure can also be used with *before*, e.g. *Before sending out invoices, I always double-check the amount* (= Before I send out …).
- Q5: *be* + adjective + infinitive. Remind learners of other adjectives used in this way (e.g. *pleased, glad, delighted, surprised, interested, sad*). Ask learners to make sentences using these structures (in the context of reacting to news if possible), e.g.:
  I was delighted to hear you'd been promoted.
  I was very sad to see her leave.

Questions 6 to 8: Vocabulary related to retirement and redundancy
- Go through the examples in the Language Notes. Check that learners can use the terms. Ask them to think how they might apply the items in their work. Note that *lump-sum payment* = a sum of money paid on one occasion in one large amount; *unemployment benefit* = (in the UK) a regular payment made by the state to people who are out of work; *natural wastage* (see Glossary); *let them go* = dismiss them; *given one month's notice* = told a month in advance that a job would be ending.
- Q6: Discuss terms related to *redundant*, e.g. *be fired* (mainly US English); *be sacked / get the sack* (these often imply some wrongdoing on the part of the employee); *leave your job* (neutral in meaning).
- Q8: Note that *golden handshake* = a large payment made to someone when they leave their job, either to compensate for redundancy or as a reward for good (and / or long) service.

Questions 9 and 10: Verbs of *saying / speaking*
- Q10: Revise the use of *speak, say* and *tell*, e.g.:
  I have to speak to Herro.
  I have to say something to Herro.
  I have to tell Herro the news.
- Note *tell* always needs an indirect object (= *tell* someone). *speak* can either be used alone or with *to* + someone. *say* cannot be followed by an indirect object (e.g. not *I have to say Herro*).
- Elicit examples and practise as necessary.

3 LISTENING

Retirement

- Lead into the exercise by asking learners to read through the retirement preoccupations and concerns listed in the box on page 46 of the Course Book, adding any others they might have.
- Point out that *making ends meet* = having enough money to pay for basic necessities.
- The speakers are: (1) a director of a charity (Scottish); (2) an ex-BBC employee who was made redundant (English).
- Speaker 1: *impoverished* = poor / lacking in money.
- Speaker 2: *turned 50* = reached the age of 50; *was eligible for* = met all the necessary requirements for; *be pensioned off* = made to leave a job (usually because of age) and be given a pension; *in lieu of* = instead of.
- Ask learners to identify the retirement status of the speakers. (Speaker 1 = anticipating retirement; Speaker 2 = made redundant and started a new business.)
- **Further step:** Ask learners to compare the speakers' thoughts on retirement with their own.

4 WRITING

A letter of regret

1
- Divide learners into two or three groups. Ask these groups to discuss the enquiry and Sue Nickson's reply on page 134, and then to present their conclusions in turn.
- Note that Sue Nickson is head of employment law at a firm called Hammonds.
- Note the following vocabulary. The enquiry: *statutory* (see Glossary); *be in breach of contract* = break an agreement in a contract. The reply: *enhanced* = more than the usual (amount); *implied* = suggested rather than stated directly.
- Ask groups to compare the views expressed with the situation in their areas.

2
- Ask learners, in pairs, to prepare a letter to a colleague who is being made redundant.
- This activity could begin with a discussion of the letters of regret learners brought to class. Identify special terms and show how they might be reused.
- There is also Useful Language on page 134.
- This activity can be given for homework.
- There is a sample letter in the answers.
- **Further step:** Pairs exchange work. Each pair reviews the letter they have received, and identifies one strength and one way in which the letter might be improved.

5 CASE STUDIES

Losing a job

- Give learners a limited amount of time to make notes on their respective texts before recounting the information to their partners. Check that they use language such as: *I was just reading ...; Apparently ...; It said in the article ...,* etc., as they recount what they have read (see the Useful Language box which accompanies the second part of this activity).
- When learners have recounted their information, ask them to check both of the texts and to comment on the information exchanged, e.g.: *You didn't tell me she had got another job. Why did you leave out that bit about ...?*
- **Further step:** Ask learners to find phrases which have similar meanings to words in the texts on pages 47 and 134, e.g. *was made redundant* = lost her job; *He didn't beat about the bush* = he came straight to the point / was very direct; *let me go* = made me redundant; *tie up all the loose ends* = do all the small jobs that still need doing.

REVIEW

- Go through the Language Notes and Useful Phrases in the Course Book, if you have not already done so.
- Check that the items listed under Vocabulary in the Language Notes in the Course Book have been covered. Encourage learners to note down the terms they found useful – especially the ones they need in their work.
- Make a note of this language for your own future reference.
- Encourage learners to practise the new language they have learnt.

Answers

1 Core practice
a i [F]   b i [F]   c i [U]   d i [T]

2 Language check
1 c   2 c   3 b   4 c   5 b
6 c   7 c   8 a   9 c   10 b

3 Listening
Preoccupations and concerns

	Speakers: 1	2
• Getting another job, working part time	✓	☐
• Starting a business, working for themselves	☐	✓
• Taking a holiday, having a rest	☐	☐
• Having time for their interests, personal schemes	✓	☐
• Earning enough, making ends meet	✓	☐
• Moving to a better / warmer area	☐	☐
• Pensions, lump-sum payments	☐	✓
• Getting bored, missing work	☐	☐

4 Writing
2 (*possible answer*)

> I was sorry / shocked to hear the sad news that you are leaving.
> It has been a great pleasure working with you. We will all miss your enthusiasm and professionalism, and your good humour.
> I hope you will take the opportunity to have a really good holiday.
> Good luck and best wishes, etc.

Audioscripts

1 Core practice
a – How did you manage during the summer? Did you have to stop any of the machines?
 – We did, unfortunately, yes. We laid off one of the machine crews and a couple of people in the warehouse. But things are picking up now and everyone is back at work. The summer was a difficult time for us all.
b Can I have everyone's attention, please? I would like, on behalf of everyone here, to wish Paul a very happy retirement. As you know, Paul has been with the company for the best part of 25 years, and I know that I speak for all of us here when I say that we will all miss him enormously. Paul, I know that you have many plans for the future, not least …
c – In this company we let people retire early at 55 – that's men and women. The policy's been very popular. There is no pressure to go, but many people have seized the chance of taking early retirement.
 – I'm not surprised. I would if I could. In my firm we have to stay until 65. If we leave before then, we lose some of our pension entitlement.
 – I opted out of our scheme. I have a private plan, which I run myself.
d – I was terribly sorry to hear what happened. How long had you been with the firm?
 – Just over two years. No one expected them to close us down. We were expecting this plant to expand if anything.
 – It must have come as a terrible shock. But I'm sure you'll find another job soon.
 – I hope so, but I'm not so optimistic. At my age it's not so easy.
 – Well, good luck – keep in touch.

3 Listening

Speaker 1
The idea of being able to take time out to start thinking and planning and doing new things is very attractive, but I think … that is a luxury in a sense because first of all I think the economic thing has to be sorted out. I would have to be very clear in my own head that … umm … I wouldn't have an impoverished retirement. I think that's probably quite important so we've got a plan for all of that. Part-time working possibilities are obviously … attractive and I guess I think about that quite a lot – although I think it has to be said that my … the thing I really like about my job is that I work with some very good and interesting people.

Speaker 2
Uhh … it's quite funny actually because I got made redundant from a large firm, having just turned 50. And that was, I suppose, at one level quite fortunate, because it meant that, number one, I was eligible for a pension. So I was in the peculiar position of having a pension every month until I die, as of that age, which seems far too early to actually be pensioned off. And also, of course, in leaving a large company I had the opportunity of a lump sum, in lieu of redundancy, which means therefore there is enough money to create an investment base if one actually wanted to start a small business, which is exactly what's happened.

UNIT 10   Conferences and exhibitions

PREPARATION

- There are three possible tracks through the unit: fast (about 1½ hours), standard (about 2 hours) and comprehensive (about 3 hours). For more information on the different tracks, see the notes in the Introduction on pages 10 and 11.
- The aims of the unit are shown in the Contents box on this page, the Language Notes at the end of the Course Book unit and the Useful Phrases below.
- Check the Self-study Guide, if it is available, for supplementary practice.
- You should also check your notes from previous classes if you have taught this unit before.

USEFUL PHRASES

I'll be in Prague next week for the Focus 49 exhibition.
Why don't we meet up?
How long does it go on?
It starts on Monday and ends on Friday.
I'll leave a pass for you at the information desk.

We saw your display – it's very impressive.
We're thinking of changing our machines.
We are looking to see what is available.
Would you like to come and sit down?
It's quieter – we can talk without being disturbed.

I'm a user – I have one of your products.
I'd like to know what upgrades are available.
I'd like to upgrade to the latest model.
We have it on display at the back of the stand.
Can we try it out?
If you leave your details, I'll get our technical people to call you.

When is your workshop?
It is due to start in five minutes.
The session on Internet selling is about to start.
Let me know if you need anything.
My pager number is on the back of your pass.
The organisers would like to take the speakers out to dinner.
I'd like that very much.

What time are we starting tomorrow?
I'll see you in the morning.
My train leaves at 7 o'clock in the evening.
The conference is going to be in Rome next year.

LEAD IN (SUGGESTIONS)

- Consider leading into the subject by discussing with learners conferences they have been involved in, either as providers or as visitors.
- Check whether they have brought to class documents relating to a conference. These can be used as a resource through the lesson.
- Check also whether they have looked at the Useful Phrases on page 52 in the Course Book (copied above). Comments from the group may indicate which areas of the target language they need to focus on and the level of interest in the topic.

Contents

Expressions
I'll be in Prague next week for the exhibition.
It starts on Monday.
I'll leave a pass for you at the information desk.
The session on Internet selling is about to start.

Language check
Future tenses: *will (I'll see you tomorrow.)*
going to (It's going to rain.)
Present Continuous: *I'm leaving at 6.00pm.*
Simple Present: *It finishes on Friday.*
due to: It's due to start in five minutes.
Vocabulary: *conference, exhibition, trade fair, lecture, seminar, workshop, speaker, exhibitor, visitor, meet up, try out, take out*

Practice
Responding to a conference mailout
Working on an exhibition stand
Coordinating a visit

---

1 CORE PRACTICE

Listening and speaking

- This exercise provides an opportunity to practise situations relating to conferences and exhibitions.
- The exercise is in two parts – listening and speaking. The listening activity (part i) provides learners with ideas and models for the speaking activity (part ii).
- In part ii, encourage learners to adapt the scenarios to their needs.
- Question a: Point out that *come over* = come; *meet up* = meet; *going on* = continuing; *(a) stand* = an area (e.g. at an exhibition) where an exhibitor's goods can be shown and where they can talk to visitors.
- Question b: The first speaker is one of the organisers; the second is a lecturer. The second speaker has an Irish accent. If necessary, point out that *(a) pager* = a small electronic device that makes a noise or vibrates to let you know that someone wishes you to contact them. The question *Would that be possible?* suggests that the lecturer already has a full schedule.
- Question c: The second speaker has a US accent. Point out that *upgrading* = improving by adding new parts or getting a newer model; *waste separator* = a machine that separates waste from other fluids, often water, so that what is left is clean; *(a) display* = examples of goods / services which exhibitors want to sell or advertising material (e.g. posters) related to the goods.

- Question d: Point out that *they are on display* = they are being shown / can be seen; *try them out* = test them.
- **Further step:** When learners have completed their individual practice in part ii, ask them to prepare and perform it to the rest of the class.

2 LANGUAGE CHECK

- The multiple-choice questions provide a starting point for the Language Check. Ensure that the related language points are explored and revised as necessary. Refer to the Language Notes and Business Grammar Guide, as required. The Specific Points section below gives you further detailed guidance.
- Adapt the points to learners' needs. Concentrate on areas where practice is needed.
- When working on vocabulary questions, introduce the specialised terms learners need, as required. Point out the Glossary on pages 158 – 160.
- For each question consider these options.
  - Identify the answer.
  - Explore why the other options are wrong.
  - Ask learners to prepare examples that relate to their working needs, e.g.:
    Question 1: *We are planning to introduce the upgrades at the New York motor show.*
    Amended version: *I'm planning to visit the trade fair while I'm there.*
- **Further step:** Ask learners working in pairs or groups to prepare a dialogue using all ten examples in the multiple-choice questions.

SPECIFIC POINTS

Questions 1 to 8: Ways of referring to the future
- Revise as necessary. Elicit examples that learners are not sure about. Clarify by referring to the Language Notes and the Business Grammar Guide as necessary.
- Q1: Use of *plan* for future intentions (BGG 2.1). Note *plan* can also be followed by the preposition *on* + *-ing*, e.g. *I'm not planning on doing much during my holiday*. It can be used in the past, e.g. *He wasn't planning to visit us* (BGG 1.4). The noun form can also be used to talk about the future, e.g. *Do you have any plans for the weekend?*
- Q2: *going to* (see BGG 2.2) is used here for a prediction based on present evidence. It indicates a strong degree of certainty (but is often used with *I think* …).
- Q3: *will* for decisions and confirming (BGG 2.2). Note this use of *will* for a spontaneous decision (often with *just*). Elicit other examples which are commonly used in telephone conversations, e.g.:
  I'll just get him.
  I'll ask her to call you.

Note in some languages the Present Simple is used in this way, so for some learners it is a common interference error.
- Q4: Present Simple for scheduled events (BGG 2.1). This is often used with the verbs *start / finish, open / close, arrive / leave*.
- Q5: See Q3.
- Q6: Present Continuous for personal plans and arrangements (BGG 2.1). Go through the examples in the Language Notes and ask learners to talk about their personal plans (including question forms, e.g. *What are you doing at the weekend?*).
- Q7: *be due* (BGG 2.6). Point out the variations in use:
  It is due to start = It is about to start.
  It is due tomorrow = It is expected / scheduled to arrive tomorrow.
  She is due back in a week = She is expected / scheduled to return in a week.
- Q8: *be about to* (BGG 2.6). Check that class members know how to use this phrase for imminent future events, e.g. *They are about to sign the contract* = They are going to sign it now. / They are due to sign it now.

Questions 9 and 10: Vocabulary and verb phrases related to conferences and exhibitions
- Go through the terms listed in the Language Notes, glossing as necessary. Ensure learners can use them correctly. Encourage learners to focus on items they are less familiar with. Ask them to give examples of how they would like to use the new items. Correct as necessary.
- Note that *a market stall* (UK) = a table or small open-fronted selling area in a market (a hall or open space where people sell things); *promotional material* = e.g. handouts, posters to promote something; *a keynote lecture* = an important lecture; *an open session* = a talk, etc. that anyone can attend.
- Q9: *how long (for)* + *go on*. Point out that the preposition *for* goes with the question words *how long* and could be omitted as it is optional. *on* cannot be omitted if *go* is used, as it is part of the verb *go on* (= last). However, *go* could be omitted: *How long is the conference on (for)?*
- Q10: exhibition vocabulary. Practise collocations with the word *stand* (e.g. *be on, run, visit, set up, put up, dismantle, take down a stand*). Practise the pronunciation of *e**xhi**bit / e**xhi**bitor / exhi**bi**tion*, concentrating on correct word stress. Note that the 'h' is silent. Point out that *a workshop* = a meeting of a small group of people to discuss and / or do practical work related to a certain subject or activity.

3 LISTENING

Internet marketing

- Prepare by going through the mailout on page 50 of the course book and glossing terms if necessary.
- Ask learners to listen to the recorded phone call and make notes. Point out that *a seasoned pro* = a

professional with a lot of experience; *an entrepreneur* (a French word) = someone who starts up a business, especially one that involves risks.
- Both speakers have non-standard accents.
- Each listening pair then decides which points on the invitation were mentioned during the call.
- **Further step:** Working in pairs, learners consider the questions they would ask if they were considering attending the conference. Then they practise calling the booking number and making a booking.

4 APPLICATION
A trade exhibition

- This is a role-play exercise involving two groups. Group A are running a stand at an exhibition; Group B are visitors to the exhibition.
- Both groups should prepare by considering the hot tips for running a stand (see page 50).
- Group A must decide what products or services they are showcasing.
- There is extra information for Group B on page 134.
- When the situation has run its course, the two groups should swap over so that Group B get a chance to run the stand.
- **Further step:** Consider videoing the events as they unfold so that you can maximise the learning opportunities presented by the exercise.

5 WRITING
Coordinating a visit

- Sonia Liddi is speaking at the Odex Conference organised by Jason Crevich in Cairo. After the conference she is flying to Damascus.
- Her timetable is as follows.
  24 November – flies into Cairo.
  25 November – speaks at the Conference.
  27 November – flies to Damascus.
- Ask learners to work in pairs or threes to read the documents, review the situation, then draft a reply.
- Point out some useful language, e.g. *on my behalf* = for me / instead of me; *e-booking* = a reservation made on the Internet. It might also be worth focusing on the way the hotel booking is requested (*for three nights, starting*) and practising alternatives (e.g. *for three nights, arriving … and leaving …* ; *for three nights, 24th to 26th Nov. inclusive*). Point out that it is always a good idea to state the number of nights to avoid confusion.
- Learners can then compare their work with the version given in the answers.
- Draw learners' attention to other useful phrases, e.g.:
  meet you in person
  Please get back to me if …
- **Further step:** Ask learners to improvise a follow-up phone call between Jason Crevich and Sonia Liddi in which both need to make changes to the arrangements.

REVIEW

- Ask learners to go through the Language Notes and Useful Phrases in the Course Book, and to note the language they need to learn.
- Make a note of this language for your own future reference.
- Remind learners that practice is the key to progress. Discuss how they can ensure that they use new language.

Answers

1 Core practice
a i [U / T] b i [U / T] c i [T] d i [F]

2 Language check
1 b 2 a 3 c 4 a 5 b
6 c 7 b 8 b 9 c 10 a

3 Listening
Points mentioned
One-day marketing conference ✓
Any tickets left? ✓
Floris Hotel ✓
Why start a website? ✓
Search engine techniques ✓
Search strategies ✓
Getting ready to sell on the Internet ✓

5 Writing
(possible answer)

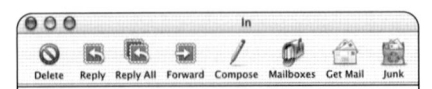

Re The Odex Conference Cairo

Dear Ms Liddi

Thank you for your message. Jason has asked me to reply on his behalf – he is out of the office today.
We are very pleased that you are able to participate in the Odex Conference. We will send a company car to meet you on 24 November. Jason regrets that he can't meet you in person but will meet up with you later.
We have made a booking for you at the Menhar Hotel for three nights, starting 24 November.
Your flight to Damascus on 27 November is by Arab Air flight no. AA312, departing 12.30, arriving 15.20 local time.
Please get back to me if you need more details.
We look forward to seeing you on the 24th.

With best wishes

Lela Arupshani

pp Jason Crevich

Audioscripts

1 Core practice
a – We have a stand at the Focus 49 exhibition. Why don't you come over and visit us?
– Where is the exhibition?
– In the Dubcek Centre. It would be good to meet up. Could you spare the time?
– I don't think I can make it today. How long is it going on?
– It ends on Friday. Why don't you come tomorrow? We could have lunch. I'd like to show you our new product range.
– OK …
– That's great. We're on stand 27 in the ground floor display area. I'll leave a pass for you with the information desk at the main entrance.

b – When is your first lecture?
– Tomorrow at 10.00.
– Have you got everything you need?
– Oh, I haven't had time to look at the room yet.
– OK, but let me know if you need anything. My pager number is on the back of your pass.
– OK, thanks.
– The organisers would like to take you out … show you some of the sights and give you dinner. Would that be possible?
– Of course – that's very kind of them.

c – Can I help you?
– I'm not sure. We're thinking of upgrading our waste separators so we're looking to see what's available. We saw your display – it's very impressive.
– Thank you. It's our latest model – the Solvex B. Can I ask what you are using at the moment?
– We have two Nemco B24s and two old Bemat Maxi machines. We produce a range of disinfectant and antibacterial products.
– Look – would you like to come and sit down? It's a bit quieter and we can talk without being disturbed?

d – I'm sorry to keep you waiting. We've been very busy this morning. How can I help you?
– I have one of your products – an SA 9,000 – and I'd like to find out what upgrades are available.
– If you come this way, they are on display at the back of the stand.
– Will I be able to try them out? Do you have them here?
– We have some – some you can check on the display screens. There's 15% discount if you order during the exhibition.

3 Listening
– Hello, Intermark. You are speaking to Carla Choudry. How may I help you?
– I'm calling about your one-day Internet Marketing Conference. Are there any vacancies left?
– Let me check – there's been a lot of interest in this. How many tickets do you want?
– Two.
– Yes, that's fine.
– And is it going to be at the address given in your mailout?
– Yes – the Floris Hotel.
– Could you tell me what level the programme is at? Will it cover the basics?
– Whether you are a seasoned pro or a new entrepreneur, the programme will have something for you.
– So it'll cover how to get started?
– Oh yes – the first session is called 'Why start a website?'.
– OK … What's the difference between 'Search engine techniques' and 'Search strategies'?
– I'm not the expert, but I guess search engine techniques are the technical details – how search engines work. The session on search strategies is more strategic.
– OK … Will you be covering on-line selling techniques?
– Let me check … Yes, that will be covered in the lecture entitled 'Getting ready to sell on the Internet'.
– OK – and what about website construction?
– Look, why don't I send you a link to the full programme? It has notes and everything.
– OK, thanks – and can I book on-line?
– Sure.

52 UNIT 10

UNIT 11 Networking

PREPARATION

- It is possible to complete this unit at different speeds, in more or less detail. The fast track takes about 1½ hours, the standard track about 2 hours, and the comprehensive track about 3 hours. For more information on the three options, see the notes in the Introduction on pages 10 and 11.
- For details of the aims of the unit, look at the Contents box opposite, the Language Notes at the end of the Course Book unit and the Useful Phrases below.
- If available to you, you can use the exercises in the Self-study Guide as extra practice.
- If you have taught this unit before, review the notes you made at the time.

USEFUL PHRASES

May I introduce myself?
I wanted to say 'hello'.
Mary Jones suggested I contact you.
I believe you know Fred White.
How do you know Fred?
We work together – we're colleagues.

It's good to meet you.
I was wondering if I could come and see you sometime.
Do you have a card?
These are my details.

Well, I think we should circulate.
It was nice meeting you.

What can you tell me about Liz Brown?
Any points I should watch out for?
She is really into sailing.
Don't discuss politics.
What's the best way to make contact with her?
It would be a good idea to send an email before you call.
Can I mention your name?

It's John Smith – we met in Mannheim.
Do you remember – we talked about anti-corrosion techniques.
You asked me to call you.
I remember – you were supposed to send me some samples.
Yes, that's why I'm calling.
Would it be possible to meet up?

LEAD IN (SUGGESTIONS)

- Check how learners have prepared for the lesson – see the Preparation section at the start of the unit in the Course Book (page 53). Have they looked at the Useful Phrases on page 56 in the Course Book (copied above)?
- Check whether learners have brought a message introducing themselves to a new contact or following up on a first meeting.
- Lead into the lesson by inviting learners to talk about their experience of developing contacts.

Expressions
Mary Jones suggested I contact you.
I was wondering if I could come and see you.
It's a good idea to send an email before you call.
It's John Smith; we met in Mannheim.

Language check
Expressing intentions: *I intend to call Maria.*
Etiquette advice: *It's best not to talk too much.*
be supposed / meant to: *I was meant to send some samples.*
Vocabulary: *network, socialise, circulate, work colleague, professional contact, business associate, custom, convention, guideline, keep in contact with, follow up with*

Practice
Corporate hospitality packages
Writing an invitation to a client
Networking tips and practice

---

1 CORE PRACTICE

Listening and speaking

- This exercise provides an opportunity to practise a range of situations relating to networking.
- The exercise is in two parts – listening and speaking. The listening activity (part i) provides learners with ideas and models for the speaking activity (part ii).
- In part ii, encourage learners to adapt the scenarios to their needs. Where possible they should introduce the realia they have brought to the class.
- Question a: The first speaker has a non-standard accent. Here *circulate* = mix with other people at the party.
- Question b: The second speaker has a US accent. Note that *compliance manager* = manager responsible for seeing that the regulations are complied with (followed); *get together* = meet; *explore common ground* = explore shared interests and concerns.
- Question c: The second speaker has a US accent. Explain that *she's really into sailing* = she's involved in and enthusiastic about sailing; *watch out for* = be careful about; *right wing* = having political views that are on the right.
- Question d: The caller has a French accent. Manheim is in Germany.
- **Further step:** Ask learners to talk about the ways in which they develop contacts and to compare experiences.

Networking 53

2 LANGUAGE CHECK

- As you go through the multiple-choice questions with the group, point out the Language Notes at the end of the Course Book unit (page 56), and the related notes in the Business Grammar Guide (see the booklet that accompanies the Course Book).
- The multiple-choice questions provide a starting point for the Language Check. Ensure that the related language points are explored and revised, as necessary. The Specific Points section below gives you further detailed guidance.
- Adapt the points to learners' needs. Concentrate on the areas where practice is needed.
- When working on vocabulary questions, introduce special terms that learners need. Point out the Glossary on pages 158 – 160 in the Course Book.
- For each question, consider the following options.
  - Identify the answer.
  - Explore why the other suggestions are wrong.
  - Ask learners to prepare examples that relate to their working needs, e.g.:
    Question 1: *When are you going to follow up the contacts you made?*
    Amended version: *When are you going to call the person you met in Dubai?*
- **Further step:** Ask learners, in pairs, to write five sentences about customs in societies they are familiar with, if possible using some of the language practised, e.g.:
  In Japan you should take off your shoes when you go into someone's house.
  In the US you are expected to leave at least a 15% tip in restaurants.

SPECIFIC POINTS

Questions 1 and 2: Intentions
- Refer to the examples in the Language Notes.
- Q1: Ask learners to correct the wrong options (*intending to follow, planning to follow*). Point out that *intend* and *plan* can be used in the simple or continuous form, e.g.: *What are you intending / do you intend to do about it? Do you plan / are you planning to work late tonight?*
- Q2: Remind learners that *not* comes before *to* in negatives (BGG 6.1). Elicit the difference in meaning between *be determined to* and *be going to* (the former is stronger in meaning).

Questions 3 and 4: Etiquette – suggestions / advice (BGG 21.1)
- Go through the examples in the Language Notes.
- Q3: This is the most commonly used structure with *suggest*. Point out there is no *to* before the verb (not *I suggest you to find out …*). To practise, ask your learners to give a specific piece of advice using the structure, e.g. *I suggest you get a tourist card if you're going to have a few free days there.*
- Q4: *should* is commonly used in questions to ask for advice. Ask your learners to imagine what questions visitors to their company / country might ask, e.g. *Should I take a gift if I'm invited to someone's house?* Point out that *evening dress* (uncountable with no article) is used for clothes worn for formal social occasions. For women this is usually a long dress; for men it is usually a black bow tie, white shirt and black suit or *a dinner jacket* (US = *tuxedo*), which is an elegant jacket – usually black. Another term used for men's formal evening wear is *black tie*. Occasionally, men's evening wear is referred to as *white tie* when the occasion demands a white dinner jacket be worn.

Question 5: Etiquette – warnings
- Ask learners to produce warnings beginning *Just to warn you*, e.g. *Just to warn you, they drive very fast there.* You could also practise other warning structures, e.g. *If I were you …* (*I wouldn't stay at the River View Hotel*). Note *asked* could be used for the second part of the sentence; *meant* is not used with *will*.

Questions 6 and 7: *be supposed to / be meant to / be expected to* (BGG 20.1)
- Q6: *supposed to* and *meant to* can be used interchangeably. Both can be used in the Present or Past Simple. When the past is used, the implication is that the opposite happened in reality. Point out that a form of *should* could be used instead, e.g. *We were supposed to take off at 11.00* = We should've taken off …; *We're not meant to use the Internet for personal things* = We shouldn't use …
- Q7: Only *expect* can be used in the continuous form. *custom* and *convention* are similar in meaning (= a traditional way of behaving in a particular society). *rule* would be a bit too strong in meaning here. It would imply something you *have to* do.

Questions 8 and 9: Socialising and networking vocabulary
- Q8: Point out that *to network* means to try to meet people who may be useful to you, particularly in your work. To *mix* and *circulate* mean to go round at a social gathering and speak to different people. Note also the phrase *to mix and mingle*.
- Q9: Note that an *associate* is a partner in a business or other undertaking. It can also refer to someone who is a member of a society or organisation but who does not have full rights, status or privileges (e.g. an associate director or a new member of a law firm). A more general word for someone to work with is *colleague*. Point out that the stress is on the first syllable.

Question 10: Verb phrases
- Try also to elicit *keep in touch (with)*.

3 LISTENING
Corporate hospitality

- The main speaker has a US accent.
- Some learners may have no experience of corporate hospitality. Clarify what it involves.
- Play the recording again as learners take notes.
- Working in pairs, learners could compare notes before they write a summary.
- Gloss as necessary: *target marketing* = marketing that is directed at specific people or markets; *tangible* = (here) a real experience; *nurtures* = carefully looks after (to allow the relationship to develop); *wining and dining* = entertaining people with wine and dinner; *losing out* = not having the advantage that other companies have; *Rolls-Royce package* = the best example of corporate entertainment.
- Learners might compare their summary with the audioscript. There is a sample text in the answers.
- **Further step:** Ask learners to talk about how corporate events such as Wimbledon tennis finals would be received in their countries. What form of corporate entertaining would they consider to be most interesting and appropriate?

4 WRITING
An invitation

- There is some idiomatic and ironic language in these two texts. Gloss as necessary.
- Wimbledon text: *are on offer* = are being offered; *a 100% turnout* = everybody will come; *hordes of teenagers* = large numbers of teenagers; *a hefty £4,000* = the big amount of £4,000; *If the sun shines, forget it* = If the sun shines, you can forget quality time with your guests; *grumpy* = bad-tempered.
- Monaco text: *the ultimate* = the best example; *serves up* = provides; *second to none* = the best.
- Ensure the Useful Phrases on page 134 in the Course Book are clear. There is a possible draft in the answers.
- **Further step:** Ask learners where they would entertain or be entertained if budget was no problem.

5 APPLICATION
Networking tips

1
- Go through the networking tips with learners, glossing as necessary: *referrals* = useful contacts or sales prospects that someone is prepared to give you because they trust you or want to help you; *sales lead(s)* = the identity of a potential purchaser; *broaden your professional horizons* = obtain more professional experience, knowledge and contacts; *explore mutual benefits* = to look for things that could help both of you; *provide an easy sight-line* (unusual usage) = be easily seen; *bone-crusher* = handshake that is too strong; *limp fish* = handshake that is too weak; *small talk* = polite friendly conversation with no deep content.
- Point out: *a valued contact* = very appreciated; and *a valuable connection* = one that could prove helpful and important.
- Elicit participants' views on networking and building contacts. Customs and etiquette vary significantly from culture to culture. Do the tips in the Course Book apply in their area? How would they adapt them?

2
- Ask learners to prepare an *'elevator' speech* (or *pitch*). What you might say in an elevator (UK English = a lift) if someone asks: *What do you do?* It has to be brief and must contain the key facts.

3
- Practice – go through the list of networking opportunities for developing contacts. Check with learners whether it includes the situations that are common in their experience.
- In pairs, ask learners to talk through a situation that is typical for them, identifying the language they need. They should refer to the messages they have brought to class, introducing themselves to a new contact or following up a first meeting.
- Learners then practise the situation in pairs.
- **Further step:** Learners discuss the messages they have brought to class. What was the outcome? Was the message a good idea? How culturally specific is it? Would it work in a wider context?

REVIEW

- Encourage learners to note down the terms they found particularly useful – especially the ones they need in their working lives.
- Make a note of this language for future reference.
- Remind learners to practise the new language they have learnt, e.g. they might write key points on a card that they carry and refer to from time to time throughout the day.

Answers

1 **Core practice**
   a i [U / T]   **b** i [F]   **c** i [U]   **d** i [T]

2 **Language check**
   1 c   2 b   3 c   4 b   5 c   6 a   7 b   8 c   9 a   10 b

3 **Listening**
   (*possible summary*)
   Corporate hospitality
   - Main benefits
     – It provides companies with the opportunity to invite potential clients to discuss new business.
     – It provides an opportunity to meet existing customers on a one-to-one basis.

- It helps to maintain and develop good business relationships.
- Range and type of events
  - A range of different events can facilitate business discussion and provide useful information.
  - The speaker mentions lunch in a wine bar at one end of the range, and the Wimbledon finals as the 'Rolls-Royce' at the other end.
- Maximum and minimum costs
  - Costs are not discussed in detail. The speaker says they are not always important. If planned properly, lunch in a wine bar can be very effective.
  - A 'Rolls-Royce' event like the Wimbledon finals might cost £4,000 per head.

4 Writing
(*possible letter*)

> Dear …
> We are organising a party on [10 July] for [the Men's Final at Wimbledon] and we hope that you will join us.
> Private facilities have been booked, and refreshments (including lunch) will be available. As usual, the tennis promises to be good.
> We would be grateful if you could confirm your acceptance by [4 May].
> Security is tight, so please bring this invitation with you. You will be escorted to [our tent]. If you have any problems, please call me on my mobile (078 —- — —).
> Hope you can make it.
> With best wishes

5 Application
(*possible answers*)

1 Possible further advice
   - Be punctual.
   - Remember details, especially names.
   - Take an interest – ask questions and listen.
   - Avoid talking about politics and religion.
   - Be aware of your body language.
   - Be sensitive to cross-cultural factors.
   - Don't gossip about other contacts / customers.
   - Don't tell lies or make false claims.
   - Don't offer if you can't deliver.

2 Possible 'elevator' speech
   'My name is Genetta Jaeger. I work for AMT – a computer applications consultancy based in Brussels. We provide management information technology to small- and medium-size companies. We work on the assumption that management information technology is like legal advice or accounting. So, we offer an alliance based on reliability and knowing somebody will be there to help at important times. Here's my card.

Audioscripts

1 Core practice
a   – I wanted to say 'hello' because Silke Ollek suggested I contact you.
    – Oh – how do you know Silke?
    – We work together.
    – Oh. I see …
    – I was wondering if I could come and see you sometime.
    – Sure! What's it about?
    – Well we have a problem, and Silke says you are a great problem solver.
    – I don't know about that – but why don't you call my office and fix an appointment?
    – I'd be glad to. Do you have a card or something?
    – Sure … here you are.
    – Thanks … and these are my details.
    – Thanks … Well, I think I'd better circulate. It was nice meeting you.
b   – So what do you do?
    – I'm a nuclear service engineer? What do you do?
    – I'm the safety and compliance manager at the plant in Rossas.
    – So you're in the business.
    – That's right. Maybe we should get together … and explore common ground.
    – Why not?
    – Here's my card.
c   – I'm planning to contact Juanita Curtiz in Mexico City. Do you have any advice?
    – Well, she's really into sailing …
    – I don't know anything about sailing.
    – You can ask questions, show an interest.
    – OK. And any points I should watch out for?
    – Well, yes … she's pretty right wing and has strong views, so it's probably best not to talk about politics or religion.
    – That's useful. Thanks. Can I mention your name?
d   – It's Gerry Atailer.
    – Sorry …
    – Gerry Atailer – we met at the conference in Mannheim.
    – You mean in June?
    – That's right. Do you remember? We talked about our new anti-corrosion techniques and you said you might be interested. You asked me to call you.
    – Oh yes, I remember. You were supposed to send me some details.

3 Listening
– What are the benefits of these corporate entertainment packages in real terms? Can firms use hospitality to help secure contracts?
– Corporate entertainment is the most direct form of target marketing there is. It's tangible and provides companies with the opportunity not only to invite potential clients to discuss new business, but also to network with existing customers and spend time running through current and future contracts. A successful company nurtures its clients in order to maintain and develop relationships and achieve good communication. Corporate entertainment provides the opportunity for such relationships to develop.
– But does 'wining and dining' really make that much difference? Are companies that don't spend money in this way, that can't afford this kind of package, losing out?
– Wining and dining provides the opportunity for relaxed discussion, and it's often during such occasions that clients provide their host with additional – and useful – business information. The matter of cost isn't always significant. A wine bar lunch can be just as effective, if planned properly to meet a specific objective.
– So how much choice is there in this market? What's the Rolls-Royce of the hospitality market?
– The Rolls-Royce package in the UK (and one of the most sought-after invitations) is probably finals day at Wimbledon All England Lawn Tennis Championships, which can cost as much as £4,000 per head for the men's final.
– Oh gosh!

UNIT 12 Security abroad

PREPARATION

- There are three possible tracks through the unit: fast (about 1½ hours), standard (about 2 hours) and comprehensive (about 3 hours). For more information on the different tracks, see the notes in the Introduction on pages 10 and 11.
- For details of the aims of the unit, look at the Contents box opposite, the Language Notes at the end of the Course Book unit and the Useful Phrases below.
- If available to you, use the Self-study Guide as a source of supplementary exercises on the key themes of the unit.
- There is a Progress Test covering Units 7 to 12 on pages 141 and 142, which can be photocopied and circulated. The answers are on page 148. For best results give learners time to prepare.

USEFUL PHRASES

Is there any sign of our luggage yet?
We've been waiting for half an hour.
I'm sorry, the baggage handlers are on strike.
It will be coming through quite soon.

How much do you usually tip?
About 100 baht – more if you think the service is good.
I'm sorry, this is all I have.

The safe in my room won't open; it's jammed.
There's something wrong with the air-conditioning.
Could someone come and have a look at it?
It won't be working again till after lunch.

I have to report a theft.
It's a brown leather wallet.
It was stolen while I was having a shower.
The police will be here in half an hour.
But I will have left by then.

I am afraid we do not accept credit cards.
I am sorry, but your card has been declined.
I'm completely out of cash and the banks are shut.

My car has been towed away.
Do you know where it was taken?
It doesn't say 'No Parking'.
How much will I have to pay to get it back?
I don't believe it. That's terrible.

LEAD IN (SUGGESTIONS)

- Check whether learners have looked at the Useful Phrases on page 60 in the Course Book (copied above). Comments from the group may indicate which areas of the target language they need to focus on.
- Check whether learners have brought messages relating to security abroad. These can be used as a resource through the lesson.
- Consider leading into the subject by talking about learners' specific experiences. If possible, tell a story of your own.

Contents

Expressions
I have to report a theft.
My car's been towed away.
There's something wrong with the air conditioning.
It won't be working again till after lunch.

Language check
Future Continuous tense: *How will you be paying?*
Future Perfect tense: *We will have left by then.*
Order of adjectives: *a brown leather wallet*
Vocabulary: *switch, plug, bulb, basin, tap, drain, pipe, fused, faulty, broken, dead, blocked, cracked, leaking, jammed*

Practice
A difficult trip to Torreon (Mexico)
Safety guidelines for San Diego (USA)
Dealing with travel hassles

1 CORE PRACTICE

Listening and speaking

- Here you can practise a range of situations relating to security and related difficulties when travelling abroad.
- The exercise is in two parts – listening and speaking. The listening activity (part i) provides learners with ideas and models for the speaking activity (part ii).
- Ask learners how they reached their answers for the comprehension questions in part i.
- In part ii, encourage learners to adapt the scenarios to their needs. Where possible they should introduce the realia they have brought to class.
- Question a: The first woman has a non-standard accent. You might ask learners why they think the woman, who needs cash, can't use her credit card in an ATM (automatic teller machine = cash machine) outside the bank to obtain cash. (Maybe she has forgotten her PIN number.)
- Question b: The woman has a US accent. Note that *baggage* is the term used in most airports, but *luggage* is also common. Both are uncountable nouns. Note also that *staff shortages* = not enough staff.
- Question c: The hotel guest has a non-standard accent.
- Question d: The man has a US accent. Note that *towed away* = taken away, pulled away (because it has been parked illegally). You might also like to point out that if a vehicle is *clamped*, it has a device fitted to the wheel (when it is illegally parked) which will be removed when the owner pays a sum of money.

- **Further step:** Video the examples and use the recordings to analyse wider communication factors such as body language.

2 LANGUAGE CHECK

- The multiple-choice questions provide a starting point for the Language Check. Ensure that the language points are explored and revised, as necessary. Refer to the Language Notes at the end of the Course Book unit and the related notes in the Business Grammar Guide (see the booklet that accompanies the Course Book). The Specific Points section below gives you further detailed guidance.
- Adapt the points to learners' needs. Concentrate on the areas where practice is needed.
- When working on vocabulary questions, introduce the specialised terms learners need. Point out the Glossary on pages 158 – 160 of the Course Book.
- Consider the following suggestions for each question.
    - Identify the answer.
    - Explore why the other options are wrong.
    - Ask learners to prepare examples that relate to their working needs, e.g.:
      Question 1: *Sorry about the delays. Your luggage will be coming through very soon.*
      Amended version: *I'm afraid Verena has been delayed. She will be joining us after lunch.*
- **Further step:** Ask participants, working individually or in pairs, to prepare extra questions using the Language Notes on page 60 and the related notes in the BGG for reference.

SPECIFIC POINTS

Questions 1 and 2: Future Continuous tense
- A time line might be useful to clarify the reason for the use of this tense. Refer to the Language Notes and the Business Grammar Guide for further explanation if necessary (BGG 2.3).
- Q1: The use of the Future Continuous here is meant to have a reassuring effect. Its use implies that the speaker is confident the luggage will come through soon and that its arrival is a routine matter.
- Q2: Here the Future Continuous is used because the verb (*not work*) refers to a situation that will last from the present until a specific time in the future (*tomorrow*).

Questions 3 and 4: Future Perfect (BGG 2.4)
- Q3: The Future Perfect is used because the action of leaving will have been completed before the police arrive. *by* phrases are often used with this tense. Again a time line may help to clarify why the tense is used.
- Q4: *by tomorrow* is the trigger here for the use of the Future Perfect. Ask learners to modify the sentence in the question so that the other two tenses can be used, e.g.:
  Have you fixed the air conditioning?
  Will you be fixing the air conditioning tomorrow?

Questions 5 and 6: Order of adjectives
- Q5: The rules for the order of adjectives are complicated. Refer to BGG 13.1 for guidelines. Here only option **b** is acceptable (size, colour, material).
- Q6: Compound nouns – nouns as adjectives (BGG 11.1). *Internet* must precede the noun (*connection*) because it is the first part of a compound noun. Elicit other examples with *Internet* (e.g. *Internet access; Internet provider*). The fact that the connection is *high-speed* is more of an inherent feature of it than the fact that it is *secure*, so *high-speed* comes nearer to the noun.

Questions 7 and 8: Vocabulary related to problems
- Q7: If something is *blocked*, other things can't pass through it. Elicit other things that can be blocked (e.g. roads, pipes, noses). If something is *jammed*, it won't move (e.g. a drawer, door, window).
- Q8: *faulty* has the most general meaning (= not working properly). A lock cannot be *fused* as it is not electrical (a fuse stops an electrical device working if the current is too high). *cracked* describes damage where something is broken but not into pieces and there are thin lines on the surface (e.g. a glass can be cracked).

Questions 9 and 10: Verbs and verb phrases
Refer to the Vocabulary section of the Language Notes.
- Q9: Note that *remote control* = a handheld device which allows you to control something like a television from a distance; *have a look* (at something) = examine it, often with the aim of fixing it.

3 LISTENING

A difficult trip

- Paul Talley's words are spoken by an actor. He has a US accent.
- Gloss vocabulary in the text, as necessary: *Lonely Planet* = a publisher that produces a popular range of guide books; *a lead smelter* = a machine that extracts lead from the raw material by heating it to high temperatures; *belching out clouds of zinc and lead dusts* = producing big clouds of zinc and lead dusts; *a migraine headache* = a very bad headache, sometimes with nausea and difficulties in seeing; *in a foul mood* = in a very bad mood; *I had my credit card declined* = the card was not accepted and it could not be used to make a payment; *sorted it out* = resolved it; *shuffled off* = walked away slowly like a very old man; *cut short* = stop.
- **Further step:** Invite learners to talk about a difficult trip – either one they have experienced or one they have heard about.

4 APPLICATION
Travel hassles

- Discuss the list of common travel difficulties on page 58 in the Course Book. Gloss as necessary: *hassles* = annoying problems; *hustlers* = annoying people who try to make money by offering 'help' and other 'services' you don't want; *overcharging* = charging too much (also *to short change someone* = not to give enough money back when something is paid for); *connectivity* = email and Internet connections; *poor mobile phone coverage* = a bad (or no) mobile phone signal in a particular area.
- Working in pairs, ask learners to identify a situation that is a major concern to them, then to think through a typical situation.
- They then prepare the dialogue that might take place in the situation.
- Ask the pairs to practise their example and present it to the rest of the group.
- **Further step:** For each situation demonstrated, discuss with the group ways to avoid the situation or to cope with it as well as possible. Supply vocabulary and phrases as necessary.

5 FEATURE
Safety guidelines

1.
   - Note that US spellings and lexis can be different. If your learners have a UK English orientation, elicit the equivalent of, e.g.:
     travelers (travellers)
     checks (cheques)
     purse (handbag)
     flashers (warning lights)
     hood (bonnet)
     freeway boxes (emergency telephones).
   - Gloss other vocabulary as necessary: *in small denominations* = coins and notes in small units (e.g. a one dollar bill); *keep track of* = know where something is; *pick up hitchhikers* = give strangers a ride in your vehicle.
   - Ask each pair of learners to choose the five most important points mentioned in the text, and to compare their choices with other members of the group.

2.
   - This activity can be undertaken individually or in pairs. It can also be done as homework.
   - Point out the Useful Phrases on page 135. There is a sample draft in the answers.
   - **Further step:** Ask learners working in two or threes to go through the messages brought to class, and to see if they can improve some aspect of these messages in the light of points covered in the lesson.

REVIEW

- Go through the Language Notes and the Useful Phrases in the Course Book, if you have not already done so.
- Ensure learners note down the terms they found particularly useful.
- Make a note of this language for your own future reference.
- Remind learners that practice is the key to progress. They need to think of ways of reminding themselves to do this, e.g. they might put key points on their computers so they come up on the screen from time to time.

Answers

1 Core practice
a i [U / T] b i [T] c i [F] d i [F]

2 Language check
1 b 2 c 3 a 4 c 5 b
6 a 7 b 8 c 9 a 10 c

3 Listening
(*possible answers*)
a He had come from Monterey.
b No, it didn't. His credit card was declined when he tried to buy the plane ticket.
c Torreon is a city in the middle of the desert that built itself around a lead smelter.
d It's hot.
e He had a migraine and was in a very bad mood.
f The clerk claimed there was no reservation for him.
g Yes, they did; they sorted out the problem.

5 Feature
(*possible answer*)

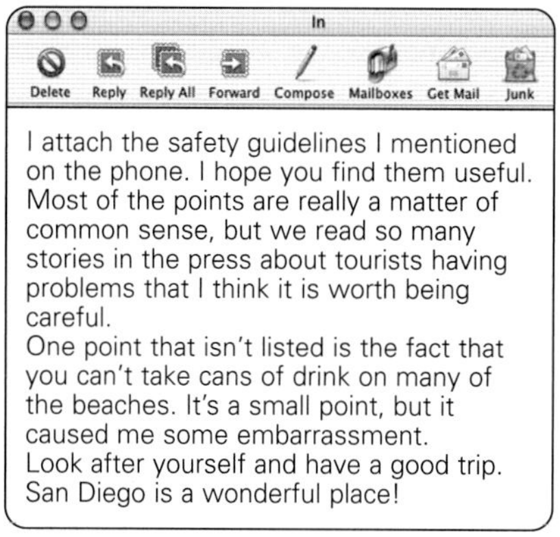

I attach the safety guidelines I mentioned on the phone. I hope you find them useful. Most of the points are really a matter of common sense, but we read so many stories in the press about tourists having problems that I think it is worth being careful.
One point that isn't listed is the fact that you can't take cans of drink on many of the beaches. It's a small point, but it caused me some embarrassment.
Look after yourself and have a good trip. San Diego is a wonderful place!

Audioscripts

1 Core practice

a
- I'm sorry, we do not accept credit cards.
- Oh, I don't have any cash. Is there a bank nearby where I can change some money?
- Yes, there's a bank at the end of the street, but I think they will have closed by the time you get there – it's lunch time. We'll be closing soon.
- So what do you suggest?
- We could accept euros, but there would be a supplement.

b
- I've been waiting half an hour for my baggage. There's still no sign of it.
- Which flight were you on, sir?
- The Athens flight.
- Yes, I'm sorry we have some staff shortages at the moment. We expect the bags will be coming through soon.

c
- Hotel security.
- Oh, come in. I have to report a theft. My wallet was stolen while I was in the shower.
- When was this?
- About half an hour ago.
- You weren't using the mini safe …?
- No it has a faulty lock; it isn't working. Are the police coming? My insurance company will need a police report number.
- Yes, they'll be here in about half an hour.
- Oh – I'll have left by then. I have a meeting.
- When will you be returning to the hotel?

d
- Your car has been towed away.
- But it doesn't say 'No Parking'.
- It was incorrectly parked.
- Oh. Do you know where it was taken?
- You need to phone this number.
- Oh, right. How much will I have to pay to get it back?
- Usually the fine is 400 US dollars.
- I don't believe it! That's ridiculous.

3 Listening

During the course of my employment with Lonely Planet I have visited some rather interesting places and many beautiful places in Mexico, which is why Torreon was a surprise. Torreon is a city that built itself around a lead smelter. Like most other mining operations, it is in the middle of the desert – the smelting operations belching out clouds of zinc and lead dusts. And it is, of course, hot.

I arrived in this charming location with a migraine headache … and in a foul mood, because I had my credit card declined when I went to purchase the plane ticket in Monterrey. It turned out to be a fraud! Then, when I got to the hotel, the clerk claimed he had no reservation for me. Nor did he have a room. We finally sorted it out, and I shuffled off to my room. To my relief my colleagues from Mexico City arrived and I was marginally better as we sat down to eat.

I have never seen steak served in so many new and interesting ways. But unfortunately dinner was cut short by the return of my migraine. In the end, my stay in Torreon was a success. Mexican hospitality worked its magic, but it was a tough trip.

(Paul Talley's words are spoken by an actor.)

UNIT 13 Salaries, incentives and rewards

PREPARATION

- Note that it is possible to go through the unit at three different speeds: fast (about 1½ hours), standard (about 2 hours) and comprehensive (about 3 hours). See the notes in the Introduction on pages 10 and 11 for more details on the three tracks.
- For details of the aims of the unit, look at the Contents box opposite, the Language Notes at the end of the Course Book unit and the Useful Phrases below.
- If you have taught the unit before, check the notes you made at the time.
- You can use the Self-study Guide as a source of exercises to supplement the unit.

USEFUL PHRASES

I work a 35-hour week.
With overtime it comes to about 43 hours.
My basic salary is quite low.
What I earn depends on my (sales) figures.
I get an incentive bonus of 2.5%.
My total package is worth in the region of 90 grand.

Everyone gets 21 days paid holiday.
I have the use of the crèche, which is subsidised.
We get a 10% discount on all company products.
We normally receive a New Year's bonus.
It's usually one week's pay.
Directors get a free car.
It's a perk that goes with the job.

When would be a good time to do my pay review?
I feel the company should recognise contributions like this.
It is easy to feel undervalued in these circumstances.
I agree, but this is a bad time.
A pay demand is very unlikely to succeed at this time.
So what would you suggest I do?
You ought to be thinking about your next step.

Taking into account the cost of living / the rate of inflation / your contribution to the bottom line, the Board have agreed to an increase of 5%.

LEAD IN (SUGGESTIONS)

- Consider leading into the subject by discussing with learners how openly people talk about money and earnings. What are the conventions in their area(s). In many cultures people will talk about non-financial benefits and incentives, possibly in general terms, but not salaries.
- Check whether learners have brought to class a job description with details of related remuneration. These can be used as resource material throughout the lesson.
- Have learners looked at the Useful Phrases on page 64 in the Course Book (copied above)? Comments from the class may indicate which areas of the target language need special attention.

Contents

Expressions
What I earn depends on my sales figures.
My total package is worth about 90 grand.
Directors get a free car; it's a perk that goes with the job.
The Board have agreed to an increase of 5%.

Language check
Modal verbs, present forms: *would, could, should*, etc.
Expressing likelihood: *bound to, likely to*
Rates and charges: *time and a half, flat-rate fee*
Symbols and numbers: +, –, =, 10K, 7½
Vocabulary: *reward, benefit, perk, salary, wage, pay rise, raise, increase, put in for, turn down, think over*

Practice
A letter about executive rewards
Benefit packages (listening realia)
A pay review

1 CORE PRACTICE

Listening and speaking

- This activity gives you an opportunity to practise a range of situations relating to salaries, incentives and rewards – see the audioscripts on page 65.
- The exercise is in two parts – listening and speaking. The listening activity (part i) provides learners with ideas and models for the speaking activity (part ii).
- As learners answer the comprehension questions in part i, ask them the basis of their answer. What verbal information have they used?
- In part ii, encourage learners to adapt the scenarios to their needs. Where possible they should introduce the documents they have brought to the class.
- Question a: The second woman has a non-standard accent. Note that *subsidised* = part of the cost is paid by the company; *bonus* (see Glossary); *workforce* = all the staff employed by a company, *a crèche* = a facility for looking after young children while their parents work; *on-site* = on the company's premises.
- Question b: The first speaker has a non-standard accent. Explain the meaning of *perks* (see Glossary); *discount* (see Glossary); *we get 7% off* = we get a discount of 7%.
- Question c: The main speaker has a non-standard accent. Gloss as necessary: *on top of that* = in addition to that; *commission* (see Glossary); *I might clear* = I might earn (in some cases it might mean: I might have earnings of X amount after I have paid taxes, etc.); *an*

incentive bonus = extra money paid to an employee if he / she does good work or achieves certain targets; *it's not a fortune* = it's not a lot of money; *get by* = survive; *overtime* = hours worked more than the contracted hours – also payment for extra hours worked. The speaker doesn't say if he is paid overtime.

- Question d: The woman has a US accent. Note that *package* (*reward package*) = all the different rewards an employee receives taken together, e.g., salary, pension contribution, health insurance, free crèche etc.; *trial period* = a limited period of time during which the effectiveness of someone or something is evaluated; *a pay demand* = a request for a pay rise; *put your request in writing* = send your request in a letter.
- **Further step:** In pairs, ask learners to playread the dialogues to the rest of the group – see the audioscript on page 65.

2 LANGUAGE CHECK

- The multiple-choice questions link to the Language Notes at the end of the Course Book unit (page 64), and the related notes in the Business Grammar Guide (see the booklet that accompanies the Course Book).
- The multiple-choice questions enable you to treat the language programme flexibly. Points that are known can be handled briefly. Points that require more remedial attention can be explored in more detail. The Specific Points section below gives you in-depth guidance for the questions.
- When working on vocabulary questions, point out the Vocabulary notes in the Language Reference at the end of the unit in the Course Book and the Glossary on pages 158 – 160. Introduce special terms that learners need, as necessary.
- Consider the following approach for each question.
  - Elicit the answer.
  - Discuss why the other suggestions are wrong.
  - If appropriate, ask learners to change the example so the wrong options can be used.
  - Ask learners to prepare examples that relate to their specific needs, e.g.:
    Question 1: *With a bit of luck, we should have a response by the weekend.*
    Amended version: *If things are like last year, we should have some information about our bonuses early next month.*
- **Further step:** Ask learners to put the examples in the questions into exchanges. What might the line before be? What could the next line be?

SPECIFIC POINTS

Questions 1 and 2: Modal verbs – present forms (BGG 7.1)
- Q1: Simple form. Only *should* is appropriate here. It is used in the sense of a present expectation (i.e. that there will be a response by the weekend) which can still be fulfilled (BGG 7.8). Try to elicit *ought to* as an alternative. Note that all the prepositions would be correct here but they have different meanings. Check that your learners know that, here, *by* = at the latest.
- Q2: Continuous forms – negative modals. The continuous is used because if there was not a modal, the Present Continuous would be the natural tense to use (*She is getting* …). Note that *can't* and *wouldn't* would both be acceptable modals here but have different meanings: *can't* conveys the idea that the increase in salary is not logically possible (which the second part of the sentence backs up); *wouldn't* indicates a prediction (slightly weaker than *won't*). Explain that *might not* indicates the speaker's opinion on the likelihood of the event happening. It does not match the second part of the sentence so well. Option **a** is the correct answer because *in* is the only correct preposition.

Question 3: Expressing likelihood (BGG 2.5)
- Go through the examples in the Language Notes. The second part of the sentence makes it clear that the speaker wants to convey the idea of certainty. Try to elicit *are sure /certain to*. Only *in* is correct here (*in the end* = after a period of time, and possibly involving some difficulty).

Questions 4 to 7: Vocabulary related to pay and benefits
- Q4: *time and a half* (= 50% more) and *double time* (100% more) are phrases that are specific to rates of pay / overtime.
- Q5: *benefits* has a similar meaning to *perks* but cannot be used here, as *benefit package* cannot follow the word *more*. An *award* is something specific, such as a prize given for achievement.
- Q6: Note that *targets* collocates better with *sales* than *goals* does.
- Q7: *gross* = before deductions (e.g. tax, national insurance); *net* = after deductions (*net pay* = take-home pay). Point out that *gross* rhymes with *close*, not *loss*. Elicit synonyms for *in the region of* (e.g. approximately, roughly, about).

Question 8: Numbers
- *two out of ten* means the same as *one in five* but would be a very unusual way of expressing the figure.

Questions 9 and 10: Verb phrases
- Go through the verbs and verb phrases in the Language Notes. Gloss as necessary: *put in for (a pay rise)* = request; *turned your request down* = didn't agree to it / rejected it; *hold out much hope* = have much hope; *Who does it have to be signed off by?* = Who has to give the final approval (with a signature)?

- Q9: *Think over* is a separable phrasal verb, so the pronoun *it* must come between the verb and the particle. *Think about* is not separable, so the preposition *about* must always immediately follow the verb. *Think over* = to think carefully about something, especially prior to making a decision.
- Q10: Note that *split the difference* = choose a figure halfway between the figure that has been offered from both sides (e.g. 5% and 10% = a split difference of 7.5%); *settled* (for something) = accepted an offer, even though it is not exactly what you wanted. If a pay increase is *backdated*, it is paid from an earlier specified time.

---

3 LISTENING
Benefits packages

- Go through questions **a** to **d** on page 62 of the Course Book to ensure they are clear. Gloss as necessary: *remuneration* = payment for work; *benefits package* = all the rewards taken together (technically *a benefit* is non-financial, e.g. the use of sports facilities, but here the word is used loosely to mean reward); *performance related* = paid / given only if certain performance targets (e.g. sales targets, finishing a job on time) are reached.
- This is an authentic recording.
- Speaker 1 is an accountant from England.
- Speaker 2 is an Irish engineer working in the construction industry.
- Gloss the recorded texts as necessary.
  - Speaker 1: *in arrears* = after the work has been done; *a non-contributory pension scheme* = a scheme to save money for an employee's retirement financed entirely by the company (the employee does not have to contribute); *everything bar petrol* = everything except petrol; *in keeping with* = as is suitable for; *accrue* = accumulate; *take up that option* = use it / accept it; *a company car* = a car provided and partly or wholly financed by the company.
  - Speaker 2: *fees* = money paid for work done by a professional person, e.g. an accountant; *prior to* = before; *be paid in a number of stages* = receive parts of a payment at different times during a process. Note also: *the call-out rate* = the minimum charge when a skilled person comes to your house, etc. to do a repair; *a flat-rate fee* = a charge that is the same for everyone / every job; *a surcharge* = an extra charge.
- **Further step:** Encourage a discussion about the kinds of benefits and rewards learners receive. If it is not culturally acceptable to discuss personal financial rewards, make the discussion more general by asking about attitudes towards salaries and benefits. Elicit other rewards and benefits such as performance-related pay, subsidised accommodation, telephone / clothing allowances, share options, luncheon vouchers.

4 WRITING
Executive rewards

- Read the text with the group and discuss it, keeping in mind questions **a** and **b** and tasks **c** and **d** on page 62 of the Course Book.
- Gloss language as necessary (**c** features some vocabulary items). Note also: *lavish* = excessively generous; *prompted* = caused / motivated / inspired; *non-executive director* = director who attends board meetings and gives advice but does not work full-time for the company; *ludicrous* = stupid / deserving to be laughed at; *unequivocally (independent)* = without any doubt or compromise – point out that this is a low frequency word.
- For **d** gloss *shareholder* if necessary (see Glossary). Note also *a company secretary* = a senior person responsible for the company's legal affairs.
- Learners can work individually or in pairs. The exercise can be given for homework.
- Go through the Useful Phrases on page 135.
- There are examples of both messages in the answers.
- **Further step:** Discuss the issue of executive rewards. What happens if they are low (e.g. they may not attract top quality people)? What happens if they are too high (e.g. other costs become hard to control, especially wages).

5 APPLICATION
A pay review

1
- Go through the items listed in the table entitled 'Elements of a reward package' on page 63 of the Course Book.
- Gloss as necessary: *allowances* = money allowed for certain expenses like clothing; *subsistence (allowance)* = money paid to cover the cost of hotels and meals when a member of staff is travelling; *long-term disability insurance* = insurance cover that provides financial support if an employee has to stop work for a long period for health reasons; *private mileage* = car travel for personal use; *sick pay* = pay received when off sick; *mentoring* = process by which a senior person helps a less experienced employee to develop their skills; *share options* = the right to buy shares at a certain price at a time in the future.
- If appropriate explain the technical differences between *a financial reward* (money), *a benefit* (a

Salaries, incentives and rewards **63**

reward that, generally, is not financial), *an incentive* (a reward designed to motivate people to work better by making payment dependent on results).

2
- Prepare to practise the core themes of the unit in an informal pay / salary review.
- This is a pairwork activity. Ask pairs to begin by agreeing the circumstances of their case. They might get some of the details from the job description they have brought to class.
- Learners playing Partner A, the manager, should go through the 'Factors to think about before the meeting' and the Useful Phrases, both listed on page 63. Gloss if necessary: *maintain parity* = keep at the same level (in different teams); *poaching ... staff* = attracting staff from another company by paying more.
- The information for learners playing Partner B is on page 135. Again gloss if required: *value added* = the extra value that you have added to the department or business; *bottom line* (see Glossary); *parity* = equality; *cost of living* = money that has to be paid for food, heating, rent, etc.
- **Further step:** Record the examples and use the playback to identify errors and increase accuracy.

REVIEW

- Go through the Language Notes and Useful Phrases in the Course Book, if you have not already done so.
- Check that the items listed under Vocabulary in the Language Notes in the Course Book have been covered.
- Encourage learners to note down the terms they found particularly useful – especially the ones they need in their working lives.
- Make a note of this language for your future reference.
- Encourage learners to practise new language outside the classroom – to bring it into their communication.

Answers

1 Core practice
a i [F]   b i [F]   c i [T]   d i [T]

2 Language check
1 c   2 a   3 b   4 c   5 b
6 c   7 a   8 b   9 b   10 c

3 Listening
(possible answers)
a The first speaker's benefits are:
- monthly salary that includes payment for any overtime done
- a non-contributory pension scheme
- paid holidays
- subsidised sports facilities
- a company car, which is fully financed except for petrol from home to work.

b The second speaker receives fees. These are sometimes based on hours worked and sometimes on a fixed price for the job. The fixed fee is paid when the job is complete or in stages through the job.

c No, they don't.

d The first speaker receives a number of perks, e.g. subsidised sports facilities, company car.

4 Writing
(possible answers)
a The tone is critical – some examples:
- fat cat
- lavish rewards
- the highly unusual payments come on top of his generous pay
- Fu will earn US$32,000 a year for working a few days a month
- magnificent pension entitlements.

c *overpaid executive* = fat cat
in the news = in the spotlight
vote = poll
non-repeatable = one-off

d **Sample message supporting**
There has been some criticism of the rewards offered to John Fu. I am writing to support the Board's position.
John Fu served the organisation well – assets grew substantially under his leadership and costs fell for 13 years running. High performance over a long period should be rewarded.
The exit package offered by the Board is not out of line with similar rewards offered by other companies to retiring chief executives. Effective leaders are difficult to find – they need to be encouraged.
The Board's policy on executive pay was rejected by 10% of the voting members. This is a significant number. However, more significant are the 90% who voted in favour of the policy.

Sample message criticising
I am writing to make clear my opposition to the rewards offered to John Fu.
He was fairly rewarded for the work he did as CEO. His pension entitlements are estimated to be in the region of £2 million. In my view there is absolutely no need to give him US$120,000 in cash and US$20,000 car on top. In addition to all the other benefits, he is to receive US$32,000 per year as a non-executive director for working a few days each month. Non-executive directors are supposed to be independent – that is their value. It is clear that Mr Fu does not qualify.
The Board clearly feel deep gratitude to Mr Fu. In my view and the view of many shareholders, he did what he was paid to do and was fully

rewarded. We demand the Board think again.

5 Application

1 (*possible answers*)
- An executive director would often not receive:
  – overtime   – shift pay
  – allowances   – subsistence.
- A politician would often not receive the following, although arrangements will vary from region to region:
  – bonus   – incentives
  – performance-related pay
- – overtime   – shift pay
  – pension
  – private health insurance
  – life insurance
  – training and development
  – mentoring and coaching
  – share options   – share of profits.
- An airline pilot would often not receive the following, but again the situation will vary from company to company:
  – childcare facilities
  – company car
- – fuel for private mileage
  – mentoring and coaching
  – share options
  – share of profits.
- An IT support manager would often not receive:
  – overtime   – shift pay
  – allowances   – subsistence
  – company car
  – fuel for private mileage
  – share options   – share of profits.

Audioscripts

1 Core practice

a – We all get a bonus at New Year. It's based on the company's results – it approximately equals one and a half week's salary.
 – Do you have child-care facilities?
 – One in three of the workforce are women, and most of them have children, so the company has to provide a crèche on-site. It's very good, but we have to pay for it.

b – Do you receive any perks?
 – The main thing we get is a discount on company products – we get 7% off. Also the canteen is subsidised – it's very good value. I'm sure the top managers get all sorts of executive perks like free cars, free health insurance and so on, but I don't qualify for those yet.
 – Do you have sports facilities?
 – Not of our own, but we have the use of the facilities at a local club.

c – My basic salary is in the region of €5,000 a month, and then on top of that I get 5% commission on sales. What I get depends on my figures. In a good month I might clear €8,000. In addition I get an incentive bonus of 3% on sales above my monthly target. After deductions, it's not a fortune but I get by. According to my contract I am expected to work a 35-hour week – in fact, it's usually more than that.
 – Do you get paid overtime?
 – No, because I'm not on an hourly contract. But when I'm away overnight, I get an allowance for unsocial hours.

d – I'm really enjoying my new supervisor role. And I think the team is doing well – we've been meeting our targets …
 – Yes, you are doing a good job.
 – Thanks – so when would be a good time to review my salary? When I accepted the extra responsibilities, you said we'd review my package after the trial period.
 – Yes I know, but I'm afraid this is not a good time.
 – Oh, I see … So what would you advise? I'm very happy to do the work, but I feel the company should recognise my contribution.
 – I agree – but right now a pay demand is very unlikely to succeed.
 – So, what would you suggest?
 – Look … put your request in writing, and I'll see what I can do.

3 Listening

Speaker 1
I get paid on a monthly basis in arrears – normally a week before the end of each month. It's quite a large salary, and so I don't get paid for overtime, etc. But that … well, my salary is … includes what I would consider a payment for that overtime. I'm also benefiting from a non-contributory company pension. They also fully finance my car, everything bar petrol from home to work. Paid holidays, I get 20 days but in keeping with my job, time is slightly more flexible and you can accrue days off because of the amount of extra hours you do during the weekends, etc. We do have sports facilities; we don't have sports facilities on-site, but we are provided with discounts for certain sports centres in the area – although I don't actually choose to take up that option. The major perk I get in my job is a company car, which, as I say, is fully financed by the company.

Speaker 2
I'm a consulting engineer … mainly involved in the domestic house market. Er … generally speaking, we're rewarded for our work in the form of fees which are sometimes based on an hourly rate. Alternatively, we can agree a fixed fee with the client prior to the work being carried out and then we are paid that, either in one full payment at the … when the work is completed, or sometimes, if the work goes on for a very long time, we can be paid in a number of stages.

UNIT 14   Personal and company finances

PREPARATION

- There are three possible tracks through the unit: fast (about 1½ hours), standard (about 2 hours) and comprehensive (about 3 hours). For more information on the different tracks, see the notes in the Introduction on pages 10 and 11.
- For details of the aims of the unit, look at the Contents box opposite, the Language Notes at the end of the Course Book unit and the Useful Phrases below.
- The Self-study Guide is a source of supplementary exercises on the key themes of the unit.
- If you have taught this unit before, check the notes you made at the Review stage.

USEFUL PHRASES

Our main overhead is the site cost – that includes rent, insurance, building maintenance, etc.
Our fixed costs come to about 40,000 per month in total.
That includes depreciation charges of 3.5 thousand.
Altogether our running costs amount to 1.7 million.
Can you give us a breakdown of this figure?
I should have brought a copy of the accounts.

My fixed outgoings include the usual things – mortgage, fixed taxes, insurance premiums, and so on.
I suppose the biggest item is my pension.
As a rough guide, I'd say our day-to-day living expenses come to about 3,000 per month, on average.
We must have been spending more on entertaining than we thought.

In the year, I exchanged my old Peugeot for an up-to-date model.
I had to sell my shares in Unicorn to pay off some debts.
On the plus side, I own some land which has gone up in value.
I got the promotion I was hoping for, which I'm pleased about.

On the work front, the outlook is very satisfactory.
Over the last year, we performed well in respect of our core activities – we met our sales targets in key markets.
Sales are up from $9.8 million last time, to $10.7 million.
Results are more or less in line with forecasts.
We made a profit of 2.2 million on sales of 20.7 million.

LEAD IN (SUGGESTIONS)

- Refer to the Preparation section at the start of the unit in the Course Book (page 65). Check whether learners have brought some accounts, personal or their company's, to the class. These can be used as a resource through the lesson.
- Consider leading into the subject by asking learners to give a simple financial overview of an organisation they are associated with – their department or company or sports club, etc. You should be ready to start the process with an example of your own, e.g. *Income is / earnings are lower than last year because a key customer went bankrupt and they owed us quite a lot of money. Costs are about the same. So profits are going to be down by about 5%. But we have some new customers, so I think the situation will improve in the next six months.*

Expressions
Altogether, our running costs amount to $1.7 million.
Sales are up from $9.8 million to $10.7 million.
We made a profit of $2.2 million on sales of $20.7 million.
I had to sell my shares in Unicorn to pay off a debt.

Language check
Modal verbs, past forms: *would have*, *would have been*
Spelling rules: *i* before *e*, except after *c*
Use of hyphens: *day-to-day expenses*
Vocabulary: *add*
Financial terms: *add up to*, *cut back on*, *go up / down*

Practice
Talking about financial performance
Talking about expenditure and assets
A news item about Caffè Nero
Writing a request for a salary increase
An article about the sale of a company

1 CORE PRACTICE

Listening and speaking

- This exercise provides an opportunity to practise a range of situations relating to personal and company finances.
- The exercise is in two parts – listening and speaking. The listening activity (part i) provides learners with ideas and models for the speaking activity (part ii).
- Ask learners to identify the verbal clues they used when answering the comprehension questions in part i.
- In part ii, encourage learners to adapt the scenarios to their needs. Where possible they should introduce the documents they have brought to class.
- Question a: The speaker has a non-standard accent. Gloss the following, as required: *performed* = did; *margin(s)* = the difference between the money received when selling a product and the costs incurred bringing it to market; *bottom line* (see Glossary); *write off a bad debt* = remove a debt from the accounts because there is no hope of it being paid; *went into liquidation* (see Glossary).
- Question b: The speaker has a US accent. Note the following: *fixed outgoings* = expenses that do not change from month to month, like rent; *a mortgage* (see Glossary); *break the figures down* = break them into detailed parts.
- Question c: The speaker has a Welsh accent. Gloss the following, if needed: *asset* (see Glossary); *setback* = something that stops progress; *a lump-sum payment* = money paid in one payment, not in several small payments; *government bonds* = contract documents issued

by a government promising to repay money borrowed (= a type of fixed-interest investment).
- Question d: The second speaker has a non-standard accent. Note the following: *overheads* (see Glossary); *costs* = money that has to be paid to run a business; *franchising* = selling a licence to trade using a brand name and paying a royalty for the right; *fixed costs* (see Glossary); *overall* = in total; *accounts* = a statement of income and expenditure in a year which shows the profit or loss made.
- **Further step:** Ask learners individually or in pairs to prepare a further question for each dialogue.

2 LANGUAGE CHECK

- As you go through the multiple-choice questions with learners, point out the Language Notes at the end of the Course Book unit (page 68), and the related notes in the Business Grammar Guide (see the booklet that accompanies the Course Book) – there are cross-references from the notes to the BGG.
- The multiple-choice questions provide a starting point for the Language Check. Ensure that the related language points are explored and revised, as necessary. The Specific Points section below gives you further detailed guidance.
- Adapt the points to learners' needs. Concentrate on areas where practice is needed.
- When working on vocabulary questions, introduce special terms not covered that learners need. Point out the Glossary on pages 158 – 160 of the Course Book.
- For each question, consider the following options.
  - Identify the answer.
  - Explore why the other suggestions are wrong.
  - Ask learners to prepare examples that relate to their working or personal needs, e.g.:
    Question 1: *These spreadsheets might have been delivered by special messenger, while we were out.*
    Amended version: *The Singapore office must have set up the arrangement without telling us.*
- **Further step:** Reinforce the vocabulary associated with personal and company finances using a simple word game. Taking the Vocabulary section of the Language Notes in the Course Book as a starting point, the class works in teams: Team 1 chooses a word or phrase; Team 2 scores a point by using it correctly in an example. Team 2 then chooses a word or phrase for Team 1 and so on.

SPECIFIC POINTS

Questions 1 to 3: Past modals for logical deduction (BGG 7.1, 7.7)
- Read through the examples of past modal forms in the Language Notes.

- Q1: Passive form. Options **b** and **c** are not grammatically correct as a past modal with a passive verb is needed here. Explain that *might have been* = the explanation (i.e. that the spreadsheets were delivered by special delivery) is a logical possibility but not a certainty.
- Q2: Continuous form (question). *could* is used to suggest a possible explanation to the situation (the high fuel costs). Option **b** is the only correct grammatical form.
- Q3: Passive form. *won't have been* has the strongest meaning: it is almost a statement of fact. A slightly weaker logical deduction would be *can't / couldn't have* (i.e. it is not logically possible that the accounts have been audited). *mustn't have* is not a possible form in standard English. Option **a** is not grammatically correct as there is no *to*.

Questions 4 to 8: Vocabulary – financial terms
- Definitions are given in the Vocabulary section of the Language Notes on page 68 of the Course Book. Ask your learners to use the vocabulary to talk about their own or their company's finances, e.g. *My outgoings were more than my income last month.*
- Q4: In **c** *head office salaries* are an indirect cost (*overhead* – see Glossary). These costs are not directly linked to the number of units of production (unlike *raw materials*). In **a** *running costs* could involve both direct costs (which vary with production levels) and indirect costs.
- Q5: Both *expenditure* and *outgoings* mean money spent, but *outgoings* is not usually used for money spent on a particular thing (as here, *developing new sites*) but rather for sums of money that have to be spent on a regular basis.
- Q6: Note that *income* is used for individuals (= money that is earned from working or investments). Point out also *income tax*.

Questions 7 and 8: Verb phrases
- Q7: Ask learners to correct the two wrong answers by changing the following preposition (= *add up to; account for*). Note also *come to*. *account for* is usually used when talking about a proportion of a total, e.g. *Exports account for about 40% of total sales.*
- Q8: Check that learners understand the meaning of *cut back on* (= reduce spending on / spend less on). Practise the verbs *be up /be down* with the prepositions *by* and *on*, e.g.:
  Sales were 10% down on last year (= compared to last year).
  Sales were down by 10% on last year.

Question 9: Use of hyphens (BGG 24.6) and numbers (BGG 24.1)
- Hyphens are usually used in numbers between 21 and 99 (e.g. *twenty-two*). Note that *million* is in the singular. It is usually only used in phrases like: *The figures are in millions of pounds*. *one-off* (= happening only once) is usually written with a hyphen. It can be used as an adjective (as in the example) or a noun, e.g. *It was a one-off*.

Question 10: Spelling (BGG 24.5)
- Revise the *ie / ei* rule and the y → *i / ie* rule.

Personal and company finances

3 LISTENING

Caffè Nero

- The listening is in the form or a radio report.
- The exercise can be done as a group activity. Ask learners to work together – each group member listening for specific information.
- Group members then pool their information and answer the questions.
- Gloss as required: *has ... exceeded analysts' forecasts* = has done better than analysts predicted; *on a same-store basis* = when comparing the performance of a store with the same store in the previous year; *excel* = do exceptionally well; *thriving* = very successful / healthy; *a favourable retail property environment* = there are lots of possible shops available at reasonable prices; *brand* (see Glossary); *self-generated funds* = funds available from the company's business activities, so there is no need to borrow.
- **Further step:** Learners prepare similar statements about an organisation they know, possibly using the accounts they have brought to the lesson. They deliver it to the rest of the group and ask one or two questions.

4 WRITING

A salary increase

- Ask learners to read the notes in the box on page 66 of the Course Book, which are about asking for a rise. Gloss as necessary: *cutbacks* = cost or budget reductions; *accomplishments* = things that have been done successfully / achievements; *business framework* = business context.
- Discuss with learners whether they agree with these suggestions. Are there any points that should be added? For example, in some areas it might be important to stress your teamwork.
- Go through the Useful Phrases on page 135.
- Consider asking learners to read the sample message in the answers before writing their request.
- **Further step:** Ask learners to check whether the sample message in the answers is in line with the suggestions on the page. (It satisfies the second and fourth suggestions; it does not satisfy the third suggestion; there is no information on the first and last suggestions.)

5 FEATURE

The sale of a company

1
- Point out that Snax in the name StraitSnax is a play on the word 'snacks'.
  - Ask learners to read the article with a view to answering some comprehension questions. They should answer the questions with reference to their notes. Possible questions include the following.
    - *How will Ragi Angshuman receive his money?* (Half in cash and the rest in shares.)
    - *Who else is involved in the deal?* (The buyer is Logan Foods. Angshuman started the company with three colleagues. They were backed by an investment group who own 28% of the company.)
    - *What is the secret of StraitSnax' success?* (Timing – they started producing adult snacks when the market was ready for them. Quality – they create products by visiting faraway places and finding genuine village recipes.)
    - *What are the financial results expected this year?* (Turnover SG$150m / US$88.54 million, profits SG$12m / US$7.1m – it doesn't say if the profit is before or after tax.)
    - *Why was StraitSnax keen to be taken over?* (They needed funding to expand.)
    - *What are the company's plans for the future?* (They intend to move into the European, Australian and US markets. They want to double turnover in the three years. They expect headcount to increase significantly.)
- Gloss as necessary: *bonanza* = a sudden opportunity to make large profits; *upmarket* = high quality; *tap into a vein of the market* = like tapping a rubber tree and extracting the rubber from the 'veins' in the tree, they identified the opportunity in the market and 'tapped' into it; *tortilla chips* = a Mexican corn snack; *titbits* = small snacks; *tracking down* = looking for and finding; *spectacular* = unusually / exceptionally good.

2
- Emphasise to your learners that there are errors of fact and errors of language in the notes they have to check.
- Review the notes on spelling in the BGG 24.5, as necessary.
- Draw attention to the informal conventions that can be used in note taking:
  - use of initials in place of names
  - omission of unnecessary words (SS was bought by → *SS bought by*)
  - use of abbreviations (US$150 million → *US$150m*)
  - use of *to* + infinitive for plans and decisions (*RA will receive* → *RA to receive* – note that on page 67, 'receive' has been incorrectly spelt).
- Ask learners, in pairs, to redraft the notes. There is a sample in the answers.

- **Further step:** Building on the activity suggested in the Lead In (page 66), ask learners to prepare notes giving key financial information on an organisation they are associated with, using note-taking techniques. This should be a fuller version of the information they gave earlier.

REVIEW

- Go through the Language Notes and the Useful Phrases in the Course Book, if you have not done so already.
- Check the items listed under Vocabulary in the Language Notes in the Course Book have been covered.
- Encourage learners to note down the terms they found particularly useful.
- Ask learners to practise the new language they have learnt, e.g. they might use Post-It notes to remind themselves of key points they need to remember.

Answers

1 Core practice
a i [F] b i [T] c i [T] d i [F]

2 Language check
1 a 2 b 3 b 4 c 5 a
6 c 7 b 8 a 9 b 10 a

3 Listening
a Caffè Nero has €5.9 million cash in the bank.
b The percentage rise in sales in the last financial year.
c The number of cafés the chain intends to open by the end of the financial year.
d The percentage rise in sales in June, July and August.
e 52 cafés were opened last year.
f Total number of cafe houses owned by Caffè Nero.

4 Writing
(*possible answer*)
Dear …
I very much appreciate the opportunity I have had during the last two years of serving as a member of the marketing and sales support team. In that time, I feel I have become an integral member of the team and contributed significantly to its success. For example, in the last six months, I have …

As you know, I'm still working for the starting salary we agreed two years ago. When I joined, you said we would renegotiate in two years, based on the quality of my work. In the light of my overall performance and the specific achievements listed above, I think it would now be fair to review my salary, as agreed, and to bring it into line with payments to people with similar responsibilities in this company and our main competitors. For the record this would involve an increase in the region of 6% on the basic rate, and an additional performance related payment of 3%.
I would like to thank you for the development opportunities you have given me. I am very much looking forward to the challenges ahead and to increasing my contribution as my knowledge and experience grow.
Please let me know if you need more information.
Best regards
Adapted from
http://jobsearchtech.about.com/

5 Feature
2 (*possible answer*)
Key financial information
- SS bought by LV for SG$150 million.
- RA will receive about SG$48 million because he owns 32% of the shares.
- His three friends / colleagues are making SG$50 million between them out of the deal.
- 28% of the company is owned by an investment group.
- Expected turnover this year is SG$150 million, profit SG$12 million.
- The company wanted a buyer because they need resources to expand.
- RA wants to double turnover in the next three years.
- The Singapore workforce of 330 is likely to increase significantly.

Personal and company finances

Audioscripts

1 Core practice

a We performed reasonably well – sales rose by 7% and we met our sales targets in all our key markets. We also achieved our quality targets in most areas. But unfortunately our financial results were a bit disappointing. We're in a very competitive field, and our margins were hit by price cuts. In addition, earlier in the year we had to pay higher-than-expected interest charges, which had an effect on the bottom line. And then in the last quarter we had to write off a bad debt when a customer went into liquidation.

b As a rough guide, I'd say last year our day-to-day living expenses came to around $3,000 a month altogether. I suppose about half of that went on the basics – I'm not sure where the rest went! I think we must have been spending more than usual on entertaining. I know from my credit card statements that our expenditure on vacations amounted to $7,000 in all. We should really cut back on that, but we're a large family and it's not easy. And, of course, all that's on top of the usual fixed outgoings like mortgage, pension, local tax and so on. I can't really break the figures down for you – my wife keeps the accounts.

c Our main asset is our house, which hasn't increased in value much during the past year but at least the value hasn't fallen. At the moment the signs are that the housing market is improving gradually, thank goodness. In June we had rather a setback when my husband was made redundant but he did receive a lump sum payment, which we put into government bonds. Er … what else? Well, we traded in our car for an up-to-date model.

d – We try to keep our overheads down to 25% of sales. That's been difficult in the last year because our core management costs are up by 4%, mainly because we've been in a period of reorganisation. We're moving into franchising, and we've been setting up a new franchise division, which has involved us in a number of one-off reorganisation costs. But these developments haven't yet led to an increase in turnover.
   – Can you tell me what your fixed costs came to overall?
   – I'm afraid I don't have the exact figure in my head. I should have brought a copy of our accounts with me.

3 Listening

Caffè Nero today revealed that not only has it avoided the downward trend in consumer spending, it has also exceeded analysts' forecasts as its sales for the financial year to the end of May rose 7.5% on a same-store basis. A spokesperson for the 230 coffee houses went further, saying that in June, July and August – when other retailers really began to feel the effect of slower consumer spending – its sales were up by 34%. Nero plans to open a further 25 cafés by the end of its current financial year next May. It opened 52 last year.

Chairman and chief executive Gerry Ford said: 'Caffè Nero is going to have another strong year. Much like last year, all the main ingredients remain in place for us to excel – a thriving retail coffee market, a favourable retail property environment with extensive availability of sites at reasonable prices, a coffee brand highly rated by UK consumers, and self-generated funds sufficient to finance the group's growth.' He added that the group now generates as much cash as it spends on expansion and has €5.9 million in the bank.

UNIT 15 Managing credit

PREPARATION

- There are three possible tracks through the unit: fast (about 1½ hours), standard (about 2 hours) and comprehensive (about 3 hours). For more information on the different tracks, see the notes in the Introduction on pages 10 and 11.
- For details of the aims of the unit, look at the Contents box opposite, the Language Notes at the end of the Course Book unit and the Useful Phrases below.
- If available to you, you can use the Self-study Guide as a source of supplementary exercises on the key themes of the unit.
- If you have taught this unit before, check the notes you made at the time.

USEFUL PHRASES

I'm calling about our invoice number AK-40 7/AZ for €450.
According to our records, the goods were delivered on time.
When can we expect to receive payment?
We charge 5% on overdue accounts.

It was passed for payment ten days ago.
You should have received our payment by now.
Apparently there's a query on this invoice.
I'm sorry about this; I'll look into it and call you back.
You'll get the money by the 10th without fail.

This account is overdue and the phone is barred.
It's a company phone. What should I do?
The only thing I can suggest is that you make a payment and sort it out with your accounts people later.
I hope this isn't going to affect my credit record.

My card's just been declined – I'd like to know what's going on.
There have been some unusual transactions on your account.
Your card has been blocked automatically.
So what do I have to do?
You should call our fraud line as soon as possible.

How can I protect myself from ID theft?
There are a number of things you can do to reduce the risk.
You need to use a shredder.
You must put your name on the anti-fraud register.

LEAD IN (SUGGESTIONS)

- Check whether learners have looked at the Useful Phrases on page 72 in the Course Book (copied above). Comments from learners may indicate which areas of the target language they need to focus on.
- Consider leading into the subject of credit fraud by discussing the stories they have brought to the class as part of their preparation – see the Preparation box on page 69.

Contents

Expressions
I'm calling about our invoice number AK-40 7/AZ.
It was passed for payment ten days ago.
My card's just been declined. What's going on?
How can I protect myself from ID theft?

Language check
Advising and suggesting: *I think / don't think you should …*
Modal verbs (criticism / regret): *You ought to have …*
Conditional sentences without *if*: *otherwise, or else*
Vocabulary: *credit limit, credit record, credit status, due, overdue, due date, look into, sort out, pay off*

Practice
Handling credit card and mobile phone problems
Querying an invoice
Writing a message about late payment
An article about ID theft

---

1 CORE PRACTICE

Listening and speaking

- Here learners have an opportunity to practise a range of situations relating to managing credit.
- The exercise is in two parts – listening and speaking. The listening activity (part i) provides learners with ideas and models for the speaking activity (part ii).
- Ask learners to identify the verbal clues they used when answering the comprehension questions in part i.
- In part ii, encourage learners to adapt the scenarios to their needs. Where possible they should introduce their examples of credit fraud, which they have been asked to prepare in advance of this lesson.
- Question a: The male speaker has a non-standard accent. Gloss language as necessary: *look into it* = investigate the problem.
- Question b: The woman has an Indian accent. Note the following: *there's a bar on your phone* = the service provider has blocked calls on the phone; *sort this out* = solve / resolve the problem; *credit record* = the history of an individual's or a company's past borrowings and payments (including details of late or non-payments).
- Question c: The man has an Irish accent. Gloss these terms, as necessary: *cloned* = the process of copying the details of a credit card to make a duplicate card; *declined* = not accepted; *transactions* = completed business activities (here = withdrawals); *sizeable withdrawals* = large amounts of money taken out the account; *fraud* (see Glossary).

Managing credit

- Question d: The woman has a US accent. Note *ID theft* = identity theft, the process of stealing an individual's personal details and using them to obtain credit facilities; *the anti-fraud register* = a service which gives added protection against credit card fraud to those who enrol.
- **Further step:** When learners have completed their individual practice in part ii, ask them to demonstrate their example to the rest of the group.

2 LANGUAGE CHECK

- The multiple-choice questions provide a starting point for the Language Check. Ensure that the related language points are explored and revised, as necessary. Refer learners to the Language Notes and Business Grammar Guide booklet that accompanies the Course Book. The Specific Points section below gives you further in-depth guidance.
- For each question, consider the following options.
  - Identify the answer.
  - Explore why the other suggestions are wrong.
  - Ask learners to prepare examples that relate to their working needs, e.g.:
    Question 1: *You should have kept us informed. Then we would have known what was going on.*
    Amended version: *They ought to have explained their terms of payment. We didn't realise the payment was overdue.*
- **Further step:** Working in twos or threes, ask learners to identify three or four examples of the language points explored in the multiple choice questions in the documents they have brought to class or in a newspaper article.

SPECIFIC POINTS

Question 1: Modal verbs expressing criticism / regret
- Go through the examples in the Language Notes concentrating on the different meanings of the various modals. It might also be worth practising the weak pronunciation of *have* in these modals.
- Use of *should have* for criticism (BGG 7.8); third conditional (BGG 3.4). Explain that *should have* indicates that a certain course of action was not taken but it would have been the correct thing to do. *ought to have* would also be possible. Both *would have* and *could have* could be used in the second half of the sentence. *You could have* means it would have been possible for you to have done something to improve the situation. As these structures need a lot of practice, encourage your learners to produce examples themselves of criticism / regret using past modals (with a consequence), e.g. *You should've let me know your car was at the garage. I could have / would have given you a lift.*

Questions 2 and 3: Advising, suggesting (BGG 21.1)
- Go through the examples in the Language Notes.
- Q2: *advise* + negative infinitive. Point out that *would* is optional with *advise / suggest / recommend*. Ensure your learners can use *suggest* and *recommend* in the example sentence (i.e. *I would suggest / recommend that you don't …*).
- Q3: Note *advise* can be followed by a *that* clause, a personal object and an infinitive, or *-ing* (when there is no personal object), e.g. *I'd advise that you protect … / you to protect … / protecting*. *suggest* and *recommend* can be followed by a *that* clause (*that* can be omitted) or *-ing* (with no personal object). Ask your learners to practise all three verbs in the example sentence and make up their own examples. All three verbs can be preceded by *would*.

Question 4: *should have* and modal verbs expressing criticism / regret
- See Q1 opposite.

Questions 5 and 6: Conditional sentences without *if* (BGG 3.6)
- Go through the sentences in the Language Notes.
- Q5: Explain that *or else, if not* and *otherwise* can all be used interchangeably. However, only **c** is correct here, as a negative verb is needed for correct meaning. Note *(to) settle* (a bill / account) = to pay.
- Q6: *as long as* – stating conditions. Try to elicit *provided / providing / on condition that* as alternatives.

Questions 7 to 10: Vocabulary – credit control
- Q7: Verb phrases and prepositions. Check that learners understand that *pay off* = to clear the balance (pay the whole sum). Go through usage of *pay* with the other prepositions, e.g.:
  I'll pay you back when I get my next pay cheque.
  I paid for it by credit card.
- Q8: Note *downgrade (your credit limit)* = reduce / lower. Your *credit status* (also *credit rating / score*) is an estimate of your *creditworthiness* (= your ability to repay money given on credit).
- Q9: *due / overdue* + verb phrases. Note *the account was overdue* = it should have been paid earlier; *due date* = the date by which something must be paid. Both *leave it with me* and *leave it to me* are possible.
- Q10: Note also *put a stop on a cheque* = to block the transaction before the cheque is cleared. Only *find out* collocates with *what the problem is*.

3 LISTENING

Querying an invoice

- Lead into the activity by discussing with class members instances when they queried an invoice. What was the problem? How was it resolved?
- Check that the situation in the listening exercise is clear.
- Diana Fry has a US accent; John Mars has an Australian accent.

- Listen with the class and elicit answers to the comprehension questions (**a** to **e**).
- Gloss as necessary: *parent company* = company which owns more than 50% of the shares of another company; *mix-up* = a mistake that causes confusion.
- **Further step:** Explore further comprehension question **d**. (John Mars was diplomatic.) How would he have communicated if he had been more aggressive? What expressions would he have used? How would his intonation have changed? The aim here is to provide a reference point, not to encourage aggressive communication.

4 WRITING
Late payment

1
- Ask learners, in pairs, to decide which of the two situations they will find most useful. If possible, have an equal number of each scenario demonstrated by group members.
- Have each pair agree the specific details of their scenario, then practise the call. Supply extra language if required.

2
- When the call is over, ask learners to work individually to prepare a brief summary of the points agreed.
- Gloss, as necessary, the Useful Language listed on page 70 of the Course Book: *a duplicate* = an exact copy; *pay by return (of post)* = pay immediately the invoice is received; *resume* = start again; *terms of trading* = conditions under which a supplier agrees to do business and allow credit; *a one-off arrangement* = will happen only once, not a regular arrangement.
- The partners in each pair then review each other's messages and decide if they are a fair record.
- **Further step:** Ask pairs to form fours, so that in each four one pair represents Scenario **a** and the other represents Scenario **b**. Ask groups to review both scenarios – the phone calls and the summary messages.

5 FEATURE
ID theft

1
- Go through the article with the group. If appropriate, ask the following comprehension questions.
  - *How do criminals steal personal data?* (They do this by going through rubbish bins, phishing, intercepting cards sent to customers – a name and address is all they need.)
  - *How can you protect yourself?* (Shred personal documents, register with an anti-fraud service.)
  - *How can a fraud prevention service protect you?* (If you register and pay the fee, companies have to carry out extra checks when they receive an application for credit in your name.)
  - *How were Anne Kemble's details stolen?* (Criminals intercepted a storecard sent out in her name.)
- Gloss as necessary: *have soared* = have risen quickly; *eightfold* = eight times; *bare (details)* = basic; *rack up (debts)* = accumulate; *scavenge through (rubbish)* = look through; *purporting (to come from)* = claiming / pretending; *bogus (website)* = false / artificial; *to pose as* = to pretend to be; *shredding* = cutting into very thin pieces or strips; *a victimless crime* = a crime where no one suffers directly; *cover customers' losses* = (in this text) do not take the 'stolen' money out of the customer's account (so the bank or card company bears any loss); *credit record* = an individual or company's payment history.

2
- Set up the pairwork exercise. Partner B's information is on page 135.
- Gloss as necessary: *crooks* = criminals; *a mail filtering service* = a service that stops unwanted mail; *card slips* = the small pieces of paper that accompany credit card transactions; *disclose your pin* = tell someone your Personal Identification Number (used in ATMs, to pay by credit card, etc.).
- The information on page 135 relates to the UK. A net search will give your learners equivalent local protection agencies.
- Ask all the Partner As to work in a group as they think through the questions they might ask. Ask the Partner Bs to work together as they prepare their role.
- **Further step:** Ask learners to think again about the examples of credit fraud they discussed at the start of the lesson, and to suggest ways the frauds could have been avoided.

REVIEW

- Go through the Language Notes and Useful Phrases in the Course Book.
- Ensure learners note down the terms they found particularly useful.
- Make a note of this language for your own future reference.
- Remind learners that practice is the key to progress. Encourage them to be systematic, e.g. they might set targets to use a particular structure or vocabulary item three times 'today'

Managing credit 73

Answers

1 Core practice
a i [U] b i [F] c i [U/T] d i [U/T]

2 Language check
1 b   2 a   3 b   4 b   5 c
6 a   7 b   8 a   9 c   10 b

3 Listening
a A duplicate invoice has been sent out by mistake, and it appears Solo Associates has paid twice.
b It's in the top right-hand corner.
c He is going to send back the duplicate invoice for them to sort out.
d He was diplomatic.
e If the invoice has been paid twice, Solo Associates will receive a refund.

4 Writing
(*possible draft messages*)
2 for 1a

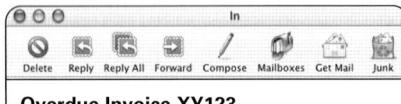

Overdue Invoice XY123
[Attachment] Duplicate invoice

Dear
Following our phone call this morning, I would like to confirm that:
- we will send you a duplicate invoice (see attached)
- you will pay by return, as this is now overdue
- we will resume deliveries as soon as we receive your payment
- you will return to normal terms of trading when settling invoices in future.

Thank you for your cooperation.
Regards

For 1b

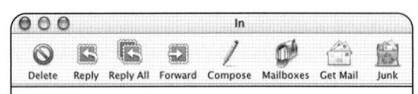

Your Invoice XY123

Dear
I would like to summarise the points we agreed in our phone call this morning. As the result of a short-term problem at this end, we would like to extend the period of credit on the above invoice by 14 days. We agreed that payment should now reach you by … .
Can I stress that this is a one-off, short-term arrangement? We will return to normal terms of trade in all other cases.
I would like to thank you for your understanding and cooperation.

Best regards

Audioscripts

1 Core practice
a – I'm calling about our invoice number AK-40 7/AZ for €450.
 – How can I help you?
 – According to our records, we haven't received payment. And it was due on the 15th.
 – Let me get the details on screen. According to this, the invoice was passed for payment ten days ago. You should have received the money by now.
 – Well, we haven't received anything.
 – I'm sorry about this. Let me look into it – I'll call you back.
b – You've come through to Customer Service because your account is overdue and there's a bar on your phone.
 – But this is a company phone. My company pays the bill.
 – I'm afraid the account is overdue.
 – Really? So, how can we sort this out?
 – You need to talk to your accounts department and …
 – But there won't be anyone there at this time and I need to use the phone.
 – The only thing I can suggest is that you make a payment now and sort it out with them later.
 – I hope this isn't going to affect my credit record.
c – My card's just been declined; I'd like to know what's going on?
 – Yes, there've been some unusual transactions on your account and the automatic fraud protection is blocking your card. Can I ask what payments you have made today?
 – I haven't made any. I had to use another card.
 – Well, there have been some sizeable withdrawals.
 – Can you give me the details?
 – 500 and 200 this morning, 700 last night.
 – Oh no! Do you know when or where?
 – No, that's not on here yet.
 – So what do I do?
 – I'll cancel the card and order a new one, and you should call our fraud line as soon as possible. I'll give you the number.
d – So, how do I protect myself from ID theft?
 – There are a number of things you can do to reduce the risk. Do you have a shredder?
 – Yes, but I only use it for confidential documents.
 – Well you need to use it more than that. If they have your name and address they can find out your previous address, your date of birth, details of your parents.
 – Does that mean I shouldn't give people my business card?
 – Well, you need to make sure you know who they are. And very important – you must put your name on the anti-fraud register.

3 Listening
– Kolmex Conference Centre. Diana Fry speaking. How can I help you?
– Oh hello, it's Solo Associates here, part of the AFC group. John Mars speaking. As you know, we had a sales conference at your place in May and I've got what looks like an invoice here for accommodation. I passed it to our parent company in Belgium and they've written back to say that in fact this was paid by our sales manager at the time. Can I give you the details that are written on it?
– Yes, please. There should be a reference number in the top right-hand corner.
– Oh, oh yes, there is, but it isn't very clear. It's 123 stroke 321, reference 'Sonya'.
– Fine. It seems we've sent you a duplicate invoice by mistake. I'm very sorry. Could you send it back to us so I can check it?
– Yes, of course, but the problem is that the person in charge of purchasing here tells me that she has also paid this to you, so it seems that you have been paid twice for one invoice.
– Look, it seems there's been an administrative mix-up. Please send us the invoice which you have there and we'll sort it out. I'm sorry about any inconvenience this has caused you.

UNIT 16 Time management

PREPARATION

- It is possible to go through this unit on three different tracks: fast (about 1½ hours), standard (about 2 hours) and comprehensive (about 3 hours). For more information on the different tracks, see the notes in the Introduction on pages 10 and 11.
- For details of the aims of the unit, look at the Contents box opposite, the Language Notes at the end of the Course Book unit and the Useful Phrases below.
- If available to you, you can use the Self-study Guide as a source of supplementary exercises on the key themes of the unit.

USEFUL PHRASES

In this job, you have to be able to work under pressure.
It's very demanding – things can get pretty busy.
It's important to delegate and prioritise.

The phone takes up a lot of time.
I have an assistant who handles routine matters.
I find it difficult to cope with interruptions.
Sometimes I wish there was less pressure.

I'm having trouble meeting the deadline.
I'm afraid the work won't be ready in time.
We've having one or two problems.
Could we reschedule the meeting?

I'd like to attend a course – it would benefit my work.
Time management is a key skill.
I can't do it unless I can take time off.
Ask HR to check it out – especially the cost.
The cost will come out of the department's training budget.
What's your schedule like at the moment?
It's OK by me, providing you can get someone to cover for you.

The course showed us how to establish priorities.
It taught us ways of dealing with stress.
It focused on ways of improving one's performance.
They stressed the importance of to-do lists.
They gave us tips for running meetings.
It helped me to handle my workload.

LEAD IN (SUGGESTIONS)

- Check whether learners have brought documents relating to a training course. These can be used as a resource through the lesson.
- Discuss the Useful Phrases on page 76 in the Course Book (copied above). Comments from the group may indicate which areas of the target language they need to focus on and the level of interest in the topic.
- You might begin the lesson by eliciting time management disasters – not hearing the alarm and arriving late for a wedding, a meeting, etc. Be prepared to tell a story of your own.

Contents

Expressions
In this job, you have to be able to work under pressure.
It is important to delegate and prioritise.
The course showed us how to establish priorities.
They gave us tips on running meetings.

Language check
More on conditionals without *if*: *or, or else, otherwise*
wish / if only: *I wish I could …*
Reflexive pronouns: *yourself, themselves*
Latin expressions: *vice versa*
Vocabulary: *planning, prioritising, delegating, workload, paperwork, backlog, problem solving, fire fighting, keep on top of, build up, get through*

Practice
Reviewing time management skills
Time management questionnaire
Organising to go on a training course
Tips on running meetings

1 CORE PRACTICE

Listening and speaking

- In this activity learners can practise a range of situations relating to time management.
- The exercise is in two parts – listening and speaking. The listening activity (part i) provides learners with ideas and models for the speaking activity (part ii).
- Ask learners to identify the verbal clues they used when answering the comprehension questions in part i.
- In part ii, encourage learners to adapt the scenarios to their needs. Where possible they should introduce the realia they have brought to the class.
- Question a: *I've (recently) been on* = I've attended; *delegating* = passing responsibility for work to someone else.
- Question b: *prioritise* (US *prioritize*) = rank jobs according to their importance; *screens my calls* = stops the unimportant calls reaching me; *The phone would take up the whole day* = I would spend the whole day talking on the phone; *an agenda* = a list of matters to be discussed in a meeting; *in the chair* = acting as chair person (the person who leads and controls the meeting); *keep on top of it* = be in control of it.
- Question c: The female speaker has a US accent. Note: *we have an export order to meet* = we have a deadline with an export order; *work something out* = find a solution to the problem.
- Question d: The man has a US accent. Explain that *cover for you* = do your work for you; *HR* = Human Resources; *check it out* = research it.

Time management 75

- **Further step:** Lead a discussion on time and time management. Attitudes vary from culture to culture and from company to company. Is it right to arrive early for an appointment? Or is it more diplomatic to arrive a few minutes late? Is it professional to start a meeting on time? Or will that alienate colleagues. Are there key differences in attitude among learners?

2 LANGUAGE CHECK

- The multiple-choice questions link to the Language Notes at the end of the Course Book unit (page 76), and the related notes in the Business Grammar Guide (see the booklet that accompanies the Course Book).
- The multiple-choice questions enable you to treat the language programme flexibly. Points that are known can be handled briefly. Points that require more remedial attention can be explored in more detail. The Specific Points section below gives you further detailed guidance.
- When working on vocabulary questions, point out the Vocabulary notes in the Language Reference section at the end of the unit in the Course Book, and the Glossary on pages 158 – 160. Introduce, as necessary, any special terms that learners need.
- For each question consider the following options.
  - Identify the answer.
  - Explore why the other options are wrong.
  - Ask learners to prepare examples that relate to their specific needs, e.g.:
    Question 1: *I can do the course as long as the company funds it.*
    Amended version: *We can go on training courses as long as they don't interfere with our work.*
- **Further step:** In pairs or groups, ask learners to prepare a dialogue using all ten examples in the multiple-choice questions.

SPECIFIC POINTS

Questions 1 to 3: More on conditionals without *if* (BGG 3.6)
- Go through the examples in the Language Notes focusing on the different meanings of the variants of *if / if not*.
- Q1: Stating a condition. Elicit alternatives to *as long as* (*on condition that / provided*, etc.).
- Q2: This sentence is about an eventuality (something – usually unwanted – that might happen in the future). Point out that **b** is not possible as it needs to be followed by a noun phrase.
- Q3: Only **b** (*If only*) has the correct meaning. It is followed by an idea which is contrary to reality (i.e. she does waste a lot of time). Point out that *providing* is wrong as it is not followed by a necessary condition. To reinforce the use of *providing*, give an example (e.g. *Providing you agree to work at weekends, we'll offer you the job*) and ask learners to give other examples.

Question 4: Conditionals, *I wish / if only* (BGG 3.2, 3.4)
- Review the examples in the Language Notes. Option **b** (*had been*) is not correct, as the sentence is about a present situation (*my new job*). Note *would* is used after *I wish* when talking about persistent behaviour (e.g. *I wish he would stop criticising me*) but is not used with the verb *to be*.

Question 5: Verb phrases
- Note that *get through the agenda* = discuss all the items in the agenda.

Question 6: Verb phrases and Latin expressions (see BGG 24.4 for definitions)

Question 7: Reflexive pronouns (BGG 12.2)
- There must be agreement between the object of the verb and the preceding pronoun / noun: *they* or *people / themselves*; *you / yourself / selves*, etc. When making a generalisation, we can use *people / you / one* (= formal) / *we*. See the examples in the Language Notes.

Question 8: Vocabulary
- Go through the Vocabulary section on page 76 of the Course Book. Note that *firefighting* = only having time to deal with crises in the workplace, due to overwork and poor planning.
- See Glossary for definitions of *backlog* and *workload*. Note that *paperwork* = the part of a job that involves dealing with letters, reports, keeping records, etc.; *the paperwork will get on top of you* = you will not be able to control / deal with the paperwork. Note that the subject and object are different in the main clause, so *yourself* is not correct.

Question 9: Verb phrases
- Note the phrases with *off* (= away from work); *have / take / ask for time off*; *be off* (e.g. *She was off all last week*); *be off sick*. Explain that *to go on* is less formal than *to attend*.

Question 10: Verb phrases and vocabulary
- Note that *demanding*, when used about something like a job, means requiring a lot of time, skill or effort (e.g. *I have a very demanding job*). When used to describe people (e.g. *My boss is very demanding*), it means that the person has high expectations, sometimes unreasonable.

3 LISTENING

Meetings

1
- Based on their direct experience, encourage learners to assess the list of tips for running meetings (see page 74 of the Course Book). Pre-experience learners should use their common sense.
- Gloss the list as necessary: *minutes* = notes of what happened in a meeting.
- Points not mentioned on the list include: punctuality, time limits, minutes and refreshments.

- Learners might like to number the bullet points in order of importance.

2
- The speaker is head of Pod, a management training organisation. He is English.
- Gloss as necessary: *the essence* = the most basic, important aspect; *motto* = a short saying that expresses a belief; *housekeeping* = (here) practical details; *Don't fall into that trap* = don't make that mistake; *with a big mouth* (slang usage) = who talks too loudly and too much, and who perhaps says things that aren't appropriate for the occasion; *taking over* = dominating; *the shrinking violets* = the quiet, shy people; *stick to* = follow exactly; *gracious* = pleasant and polite; *ruthless* = very hard and determined.
- **Further step:** Learners prepare and then deliver a short summary of the key points. This can be written or spoken. Useful language:
  The key points were …
  Other points he made include …
  He stressed the importance of …
  He warned against …
  He didn't mention …
  In my view …

4 WRITING
Allocating your time

- Ask learners to consider pie charts **a** and **b** in the Course Book (page 74) and the accompanying texts.
- Gloss as required: *allocate* (in the task instructions) = divide up. In text 1 *subordinates* = people with a lower ranking job; *fit in* = find time (to attend); *merely* = only. In text 2 *responsive approach* = mainly responding, not initiating; *is indicative of* (serious problems) = shows that there are (serious problems).
- Pete Drucker, referred to in text 2, is a well-known writer on management techniques.
- Ask learners to think about the way they divide their time and to prepare a pie chart showing the result.
- Ask them to write a text to accompany their chart. Encourage learners to write in a way that is simple and direct. You might offer an example showing how you allocate your own time.
- **Further step:** Collect the work that learners have prepared. Ask them to remove names. Number the documents and ask learners to identify which chart / text relates to which learner.

5 FEATURE
A course for managers

1
- Time Manager International (TMI) is a worldwide training consultancy.
- Lead into the pairwork activity by discussing with learners any time management courses they have done. They can refer to any documents about courses they have brought to class. Ask learners questions about what these courses covered, how they were organised and when they took place.
- Gloss the advertisement on page 75 of the Course Book as necessary: *implementing* = putting into operation; *a 'tune-up' day* = a day when you review and refresh your learning, like tuning a guitar; *a telephone hotline* = an emergency line you can use if you need help; *turn work away* = not accept work; *put your job on the line* = put your job at risk / make it possible that you will lose it.

2
- Note that the information for Presenter B is on page 136.
- Gloss as necessary: *non-residential* = does not involve staying overnight at the course centre; *a back-up service* = a support service.
- Ensure learners practise both sides of the interaction.
- **Further step:** Learners request permission to attend a TMI course using information they have been given in the activity. The request may be spoken or written. Useful language:
  I would like permission to attend …
  The next course is …
  The training covers …
  The cost includes …
  … has an excellent reputation
  … teaches techniques that will be useful.

REVIEW
- Encourage learners to note down the terms they found particularly useful.
- Make a note of this language for your own future reference.
- Go through the Language Notes and the Useful Phrases in the Course Book.
- Encourage learners to practise the new language they have learned. Suggest that they monitor themselves. For example, at the end of the day they might assess how well they have used the target language.

Time management

Answers

1 Core practice
a i [T]
b i The speaker is under pressure [T], but the job is not a nightmare [F].
c i [T]   d i [U]

2 Language check
1 c   2 c   3 b   4 a   5 b
6 b   7 a   8 a   9 c   10 c

3 Listening
Running time-efficient meetings
- Make sure everyone is informed of time and place. ✓
- Ensure the facilities are right (size of room, enough chairs, etc.).
- Allow enough time for your agenda. ✓
- Restrict the numbers present. ✓
- Distribute copies of working documents in advance.
- Circulate a clear agenda in advance.
- Make sure the person in the chair has experience. ✓
- Stick to the agenda.
- Make arrangements for calls to be held.
- Take and circulate clear minutes of the meeting.

4 Writing
a 2
b 1

Audioscripts

1 Core practice
a – This company is very keen on training – so, I've recently been on a time management course.
 – Was it useful?
 – Well, you know, on these courses you usually don't learn anything you don't already know. What they do is remind you of the techniques you should be using anyway.
 – So what did the course focus on?
 – How to establish priorities, how to handle interruptions, the importance of delegating. All useful points.

b – I'd say I have a fairly high-pressure job. It's rewarding but we're under a lot of pressure. The secret is to stay calm and to have clear aims – you have to prioritise. However many interruptions there are, I try to do the important things first. I'm fortunate because I have a good assistant who screens my calls and handles routine matters. The phone would take up the whole day, if I let it. But the biggest time-waster, in my experience, is meetings. I now insist on an agenda, and if I'm in the chair I set time limits for each item. I like the job, but it's very demanding; I have to keep on top of it, otherwise it's a nightmare.

c – Look, I'm afraid we're having problems meeting the deadline on that consignment of water-filter parts for you. I know time is critical at your end.
 – It is. What's the problem?
 – I'm afraid the changes in specification have caused more problems than we expected. We're not going to be able to complete on time.
 – Well, that leaves us with a big problem – we have an export order to meet.
 – I know, I'm sorry. I'm calling to see if we can work something out.

d – I think the course would benefit my work – not just my work but the department as a whole. RTL Training has a good reputation. Its courses are supposed to be good.
 – What's our schedule like at the moment?
 – Not too bad; we've just finished stock-taking. I thought it might be a good time.
 – Well, it's OK by me providing you can get someone to cover for you. Ask HR to check it out, especially the cost; it'll come out of my training budget.

3 Listening
– What do you do to prepare for a successful meeting?

– Well it is a very interesting question because, of course, we need to make meetings as efficient and effective as possible because statistics show that 1% more of business people's time is spent in meetings each year. So how do we prepare for an effective meeting? And the essence of it is planning. And I quote you the old motto of 'Failing to plan is planning to fail'. So how do we plan for a meeting? We make sure, first of all, that everybody knows where it is, the sort of housekeeping details, where and when and ideally what time it is going to finish as well. The third thing is the agenda, a most important tool, but have we got too many things on the agenda?
The fourth thing is, don't be tempted to include too many people in your meeting. Sometimes people want to just be in the meeting to be seen. Don't fall into that trap. Have the decision-makers and the people with the right information in that meeting. The other very important aspect is the chair person. Now it is no good just suggesting that somebody is the chair person; we have to make sure that that chair person has the experience and the authority with which to control that meeting. Otherwise we'll get somebody with a big mouth and lots of ideas and lots of enthusiasm taking over and the shrinking violets, shrinking into the corners and feeling that their time has basically been wasted. So that person with authority needs to stick to that agenda. There's a saying that goes with this: 'Be gracious with people, but be ruthless with time.'

UNIT 17 Delivering quality

PREPARATION

- There are three possible tracks through the unit: fast (about 1½ hours), standard (about 2 hours) and comprehensive (about 3 hours). For further information, see the notes in the Introduction on pages 10 and 11.
- For details of the aims of the unit, look at the Contents box opposite, the Language Notes at the end of the Course Book unit and the Useful Phrases below.
- The Self-study Guide has a range of supplementary exercises.
- If you have taught the unit before, check the notes you made at the time.

USEFUL PHRASES

What we sell is quality and service.
We attach great importance to our customers' needs.
The company is committed to raising standards.
raising standards   improving quality   reducing errors

We need to update our system for dealing with returned goods.
It would improve our performance if we had better procedures for logging faults.
It would help us to identify areas of weakness.
We encourage best practice in all areas.

Our experience is that customers insist on quality certification. Some won't deal with you if you don't have it.
A quality certificate shows that you have good systems in place, and that they're working properly.
It's good from a marketing point of view.
It would undermine our position if we didn't have it.

We have a problem with lack of communication between departments.
Each department records complaints separately.
The system needs to be centralised, and made more efficient.
Quality suffers because nobody knows what is going on.
I'd streamline our internal information systems.

We're selling against a product called Softcell.
It's cheaper, but we believe we're more cost effective.
The secret is to listen to what your clients say.
It's usually not a question of better or worse, but what fits the client's requirements.

LEAD IN (SUGGESTIONS)

- Check whether learners have brought to class a complimentary message and a complaint. These can be used as a resource.
- Check also whether they have looked at the Useful Phrases on page 80 of the Course Book (copied above). Comments from learners may indicate which areas of the target language they need to focus on.
- Consider leading into the subject by eliciting stories about good and bad quality – if possible based on personal experience. Be prepared with a case of your own.

Contents

Expressions
What we sell is quality and service.
It would improve our performance
… if we had better procedures for logging faults.
We encourage best practice in all areas.
The secret is to listen to what your clients say.

Language check
More on conditionals (2nd / 3rd conditionals)
Alternative sentence structures
prevent vs. *avoid*
Vocabulary: *high / low quality, well / poorly made, very / not very good, really first class, user-friendly, value for money, be above / below / up to standard*

Practice
Talking about quality performance
Handling compliments and complaints
Writing a letter of apology
A customer care questionnaire

1 CORE PRACTICE

Listening and speaking

- This activity gives you an opportunity to practise a range of situations relating to quality issues.
- The exercise is in two parts – listening and speaking. The listening activity (part i) provides learners with ideas and models for the speaking activity (part ii).
- Ask learners to identify the verbal clues they used when answering the comprehension questions in part i.
- In part ii, encourage learners to adapt the scenarios to their needs. Where possible, they should introduce the realia they have brought to the class.
- Question a: The woman has a non-standard accent – she sounds Indian. See Glossary for *quality certificate*. Note that *a manual* = a handbook with detailed information such as the steps in a procedure or instructions for operating a machine; *laid down* = established / agreed.
- Question b: The speaker has a US accent. Note that *compete on price* = offer lower prices than competitors; *a lower cost base* = basic costs that are lower; *sell at a slight premium* = sell at a slightly higher price; *our reputation for* = being known for; *aftersales service* = service received from the supplier after the sale (when the customer is using the product).
- Question c: The speaker has an Irish accent. Note that *on the retail market* = for sale to the

Delivering quality 79

general public; *our range* (of products) = the number of different products we offer; *beat us on price* = sell their goods at lower prices; *back up* = support.
- Question d: The speaker has an Australian accent. Explain that *we let a job go out* = we allowed an order to be sent out; *a rushed job* = an urgent order which was produced quickly; *let down by someone* = someone broke a promise; *were screaming for it* = were pressurising us (to send the order); *an important account* = an important customer (who has an account with us); *hassle* = trouble.
- **Further step:** Record some of the situations practised in part ii and analyse the accuracy of the language used.

2 LANGUAGE CHECK

- As you go through the multiple-choice questions with the group, point out the Language Notes at the end of the Course Book unit (page 80), and the related notes in the Business Grammar Guide (see the booklet that accompanies the Course Book).
- The multiple-choice questions provide a starting point for the Language Check. Ensure that the related language points are explored and revised, as necessary. The Specific Points section below gives you further detailed guidance.
- Adapt the points to learners' needs. Concentrate on the areas where practice is needed.
- When working on vocabulary questions, introduce special terms that class members need. Point out the Glossary on pages 158 – 160 of the Course Book.
- For each question consider the following options.
  - Identify the answer.
  - Explore why the other options are wrong.
  - Ask learners to prepare examples that relate to their working needs, e.g.:
    Question 1: *If we had known about the scheme, we would have applied to join.*
    Amended version: *If we had spent more time planning, the project might have succeeded.*
- **Further step:** Ask learners, working individually or in pairs, to prepare extra questions, using the Language Notes and the related notes in the BGG.

SPECIFIC POINTS

Question 1: Second and Third Conditionals (BGG 3.2, 3.4)
- Go through the examples in the Language Notes to revise the conditionals.
- Only **c** (the Third Conditional) is both grammatically correct and makes sense. It refers to a situation where the opposite happened in reality (i.e. they did not know about the scheme so did not apply). The Second Conditional would not make sense because they obviously do know about the scheme as they are talking about it. Ask your learners if they could modify the example in any way to make a Second Conditional fit (e.g. *If we knew more about the scheme, we might apply to join*).

Questions 2 to 5: Other conditional forms (BGG 3.6)
- Q2: Second Conditional. Note that *shoddy* = poorly made / bad quality. Only **a** makes sense. Explain that *even* is essential for correct meaning here: it conveys the idea of *it wouldn't make any difference if …*
- Q3: This is an abbreviated form of a negative *if* clause (*If you don't have a manual …*). It avoids repetition (BGG 3.5).
- Q4: First Conditional (BGG 3.1). Both *supposing* and *what if* would be possible here for this hypothetical question. However, only **c** (*performance improvements*) collocates with the verb *finance*.
- Q5: Explain that *if it wasn't / hadn't been for your help* was the most important reason for not losing the order. Note *if it hadn't been for* could also have been used here.

Question 6: Alternative sentence structures (BGG 19.1) for emphasising specific parts of a sentence (cleft sentences)
- In this example, *What … is …* is used to transform the basic structure (*We provide top quality service*) in order to highlight the object (*top quality service*).

Questions 7 and 8: Vocabulary related to quality
- Go through the Vocabulary section on page 80 of the Course Book. Note *sloppily finished* = finished in a careless way; *atrociously designed* = very badly designed.
- Q7: Note *rock bottom* (usually used with prices) = very low; *best practice* = a working method (described in detail) which is officially considered the best in a particular business or industry.
- Q8: Explain that *committed (to doing something)* = giving time and energy to achieve something.

Question 9: *prevent / avoid* (BGG 20.3)
- Both could be used here (*people working late* functions as a noun phrase so can be used after *avoid*), but with slightly different meanings; *prevent* would be stronger because it implies more action on the part of the company to stop the situation happening.
- Note *to fall short* = not be good enough.

Question 10: Verb phrases
- Ensure all the verb phrases on page 80 have been understood: *take pride in* = do well (so that you can feel pleased and satisfied); *come to light* = are noticed / discovered.
- Note *set out* = describe something formally and in detail, usually in writing. It is a separable phrasal verb. Note also *operating procedure* = a set of fixed instructions or steps for carrying out routine activities.

3 LISTENING

Handling technical complaints

1. - Lead a discussion on how complaints are handled in learners' organisations. Ask questions such as:
     What record does your organisation keep of complaints?
     Do they to relate to one area – product quality, accounts, distribution, aftersales service, etc.?
     What are the solutions? Better training, staffing levels, investment in plant / machinery / IT infrastructure, etc.?
   - Pre-experience learners should talk about an organisation they belong to – a college perhaps.
   - Ask learners to refer to the realia they have brought to class, if relevant.

2. - The speaker is a technical service assistant working in an electrical engineering company specialising in thermostats. He is Dutch.
   - Prepare for the exercise by going through the true / false statements listed on page 78.
   - Consider reinforcing the activity by having learners read the audioscript (page 149 in Course Book). Answer vocabulary questions if required: (*our sales managers*) *in the field* = working away from the factory and having contact with customers; *gain authority* (non-standard usage) = seek / get authority; *a credit note* = a document given in place of a refund which acknowledges that the holder is entitled to goods / services to the value of those returned; *break down* = separate; *process areas* = the various stages involved in producing a product – moulding, assembling, quality checking, etc.; *Quality Assurance* = providing evidence that the quality-related activities are being performed effectively – including design, development, production, installation, servicing and documentation.
   - **Further step:** Ask learners to summarise what the speaker's job involves – technical evaluation of complaints, organising credit notes / refunds, etc.

4 WRITING

Responding to feedback

1. - Go through the tips listed in the Course Book (page 78). Gloss as necessary: *to rectify* = to put right; *to the point* = relevant to the subject being discussed; *considerate* = showing concern for your customers' rights and feelings. Note that *overly dramatic* is low frequency usage. More common would be *over dramatic*.
   - Ask learners if they agree with the tips. Some might say that you should never apologise because it suggests liability. Others might point out that well-handled complaints increase customer loyalty.
   - Discuss the form of the response – letter, email, phone call?

2. - Ask learners, working in pairs, to draft a response to a letter of complaint. If possible, they should refer to one of the letters they have brought to class. There is a sample in the answers.
   - This activity can be given as homework.
   - **Further step:** Learners go through the sample letter in the answers and check whether it follows the advice in the exercise. Possible answers:
     Write as soon as possible – no information.
     Focus on actions to rectify the situation – yes.
     Be brief – the sample is quite long.
     Be sincere in a clear simple way – yes.
     Be respectful and considerate – yes.
     Take responsibility – yes.
     Follow-up – no information.

5 FEATURE

Customer care

1. - The advertisement is put out by the Institute of Customer Care (IOCC), an organisation that assists customer care professionals.
   - Go through the advertisement and gloss as necessary: *TQM* = total quality management (see Glossary); *increase your customer loyalty* = increase the chances of your customers continuing to do business with you; *refining* = improving (by making small changes); *impartial advice* = neutral advice; *sustain the momentum* = keep moving forward (with the customer care improvement programme); *networking service* = a service where members can contact each other when they need advice / assistance.
   - Note that the text includes an ironic statement – point out the exclamation mark: *Contact us. It sounds interesting!*
   - Possible pre-questions include the following.
     What is the key message of the advertisement? (Customer care is a key part of any business strategy; without customers you have no business.)
     What is it offering? (A number of free services – see the summary in the answers for details.)
   - Ask learners to summarise how the IOCC supports its members – see answers.

Delivering quality

2
- Ask learners to discuss their experience of customer care, if possible with reference to the organisation they work for.
- As individuals tell their stories, ask the rest of the group to identify examples of good and bad customer care, and the ways in which the level of care can be improved.
- Ask them to match the needs they have identified with the support offered by the IOCC in its advertisement.
- **Further step:** Have learners use the flowchart as the basis for a guided discussion. Partner A represents the IOCC and asks the questions. Partner B replies on behalf of his / her organisation (or an organisation he / she knows about). Encourage learners to improvise and use the chart flexibly.

REVIEW

- Go through the Language Notes and the Useful Phrases in the Course Book, if you have not done so already.
- For future reference, make a note of the language that class members have found particularly relevant, especially if you have introduced it in response to the specific needs.
- Encourage learners to work on their language development outside the class in an organised way, e.g. they might consider rewarding themselves in some way when they use target language correctly.

Answers

1 Core practice
a i [U]   b i [T]   c i [T]   d i [T]

2 Language check
1 c   2 a   3 b   4 c   5 b
6 a   7 c   8 b   9 c   10 b

3 Listening
a [T]   b Not given.   c [T]   d Not given.
e [F]   f Not given.

4 Writing
(*possible answer*)
2

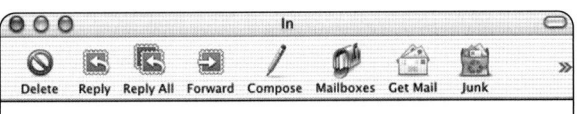

Dear Ms Navage

Installation delays

I am writing to offer my sincere apologies for the inconvenience you have experienced in connection with the high speed Internet service you requested in your letter of 20 May.
Your file has been passed to me because we would like to put right the mistakes that have been made and to give top priority to your request. It is clear that your case somehow slipped through the net. I'm afraid there have been a number of key staff changes in our customer service team and this may explain how your letter was overlooked.
I have directed our Installation Team to contact you immediately to set up a time convenient to you when they can come to your house and install the new router and make the necessary adjustments to your software.
As a sign of our concern and of our appreciation of you as a customer, we would like to offer you the first three months of the high speed service free of charge. Therefore, your account will not be billed until October.
Can I stress that what happened in this case is not typical of CableNet's level of customer service. We are committed to providing you and all our customers with the highest standards at all times.
If you have any questions, please do not hesitate to call me on 754-9785.
With best wishes
Manager, Customer Solutions

Adapted from WritingHelp

5 Feature
(*possible summary*)
1
- IOCC helps companies to achieve better products / results by improving customer care / TQM.
- It offers the following services free of charge:
  - impartial advice and support
  - practical assistance with developing customer care strategies
  - regular site visits
  - advice with selecting appropriate specialists
  - a networking service and the chance to see solutions in practice
  - guidance on how to stay ahead of the competition by offering better products and services
  - information on how customer care improves profitability.

Audioscripts

1 Core practice

a
- We find that many customers insist that suppliers have a quality certificate. You have to have one; if not, they won't deal with you. So from a marketing point of view, they're important.
- But they don't guarantee quality, do they?
- Not exactly. What they mean is that you've reviewed your systems and prepared a manual, and that you're keeping to the standards laid down. If you like, it shows that your systems are working properly.

b
- We believe we have high production standards. Everyone in the company from top to bottom accepts the importance of quality in our work. We're always improving and updating our quality-check procedures. It's difficult for an American company to compete on price. Our main competitors tend to have a lower cost base, so generally our products sell at a slight premium. What we depend on is our reputation for excellence, not just of our products themselves, but also the aftersales service and so on.

c
- Our best-selling product is a low-cost mouthwash called Aquarinse. We supply it direct to dentists – it's not available on the retail market. It's part of our range for the dental profession. We specialise in offering a complete 24-hour service. A dentist can call us at any time before 5.00pm and we guarantee next-day delivery. Our competitors may be able to beat us on price; some have particular lines that they claim are superior to ours, but none of them can offer the range and the service we offer. Our customers are prepared to pay a little extra in order to have the back up we provide.

d
- A couple of months ago, we let a job go out that was below standard. Never again. What we should have done was re-run it, but we didn't. It was a rushed job that came in at the last minute – the customer had been let down by someone else. So they were screaming for it, and they told us to send it as it was, which we did in the end – because the customer is always right. But then the complaints started to come in and, of course, they blamed us. We lost an important account – and we didn't get paid. It was a lot of hassle for nothing.

3 Listening

INT = Interviewer
TSA = Technical Services Assistant

INT: Can you tell me something about what you do?
TSA: My official title is Technical Services Assistant and I deal basically with complaints, technical complaints and to a limited extent non-technical complaints.
INT: How does the system work exactly?
TSA: Well, basically we use our sales managers in the field to process complaints, which are then handed on to me for technical evaluation. And then, after dealing with the technical evaluation … evaluation side of the complaint, I gain authority from my superior Charles Eden. And with this authority I then produce a credit note for the customer, in the case of justified complaints. If it's a one-off contract, I might have to organise a refund. That's about it.
INT: Um, what kind of record do you keep of complaints?
TSA: We produce a monthly report which tries to break down all the complaints into our process areas so that we can try to analyse them. Our major problems come from development work, some problems are inherent in the products and not produced by the machines or whatever.
INT: Can you give an example?
TSA: Well, when things go wrong it's often a design problem, not a quality control problem – there are design faults which need sorting out.
INT: So is quality assurance part of the technical department?
TSA: Yes, in a way – I actually work in the technical service department, which is just myself and Charles. Technical Service sits halfway between Quality Assurance and Research and Development.

UNIT 18 Working practices

PREPARATION

- Note that you can go through this unit at three different speeds: fast (about 1½ hours), standard (about 2 hours) and comprehensive (about 3 hours). For information on the different tracks, see the notes in the Introduction on pages 10 and 11.
- Check the Contents box on this page, the Language Notes at the end of the Course Book unit and the Useful Phrases below for the aims of the unit
- The Self-study Guide is a source of supplementary exercises.
- If you have taught the unit before, review the notes you made at the time.
- There is a Progress Test covering Units 13 – 18 on pages 143–144, which can be photocopied and circulated. The answers are on page 148. For the best results, give learners time to prepare.

USEFUL PHRASES

Our management style is very informal.
informal   traditional   progressive
The emphasis is on what works.
We are having to adapt to the demand for flexitime, as are our competitors.
We don't like the new legislation, and neither do they.

We are very customer focused.
Were one of our customers to complain, the people responsible would probably lose their jobs.

Our switchboard lets us down badly.
They make a bad impression.
Had we known about the problem, we would have sorted it out.

Health and Safety comes under Compliance.
It's part of the Building Manager's job.
He has to ensure the regulations are being applied properly.
We have to comply with the regulator's requirements.

The regulations are updated every so often.
Who checks if they are being applied?
The inspectors do spot checks from time to time.
Very seldom do they give you a second chance.

I used to have an administrative assistant.
Now, we work online and handle our own filing.
The main changes have been in the area of technology.
There is more competition – the pace is faster.

LEAD IN (SUGGESTIONS)

- In line with the suggestions in the Preparation section, check whether learners have brought to class samples of regulations or guidelines that apply to their work.
- Consider leading into the lesson by discussing such guidelines and working practices. Are they expressed in writing or are they more informal?
- Check whether learners have looked at the Useful Phrases on page 84 in the Course Book (copied above). Comments from the group may indicate which areas of the target language they need to focus on and the level of interest in the topic.

Contents

Expressions
Our management style is very informal.
We are very customer focused.
We have to comply with the regulator's requirements.
The main changes have been in the area of technology.
There is more competition – the pace is faster.

Language check
More on conditionals: *should they*, *were they to*, etc.
Expressions of frequency: *three times a year*, *very seldom*, etc.
Accord, indicating parallels: *X does* and *so does Y*
Terms relating to compliance: *comply with*, *enforce*, etc.
Vocabulary: *flexitime*, *job sharing*, *equal opportunities*, *requirements*, *guidelines*, *procedures*, *industrial / staff relations*, *do spot checks*, *give a good / bad impression*

Practice
Talking about dress and behaviour codes
Interview with an employee relations manager
Article on managing paperwork
Questionnaire on company culture

1 CORE PRACTICE

Listening and speaking

- In this activity learners can practise a range of situations relating to working practices. The exercise is in two parts – listening and speaking.
- The listening activity (part i) provides learners with ideas and models for the speaking activity (part ii).
- Where possible, ask learners to explain how they have reached their answers to the comprehension questions in part i.
- In part ii, encourage learners to adapt the scenarios to their needs and experience.
- Question a: The second speaker has a US accent. Note that *customer focused* = paying close attention to the customer's needs; *letting us down* = not giving a good impression of the company; *crucial* = very important and necessary.
- Question b: The second speaker has a non-standard accent. Note that *Health and Safety* = the department responsible for health and safety matters; *comes under* = is part of / is a sub-section of; *Compliance* = the department responsible for compliance matters (see Glossary); *evacuation procedures* = the instructions for leaving the building when it is not safe; *fire drills* = a safety exercise to practise what to do if there is a fire or other emergency and you need to leave the building quickly; *spot checks* = checks made without warning.

- Question c: The female speaker has a non-standard accent. Note *a dress-down policy* = a dress policy where employees can wear casual clothes; *pull your weight* = to do your share of the work properly; *an estate agent* = a professional who arranges the sale or letting of property.
- Question d: The man has a slight Scottish accent; the woman has a US accent. Note *in a back-up capacity* = in a support role; *terminals* = keyboards and screens (linked to the main computer network); *intermediaries* = people like agents who link the customer and supplier; *flexitime* (see Glossary); *job sharing* (see Glossary); *pace* = speed.
- **Further step:** Video the scenarios practised in part ii and use the recordings to analyse wider communication factors such as body language. Draw attention to the fact that in different cultures body language may be interpreted in different ways. Are there any local behaviours that might be misunderstood in a global context?

2 LANGUAGE CHECK

- The Specific Points section below gives you detailed guidance for the questions.
- When working on vocabulary questions, introduce the specialised terms learners need as required.
- Consider the following options for each question.
    - Identify the answer.
    - Explore why the other options are wrong.
    - Ask learners to prepare examples that relate to their working needs, e.g.:
    Question 1: *Should the inspectors do a spot check, we will be in serious trouble because we aren't complying with the regulations.*
    Amended version: *Should the worst happen and somebody gets hurt, the company would be liable.*
- **Further step:** Ask learners to put the examples in the questions into exchanges. What might the line before be? What could the next line be?

SPECIFIC POINTS

Questions 1 and 4: Inversions
- Q1: Inverted conditionals with *should* (BGG 3.5). Review the examples in the Language Notes. Explain that *should* + infinitive can be used in a hypothetical situation (*If the inspectors should do …*). Here the structure is also inverted and there is no *if* (*Should the inspectors do …*), which gives the sentence a more formal feel. It can be followed by *will* or *would* + infinitive in the main clause. The choice would depend on how likely the *spot check* was thought to be. Ask learners to produce other variants of this sentence (e.g. *If the inspectors do / did / were to do …, we will / would …*).

Question 2: *if / in case* (BGG 3.6)
- For the first gap, both *required* and *supposed* are correct. However, *if* would not make sense in the example as this would mean that hard hats only need to be worn *if* an accident occurs. Obviously they have to be worn as a preventative measure to avoid problems in the event of an accident, so *in case* (a) is correct.

Questions 3 and 4: Expressions of frequency
- Q3: To *dress up* means to wear formal clothes (usually for a special occasion). For *dress code*, see Glossary. Note *more often than not* = most of the time.
- Q4: See the examples in the Language Notes and BGG 19.2. This is an example of an inversion after *only*. It has the effect of emphasising the fact that the check happens on just one day a week. Ask your learners to transform the sentence back to normal word order (*There is only time on Wednesdays to check …*). Note *daily* is in contrast to *on Wednesdays* (once a week / weekly).

Questions 5 and 6: Accord (indicating parallels) (BGG 18.4)
- Go through the examples in the Language Notes.
- Q5: Note *so* with inversion. The use of *so* here avoids repetition of the verb phrase (with a positive verb) from the previous clause. Note that *do* represents *have an agreement with the union* here, but *have* could also be used (*and so have …*). It would be possible to use *as* if there were no *and* linking the clauses. If *also* were used it would have to come after the subject (*… also do*). However, *too* would be more natural (*… do too*). Note *no-go* (as in *no-go area*) = something not to be entered into.
- Q6: The second sentence needs *don't do* for it to logically agree with the first. Note *neither* is used instead of *so* to avoid repetition when the verb in the first clause is negative (*don't do the payroll …*). Ask learners to suggest alternatives to *neither* (e.g. *nor does; doesn't either; and the same is true for*).

Questions 7 and 8: Terms relating to compliance
- Q7: Only *ensures* (= makes sure) can be followed by a *that* clause. All three of the passive verbs could be used with *procedures*. Try also to elicit *complied with*.
- Q8: Elicit *illegal* for *against the law*. Note that *legislation* (uncountable) can refer to an individual law or a set of laws. *A penalty* can be used synonymously with *a fine* (a punishment for breaking the law which involves paying a sum of money) but can be used more generally to mean a punishment (e.g. *Illegal dumping carries a penalty of up to three years' imprisonment*). Teach / elicit some collocations: *pay a fine / penalty; take / be awarded a penalty* (football); *a penalty clause* (in a contract – for non-delivery); *a £100 fine*. Point out that only *fine* can be used as a verb (e.g. *We were fined for exceeding permitted emission levels*).

Questions 9 and 10: Vocabulary
- Check that all the vocabulary items in the Vocabulary section on page 84 of the Course Book are clear. Note *job rotation* = moving employees to different tasks or departments to broaden skills and experience and to

Working practices

avoid boredom; *cross training* = to undergo or provide training in different tasks and skills, either in a different department or within the same department; *clock watching* = constantly looking at the clock to see how much longer you have to work.
- Q9: To *pull rank* = to use your superior position in order to gain an advantage or make someone do what you want.
- Q10: Note *let off* = allow to escape punishment; *let (someone) go* can be used in the sense of making someone redundant (e.g. *We're going to have to let you go*). Only *impression* collocates with *bad*. Note *to make a bad impression* = to cause people to have a bad opinion (of the company).

3 LISTENING

An Employee Relations Manager

- The speaker has a French accent and refers to a French working environment.
- Alyces is a fictitious company, but the audioscript is based on an authentic recording.
- The exercise requires learners to summarise the information for their boss.
- Comprehension questions that might be used as preparation for the summary include the following.
  - *What three adjectives describe the management style?* (Open, informal, flexible.)
  - *How successful is this management style?* (Generally, Alyces avoids industrial relations problems.)
  - *What is the Comité d'Enterprise?* (A staff committee, elected by the workforce.)
  - *What kind of relationship do the management have with the Comité?* (They have a very close cooperation. They try to involve them in decision making.)
  - *What is the position with regard to single-union and no-strike agreements?* (They don't exist; they are illegal.)
- Gloss the audioscript as necessary: *distinctive* = unusual in a positive way; *industrial relations' problems* = problems between companies and their workforce; *went out of business* = ceased trading; *a single-union agreement* = an agreement between management and one union that it will represent all the workers; *affiliated to* = connected to; *no-strike agreements* = agreements by the union and workforce not to go on strike.
- **Further step:** Ask learners to make comparisons between Alyces and their own organisations, and to discuss the differences.

4 READING

Dealing with paper work

1
- Ask learners to work in pairs. Check the instructions are clear.
- Gloss language in the text as required: *in-tray* = an open container (tray) on your desk for keeping papers that you haven't dealt with yet; *got round to* = found time to deal with; *accumulation* = growing quantity; *colossal* = very big / huge; *a hard copy* = a copy made onto paper; *cluttered desks* = untidy desks with many items on them; *lurch from job to job* = move from job to job in an uncontrolled way; *procrastinate* = delay doing jobs; *end up stressed* = finally become stressed; *bin it* = throw it in the rubbish bin; *a heavy bias towards* = a big preference for.

2
- Have learners work individually for this part of the exercise.
- Ask them to read out their written responses. Lead a discussion on desk / paper management based on the information learners give.
- **Further step:** Ask learners to review the three rules in the article. Ask them to customise the rules for this group, revising them as necessary. The aim is to identify the rules that will help learners most in the area of paper management.

5 QUESTIONNAIRE

Company culture

- The questionnaire assesses how well contacts / clients are treated. For scoring / interpretation, see page 136 of the Course Book.
- Gloss terms as necessary: *the front line* = the first point of contact; *a ploy* = a technique, strategy; *show the visitor out* = go with the visitor to the door / exit; *conference labels* = name tags.
- Dale Carnegie wrote the best-selling book *How to Win Friends and Influence People* – one of the first and most famous books on business practice.
- In the follow-up discussion, encourage learners to use the information they have brought to the class about their organisation. Pre-experience learners should talk about an organisation they have an association with, e.g. a college.
- Do learners agree with the interpretation? The questionnaire supports a certain type of culture. Does this ideal apply in their business?
- When listing strengths and weaknesses, learners should use the text for ideas and sample sentences.
- **Further step:** The focus in the questionnaire is on company treatment of visitors and contacts. Ask learners to think now from the point of view of the visitors or contacts – to advise them on best

practice. Divide class members into pairs and ask each pair to consider one of the questions, from the visitors' point of view and to make recommendations on how to behave.

REVIEW

- Check that the items listed under Vocabulary in the Language Notes in the Course Book have been covered.
- Encourage learners to note down the terms they found useful – particularly the ones they need for their work. You should make a note of this language for future reference.
- Encourage learners to practise the new language in a professional way, e.g. they might practise new language by using it in a specific presentation or report.

Answers

1 Core practice
a i [F] b i [T] c i [F] d i [T]

2 Language check
1 c   2 a   3 c   4 c   5 b
6 a   7 b   8 c   9 c   10 a

3 Listening
(*possible answer*)
- Management style
  The style is informal, flexible and progressive. The company does not have industrial relations problems.
- Relations with the trade unions
  The company has good relations with the Comité d'Enterprise – the staff committee. In France, any company with more than 50 employees must have a Comité. These are elected by the workforce and usually include candidates from the national unions. Generally, no-strike agreements do not exist – they are not legal in France.

Audioscripts

1 Core practice
a – If your organisation is customer focused, the contacts and clients are well treated not out of politeness, but as part of your standard working practices. That's the situation in this company; in fact, were one of our customers to complain the person responsible would probably lose his or her job.
 – Do you maintain these standards in all areas?
 – We try to; we don't always succeed. At the moment our switchboard is letting us down a bit. We can't get the right kind of staff. It's a crucial job, but it's a bit repetitive.

b – Health and Safety comes under Compliance. It's part of the Building Manager's job. He has to ensure that the regulations are properly applied – for example, that the fire alarms are tested regularly, that the evacuation procedures are clearly displayed – and he has to organise fire drills on a regular basis. He ensures we comply with all the legal requirements.
 – Who checks if they are being applied?
 – The inspectors do spot checks from time to time.

c – The atmosphere in my company is pretty easy going. The managers are all fairly young – the MD is only 36. The management style is generally informal; we all use first names and we have a dress-down policy. But they do expect you to pull your weight. The emphasis is on what works.
 – It wouldn't work in my business.
 – Why's that?
 – I'm a sales demonstrator with an estate agent. My bosses wouldn't want me to wear jeans, and neither would the customers; they expect us to be a bit traditional.

d – The main changes have been in the area of technology. I used to have an administrative assistant who worked with a number of us in a back-up capacity. Now we work on-line with terminals on our desks. We handle our own typing and filing. I have a few work-in-progress files, but most of our data is stored electronically. Another big change is that we no longer have agents or intermediaries – customers from around the world contact us direct, by email or phone. The connection is direct.
 – Do you have much flexitime or job sharing?
 – Yes, because we have a lot of women. But the main changes have been in the area of technology. We have to work harder and the pace is faster.

3 Listening
ERM = Employee Relations Manager INT = Interviewer
INT: Could you tell me something about the style of management here at Alyces?
ERM: I think what we have tried to do here is to develop a distinctive Alyces style of management which is very open, informal, very flexible. French industry is sometimes troubled by industrial relations' problems. Some companies experienced difficulties and some of them went out of business because of these problems. But we've overcome that by having a very progressive style of management which, as I've said before, is very open and informal.
INT: And what about your relations with the unions?
ERM: Well, we have a very close cooperation with the staff Comité d'Enterprise – the equivalent to the staff committee. We try to involve them in the decision-making process.
INT: Does that mean you have a single-union agreement?
ERM: No, generally they don't exist in France; by law, companies with more than 50 employees must have a Comité d'Enterprise. These committees are elected by the workforce – and candidates are put forward by the national unions and there are also candidates who are not affiliated to any union.
INT: What about no-strike agreements?
ERM: Again, this type of agreement does not generally exist in France. All workers have the right to go on strike. This means that an agreement in advance not to strike would be illegal or non-legal.

UNIT 19 Advertising and promotion

PREPARATION

- You can go through this unit at different levels of thoroughness. The fast track takes about 1½ hours, the standard track about 2 hours and the comprehensive track about 3 hours. For more information on the different tracks, see the notes in the Introduction on pages 10 and 11.
- For the aims of the unit, see the Contents box on this page, the Language Notes at the end of the Course Book unit (page 88) and the Useful Phrases below. Remember to check any notes you have from the last time you taught this material.
- If you have it, you can use the Self-study Guide for extra study between classes.

USEFUL PHRASES

The service is promoted over the Internet.
The company pays for a number of sponsored links.
Do you get much spam?
junk mail   nuisance calls
Are you targeted by nuisance callers?

We also use a mail order catalogue.
We tried a corporate advertising campaign but it wasn't worth the £200,000 we spent on it.
The feedback we got from focus groups was not encouraging.
We want to create an image of reliability and technical excellence.
We have a glossy brochure that promotes the company as a whole.
And there are a number of product brochures, which highlight product details.
Our products are aimed at low-income consumers.
The message is that when you buy this, you're buying style.

This leaflet tells you about the company.
Could you tell me a little about your micro pumps?
Do you have a sample I can see?
The specifications are on this sheet.
The price list is on the back.

Our research indicates that there is a large potential market for your product among young people.
Why don't we do a campaign based on radio ads?
Properly handled the campaign could be very successful.

LEAD IN (SUGGESTIONS)

- Check how learners have prepared (see the Preparation section in the Course Book). Have they brought a sample of promotional literature relating to their work?
- Check also whether they have looked at the Useful Phrases on page 88 in the Course Book (copied above).
- Consider leading into the lesson by discussing with learners how their organisations or teams promote themselves.

Contents

Expressions
The service is promoted over the Internet.
We depend a lot on personal recommendation.
Do you have a leaflet or something?
The price list is printed on the back.
We should try a campaign based on radio ads.

Language check
Passive verb forms: present, future, past
Omissions in clauses: *being the client* vs. *as we are the client*, etc.
Vocabulary: *advertising agency / campaign / slogan, focus group, market survey, sponsored link, brochure, leaflet, flyer, junk mail, nuisance calls, spam, highlight, target, put across*

Practice
Talking about your advertising
Promoting a company / a product
Preparing promotional literature
An article on spam and nuisance calls

1 CORE PRACTICE
Listening and speaking

- The exercise is in two parts – listening and speaking. The listening activity (part i) provides learners with ideas and models for the speaking activity (part ii).
- Question a: The second speaker has an Australian accent. See Glossary for *focus group*. Explain that *campaign* = an advertising programme; *we can target fairly closely* = we can aim fairly accurately at a specific part of the market; *various listener profiles* = groups of listeners with different characteristics (e.g. teenagers, females over 30).
- Question b: The second woman has a US accent. Gloss language: *retail outlets* = shops that sell to the public; *promotions* = advertising activities; *leaflet* and *poster* (see Glossary); *tear-off, money-off-your-next-purchase* = a part of a leaflet that you can tear off and give to the supplier that entitles you to a reduction on your next purchase; *a glossy brochure* = a publicity booklet printed on bright, shiny paper with lots of coloured photographs; *point-of-sale* = place where a product is sold (e.g. a shop).
- Question c: Explain that *brand advertising* = advertising that promotes the brand (see Glossary); *upmarket* = relating to products that are relatively expensive and superior in quality; *lifestyle magazines* = consumer magazines that feature the way certain people (usually rich and successful) live; *one-off promotions* = promotions that happen only once, not repeated; *a mass market* = a large group that includes the majority.

- Question d: The second man has a non-standard accent.
- **Further step:** Identify words, phrases or sentences in the dialogues that your learners find difficult to say clearly and use the recording as a basis for detailed pronunciation practice.

2 LANGUAGE CHECK

- These questions enable you to treat the language programme flexibly. Points that are known can be handled briefly. Points that require more remedial attention can be explored in more detail. The Specific Points section below gives you further detailed guidance.
- Consider the following options for each question.
  - Elicit the answer.
  - Discuss why the other choices are wrong.
  - Ask learners to prepare examples that relate to their specific needs, e.g.:
    Question 1: *If the ad hadn't been shown on TV, we would have had less exposure.*
    Amended version: *If the copy hadn't been checked and corrected, the wrong figures would have been posted on our website.*
- **Further step:** Reinforce vocabulary associated with advertising and promotion using a simple word game. Taking the Vocabulary section of the Language Notes in the Course Book as a starting point, learners work in teams: Team 1 chooses a word or phrase; Team 2 scores a point by using it correctly in an example. Team 2 then chooses a word or phrase for Team 1 and so on.

SPECIFIC POINTS

Questions 1 to 4: Passive forms (BGG 4.1, 4.2)
- Q1: Past forms. This is a third conditional with a passive verb in the *if* clause (*hadn't been shown*). Note that here *exposure* = publicity.
- Q2: *should have* + passive verb. Option **a** strictly follows the rule for tense agreement in reported speech: the verb tense in the second clause (*was going to be changed*) agrees with the past form in the first clause (*should have been told*). However, for many speakers, in everyday usage, **b** (*is going to …*) is also acceptable – if the brief has still not been changed at the time of speaking. Note *the brief* = a set of instructions about a task.
- Q3: Present Simple passive. Note the preposition *over* with *the Internet*; *on* would also be possible. A *sponsored link* = when one website directs users to another website, for which they are paid a fee.
- Q4: Past Simple passive. The past has to be used to agree with the tense in the second sentence. For *junk mail*, see Glossary; *spam* = unwanted emails (usually advertising); *a nuisance call* = an unwanted telephone call (usually from someone who is trying to sell you something).

Questions 5 to 7: Omissions in clauses (BGG 19.3)
- Refer to the examples in the Language Notes.
- Q5: *as*, *-ing* forms (BGG 6.4, 19.3). After *As*, *I am* can be omitted – *As (I am) the Account Director …* Another possibility is: *Being the Account Director* (instead of *Because / As / Since I am*). An *account director* = someone who looks after a specific client.
- Q6: *-ing* forms (BGG 6.4). Both *Having heard …* (the perfect *-ing* form) and *Now I have heard …* are correct. It is possible to use *the new corporate brochure*, but *the new corporate market research* is not a possible combination. Note that *the* is not used with *market research* (e.g. *do market research*) unless it is followed by a qualifying phrase (e.g. *The market research we did last year…*). Explain that *corporate image* = how a company is seen and thought of by the public. Elicit other collocations with *corporate*, e.g. *corporate finance, culture, executives*.
- Q7: After *If* the pronoun and form of *to be* can be omitted; *If* could also be left out, just using the past participle. Here, the correct preposition after *aimed* is *at*. Note that *flyer* can also be spelt *flier* (see Glossary for definition).

Questions 8 to 10: Vocabulary
- Explain that *direct mail advertising* = companies writing to people to try to persuade them to buy something; *a market survey* = a series of questions designed to establish people's behaviour and opinions; *has a good track record* = has done a lot of good work in the past.
- Q8: Explain that *come up with* = suggest / produce (an idea or plan). Note the use of *fresh* here for *new / different*.
- Q9: Note that here *behind* means to be responsible for.
- Q10: Note *to put across* = to communicate; *slogan* (see Glossary).

3 LISTENING

Advertising slogans

- Discuss the slogans on page 86 of the Course Book. Gloss as necessary: *no strings attached* = not linked to any responsibilities or liabilities; *running costs* = costs of running a business or machine; *CFCs* = chlorofluorocarbons (used in refrigerators and aerosol sprays, and said to damage the ozone layer); *Never knowingly undersold* = We will never sell goods at a higher price than our competitors – if we are aware of these prices.
- Elicit other famous slogans. Do learners' companies have marketing slogans?
- The words, based on actual recordings, are spoken by actors. Speaker 1 has a US accent; Speaker 2 is non-native, non-standard; Speaker 3 is native, non-standard.
- Ask learners to work in pairs as they match the recordings to the slogans.

- **Further step:** Working in pairs, ask learners to write a slogan for their main product or for their function: e.g. accountants – 'Accurate and reliable'.

4 WRITING
Promotional literature

- As a group go through the text of the advertisement.
- Discuss terms and phrases: *suites* = usually a sofa and two chairs; *renovate* = repair and renew; *100% tax relief* = 100% of the cost can be set against tax; *on-site quotations* = able to visit your site and give a price for the job; *flame-retardant* = materials treated so they are difficult to burn and burn slowly; *warranty* (see Glossary); *undertake* = promise.
- Ask learners to work in pairs. Guide them by discussing what the brief should include, e.g. the main selling points, interesting features, key benefits to the customer and so on.
- There is a possible draft in the answers. If the exercise is difficult for your learners, consider letting them read the draft before they start work on their own version.
- **Further step:** Have each pair look at the submissions of other pairs and select the one they think is the best brief.

5 CASE STUDY
Spam and junk

1
- Lead in by discussing spam and junk mail generally. Is it a problem for group members? What do they do about it?
- Ask learners to read the article on page 87 of the Course Book. Check they understand the business of the woman featured: *patchwork* = sewing pieces of different materials together to create, e.g., a cushion cover or bedspread; *quilting* = thick warm layers of fabric filled with soft materials, usually for a bed cover.
- Ask questions a to f, listed opposite the article.
- Gloss vocabulary as needed: *get them off her back* = get someone to stop them bothering her; *bombarded* = contacted repeatedly; *a ruse* = a trick intended to deceive someone.

2
- Ask learners to brainstorm a list of 'do's' and 'don'ts' for dealing with spam, junk mail and nuisance calls. These should be based on learners' experiences or on stories they have heard. If possible they should include details of local agencies that can help.
- **Further step:** Practise dealing with unwanted calls. Using information in the article and their own experience, ask learners to list the kinds of things nuisance callers say, e.g.:

I called you yesterday.
50% of the price goes to charity.
Then list possible responses, e.g.:
Who did you speak to?
You didn't speak to me.
Please don't call this number again.
I am going to put the phone down.
Finally, in pairs, learners practise dealing with nuisance calls: Partner A is the caller; Partner B has to block the call.

REVIEW

- Check that learners note down the language they need in their business life, especially if there are special terms you have introduced to meet the needs of the class.
- Remind learners that practice is the key to progress. Encourage them to be systematic in the way they work on this project outside the classroom. For example, they might use Post-it notes to remind themselves of points they must use.

Answers

1 Core practice
a i [F]   b i [T]   c i [T]   d i [F]

2 Language check
1 c   2 a   3 a   4 b   5 b
6 a   7 c   8 c   9 a   10 b

3 Listening
(*possible answers*)
a Software packages
   The right solution at the right price
b Forklift trucks
   Running costs worth rushing for
c Fast-food chain
   A friendly welcome for all the family

4 Writing
(*possible answer*)
Phoenix specialises in supplying or renovating office furniture, seating, suites and antiques. We offer a competitive alternative to buying new, replacement furniture. The savings are significant. And our charges can of course be set against tax – in full.
We offer on-site quotations, collection and delivery – all free of charge. Customers can choose from the full range of colours and materials normally available on the market. In particular we only use the latest flame-retardant materials and foam.
We undertake to complete all work within 10 – 14 days. Clients also receive a 12-month guarantee and a first-class after-sales service.
Recently we have expanded our service to include a wide range of office furniture made by Phoenix. We also supply other reputable brand names at competitive prices.

5 Case study
(*possible answers*)
1 a To outline the nuisance of junk mail and spam, using the story of one person – Christine.
  b The number of calls eventually decreased.
  c She had to pay to be removed from various lists that companies used to cold-call. She still receives junk mail.
  e Because people are paid to use the techniques and generate sales.
  f Register with the agencies and services which stop unwanted communication. Get your name taken off the lists that are sold to companies.

2 (*possible answer*)
Do's
- Register your phone number with a national 'do-not-call' registry.
- Tell companies, 'don't sell or share my name'.
- Ask the direct marketing associations to tell their members not to mail or call you.
- Ask list vendors and credit reporting agencies not to sell your name.
- In many areas junk faxes are illegal; tell senders they are risking prosecution.
- Delete junk email messages without opening them.
- Think twice before opening attachments or clicking links in email.

Don'ts
- Don't reply to spam.
- Don't give personal information in an email.
- Don't buy anything or give to any charity promoted through spam.
- Don't forward chain email messages.
- Don't throw credit card information in the rubbish.
- Don't give your business card to people you don't know.
- Don't allow your details to be published in a public directory.

Audioscripts

1 Core practice
a – The draft report from the focus groups indicates that the main problem you face is that your potential customers don't realise that what you provide is different from what they can get at the local supermarket.
 – That's the conclusion we've come to.
 – I think we should try a campaign based on radio ads. It's a low-cost medium, and the great thing is that we can target fairly closely, because we have a variety of radio stations with various listener profiles. Organised properly, the campaign should work.
 – When will your report be circulated?
b – We sell a range of pre-packed frozen meals to the domestic market through retail outlets, and also to places like hospitals and canteens. For the domestic market we do promotions in shops and supermarkets, where we give away free samples and hand out information leaflets which have a tear-off, money-off-your-next-purchase section.
 – Do you have anything promoting the brand?
 – Yes, we have a glossy brochure that promotes the company as a whole, which has just been redesigned. And we have point-of-sale display posters.
c – In our business, reputation is crucial. We try to promote an image of quality and excellence. Whatever people spend, they don't want a piano that sounds cheap. So we do quite a lot of brand advertising, usually in upmarket lifestyle magazines. But it's expensive, and it's difficult to measure the results. More recently we've tended to concentrate more on special offers and one-off promotions in the musical press.
 – Are you being advised by anyone?
 – Yes, we are …
 – Well, you should have been told this won't work if you want to reach a mass market.
 – I know; we depend a lot on personal recommendation.

d – This is our company brochure; as you can see we're part of the Tango Group of companies.
 – Can I take a copy?
 – Yes, of course. What are you particularly interested in?
 – I see you make micro pumps.
 – Yes, it's an area we specialise in.
 – Do you have a leaflet or something?
 – Yes, here. These are the specifications for the standard C17 model – they give an idea of the products' capabilities. The price list is printed on the back.
 – Umm … Considering what your competitors charge, these seem quite high.

3 Listening

Speaker 1: a computer software developer
The flexibility of our products is what makes a key selling point for us. And really that's because it allows us to deliver, as a whole package, solutions that meet business needs. And that's where the money's coming from and after all it's from the business user, not the IT department. And they want something competitive.

Speaker 2: a production director of a fork-lift truck manufacturer
We build a quality product with … high reliability, and this leads to improved profitability for the customer due to extremely low running costs.

Speaker 3: the manager of a fast-food chain
Key selling points of our product must be the nice environment in which you can sit and eat, the high standards of cleanliness, the friendliness of the staff – also, especially, the value for money. The staff are carefully chosen so they're nice, friendly, outgoing personalities that get on with people. As I say, the restaurant itself is maintained well. I mean, where else can you get a meal at this kind of price?

UNIT 20 Offers and orders

PREPARATION

- You can go through this unit at different speeds in more or less detail. The fast track takes about 1½ hours, the standard track about 2 hours and the comprehensive track about 3 hours. For more information on these three options, see the notes in the Introduction on pages 10 and 11.
- For details of the aims of the unit, look at the Contents box on this page, the Language Notes at the end of the Course Book unit and the Useful Phrases below.
- If available, use the exercises in the Self-study Guide as extra practice.

USEFUL PHRASES

The unit weighs 2.5 kilos.
It has a volume of 1.5 cubic metres.
The screen measures 17 centimetres by 5.
The surface area is 85 square centimetres.
We offer a quantity discount and generous credit terms.

I can let you have them for $62.
They are on special offer.
Can you supply them on sale or return?

I'm calling to place an order.
We'd like to take you up on your offer.
You quoted us $9 per hundred.
I'll check if we have them in stock.

Our quote was subject to the cost of raw materials.
We had to put our prices up.
That wasn't made clear.
We ought to have been informed.
Our margins are very tight.

I'm afraid we're not going to be able to deliver on time.
But time is critical at this end.
Our instructions seem to have been ignored.
We are being given unrealistic delivery dates.
We rely on being given the facts.
We could batch through part of the order on Wednesday.

Sometimes customers order on-line (in order) to cut costs.
That's the reason. That's why.

LEAD IN (SUGGESTIONS)

- Point out that the language related to offers and orders is relevant to most aspects of business activity, not only to people who are 'customer facing'. Back office support functions (e.g. Accounts, Security) have internal customers – people whose needs and requirements have to be satisfied.
- Consider leading into the subject by asking learners to talk generally about goods and services they supply and those they buy. Be prepared to lead with an outline of your own place in the supply chain, e.g.: I supply ____ and ____ , and the main products I buy in order to do this are ____ and ____ .

Contents

Expressions
The unit weighs 2½ kilos.
I'm calling to place an order.
We had to put our prices up.
We ought to have been informed.
Some customers order on-line (in order) to cut costs.

Language check
More on passives: continuous, infinitive, -ing forms
Giving reasons: *because*, *in order to*, *so that*, etc.
Measurements: dimensions, volume, capacity, etc.
Vocabulary: *retail*, *retailer*, *wholesale*, *wholesaler*, *quantity / trade discount*, *take someone up on an offer*, *put prices up / down*, *place an order*

Practice
Taking / placing / confirming an order
Product enquires – written and by phone
Querying an invoice
Dealing with late deliveries

1 CORE PRACTICE

Listening and speaking

- Here learners can practise a range of situations relating to buying and selling.
- The exercise is in two parts – listening and speaking. The listening activity (part i) provides learners with ideas and models for the speaking activity (part ii).
- In part ii, encourage learners to adapt the scenarios to their needs. Where possible they should introduce the realia they have brought to class.
- Question a: The first speaker has a non-standard accent. Point out the language used in this negotiation, how the buyer and the seller both move their positions. Gloss as necessary: *take you up on* (your offer) = accept; *You quoted us* = you gave us the price of; *fair enough* = I accept your point.
- Question b: The first speaker has a non-standard accent, possibly Asian. Note that *querying* = asking questions to check something you think may be wrong; *was subject to* = was conditional on; *We've quoted our clients* = we've given them a price; *without notice* = without informing people. How do learners think this discussion will end? Will the caller get a reduction in price?
- Question c: The woman has an Australian accent; the man has a non-standard accent. Note that *glare filters* = filters used in front of a computer screen to reduce the brightness; *the courier* = the person or company responsible for delivering the goods.

- Question d: The man has a non-standard accent. The woman has an East European accent. Note *the supplier is not to blame* = the supplier is not responsible for; *critical* = very important; *ignored* = not paid attention to; *a hold up at your end* = a delay at your company; *batch through* = send part of the order; *track (the order)* = follow.
- **Further step:** In pairs, ask learners to playread the dialogues to the rest of the class. Make a sound recording of the readings and use it to analyse and improve pronunciation. In particular, point out incorrect stress patterns in words – a common cause of misunderstanding.

2 LANGUAGE CHECK

- As you go through the multiple-choice questions, point out the Language Notes at the end of the Course Book unit (page 92), and the related notes in the Business Grammar Guide (see the booklet that accompanies the Course Book); there are cross-references from the notes to the BGG.
- The multiple-choice questions provide a starting point for the Language Check. Ensure that the related language points are explored and revised, as necessary. The Specific Points section below gives you further detailed guidance.
- Adapt the points to learners' needs. Concentrate on the areas where practice is needed.
- When working on vocabulary questions, introduce special terms the class need. Point out the Glossary on pages 158 – 160 of the Course Book.
- For each question consider the following options.
  - Identify the answer.
  - Explore why the other options are wrong.
  - Ask learners to prepare examples that relate to their working needs or experience, e.g.:
    Question 1: *The goods were being loaded when the buyer called to cancel the order.*
    Amended version: *The order was being checked when the fire broke out.*
- **Further step:** Ask learners to prepare an example of a point they often get wrong. The rest of the group say if it is correct.

SPECIFIC POINTS

Questions 1 to 3: Passive forms (BGG 4.1)
- Review the examples in the Language Notes.
- Q1: Past Continuous passive (BGG 1.4, 4.1). This is an interrupted action in the past. The longer action is in the Past Continuous (*were being loaded*). The infinitive used in the second clause is an abbreviated form of *in order to*.
- Q2: Passive infinitive. In this example a past infinitive is needed after *seem* (= *to have been forgotten*).
- Q3: Present Continuous passive and *-ing* passive. Here *being let down* = being promised something (delivery dates) which fails to happen.

Questions 4 and 5: Giving reasons (BGG 18.1)
- Q4: Note the use of a *that* clause after *The reason ... is*. Although *The reason is ... because ...* is considered to be technically incorrect, for many speakers this is also an acceptable form. Elicit *a delay* for *a hold up*.
- Q5: Purpose. Only *so that* is grammatically correct here; *in order to / so as to* need to be followed by an infinitive (e.g. *in order to be able to track*). Try to elicit this from your learners. To *track* = to follow the progress of the order, e.g. Has it left the warehouse? Is it in transit?

Questions 6 and 7: Measurements (BGG 24.3)
- Go through the examples in the Language Notes.

Questions 8 to 10: Vocabulary related to ordering and sales
- Go through the Vocabulary in the Language Notes on page 92. Make sure learners understand and can use all the items. Note *to be reduced to clear* = to be reduced in price in order to be sold.
- Q8: Elicit *accept* for *take (you) up on*. Note the use of *open* here for *available*. If an offer is *on the table* it is open for negotiation. Explain that *good* could possibly be used in the sense of *valid*.
- Q9: Ensure learners understand *place an order* (the customer does this) and *take an order* (the supplier / sales person does this). Point out that we cannot use *make* for *place* with *order*. Note also that *place* can be used in a similar way with *a bet* and *an advertisement* (e.g. in a newspaper).
- Q10: A *trade discount* = a reduction in the standard price of something given to other business people (especially if they are in the same trade); *bulk* and *wholesale* (see Glossary).

3 LISTENING

In a sales office

- The exercise consists of two short dialogues with questions for each. Go through the questions and check they are clear.
- Dialogue a: the man has a slight Australian accent; the woman has a US accent.
- Dialogue b: the woman has a US accent, the man a non-standard accent, possibly mid-European. Note *the initial delivery* = the first delivery; *at our expense* = we will pay for it.
- **Further step:** In pairs, ask learners to read the audioscripts and, using them as models, write a new dialogue that relates to their own business and products. Learners should refer to emails they brought to class (as part of the preparation). Pre-experience learners should refer to the business area they know most about.

4 WRITING

A home page

1. - Conversis offer translation services and cross-cultural advice so that materials they work on for clients work effectively in a global context.
   - Go through text taken from the company home page. It contains a number of specialised terms and phrases. Ask learners to suggest explanations. Then gloss as necessary: *full-service translation* = this probably means they offer a full translation service, including cultural adjustments; *localisation company* = this probably means they help to 'localise' messages, to change them so that they are comprehensible in a local context; *suite* = range; *website and branding globalisation* = this probably means helping customers to review and modify their website and brand image so that they work globally; *desktop publishing* = designing and printing documents in an office, using a computer and special software; *quality assurance* = providing evidence that the quality-related activities are being performed effectively, including design, development, production, installation, servicing and documentation.

2. - Ask learners to write a message to Conversis as required in the question.
   - Point out the Useful Language on page 136: *testimonials* = formal written recommendations given by former clients. There is a sample text in the answers: *lead times* = the time between ordering and delivery.
   - **Further step:** Discuss with learners their reaction to the language used in this promotional text. Ask them to rephrase the messages so that they are more accessible.

5 APPLICATION

Contact with a possible supplier

- The company featured here provides public information systems. These might be screens that show which platform trains leave from or that indicate which window in a bank is free, etc.
- Lead into the exercise by discussing with the class display systems in general. Do learners use computerised systems in their organisation? Or do they rely on non-electronic systems – traditional signs, flipcharts, etc.?
- Go through the task and website information glossing as necessary: *prospects* = possible customers; *intelligent queuing* = the electronic systems used in banks and sales outlets that indicate which window is free; *meeting agenda systems* = screens that show the name, purpose and room number of a planned meeting; *leading edge* = the latest; *integrated information platform* = computer software that combines all the information systems required in the process; *we offer full project life-cycle management* = we manage projects closely at every stage of their development; *face-on monitor display* = a simple display with a local message (e.g. a message on a TV screen welcoming a guest to his / her room); *fully integrated transport infrastructure management system* = a complex system with screens in many places linked to a transport network that enables travellers, staff and managers to see clearly what is happening; *outcomes* = results.
- The information on the website (page 91 of the Course Book) and the mail-out for Partner A (page 136) focuses on applications of Customer Information Systems in the field of transport. Point out that information systems can be used in other fields (e.g. companies, conference centres, universities, hospitals).
- The easiest task would be for learners to negotiate the purchase of an information display system for a conference centre. If you think your learners are capable of a more challenging task, they can choose another field. Guide them as appropriate.
- There is information for Partner A on page 136 – a mail-out from Guidex. Gloss as necessary: *expertise* = a high level of knowledge and skill; *operator interface design* = the design of the screen, commands, etc. that allow the user to communicate with the system; *readily extendable* = can be easily added to; *configured* = set up / designed. Before beginning the task, Partner A should think about what type of features are important for their particular needs.
- Partner B works in a call centre processing first enquiries (see page 137 for information). Note *can be scrolled* = can be made to appear on the screen by moving the text up or down; *ex-stock* = available from existing stock; *site proven* = tested on-site.
- **Further step:** Ask learners to report back to the class. Potential buyers say what they have found out and whether they intend to go further; call centre staff report the status of the potential sale.

REVIEW

- Check the items listed under Vocabulary in the Language Notes in the Course Book have been adequately covered.
- Go through the Language Notes and the Useful Phrases in the Course Book.
- Encourage learners to use a variety of techniques to help them practise the new language they have learned, e.g. they might put key points on their screen savers.

Answers

1 Core practice
a i [U]   b i [F]   c i [U]   d i [T]

2 Language check
1 b   2 a   3 c   4 c   5 b
6 b   7 a   8 b   9 a   10 c

3 Listening
(*possible answers*)

a i They are colleagues on the marketing side.
  ii It's difficult to say because we do not have production details, but it sounds as if production will have to be increased.
  iii 'but there isn't much cushion' can also be phrased 'but this doesn't give us much time' or 'but the deadline is very tight'.

b i The customer is threatening to cancel because he is not happy with the weight specifications in the initial order.
  ii By sending one of their technical people over.
  iii 'let's keep our fingers crossed' can also be phrased 'let's hope that everything goes to plan' or 'let's hope that everything turns out all right'.

4 Writing
2 (*possible answer*)

> We are an Egyptian trading company with offices in Calcutta. We often need to have documents translated to and from Arabic, Hindi and English. We have our own in-house translators but we frequently have a large volume of documents which have to be translated at short notice.
>
> Please send details of your charges, and lead times.
>
> Regards

Audioscripts

1 Core practice

a – We'd like to take you up on your offer; I'd just like to check the details. You quoted us £57.20 each.
  – I'm afraid that was old stock – we now have the new stock in and the prices are higher.
  – But we left it that we'd get back to you before the end of the month. You knew that when you gave us the quote.
  – OK, fair enough; I can let you have them for £61 – I can't let you have them for less than that.
  – £61; it's still a big increase.
  – How many are you taking?
  – Seven.
  – OK, look, I'll tell you what I'll do – we're offering a quantity discount on this one. If you take ten, I can reduce the price to £58.

b – There seems to be an error in your invoice. You quoted us $9 per hundred, but you've charged us $13 per hundred.
  – Our quote was subject to the costs of raw materials. As you know, paper is up by 19% since the beginning of the month. That's why our margins are very tight – we've had to put our prices up.
  – But this was all agreed at the time. We've quoted our clients on the basis of the price you gave us.
  – Well, all our quotes are subject to market variations. In our terms of trade, it says that we can increase prices without notice.

c – We're hiring 30 plasma screens from you and they're due to be delivered on Friday. I'm just ringing to see if I can increase to 35 screens and include glare filters.
  – Let me just check if the courier has gone. No, apparently your order still being loaded. It should be OK. I'd better check with the warehouse if they have them in stock. If they haven't, I'll call you back immediately.
  – OK thanks. Will they be at the same price?
  – No that was a special offer – you got 15% off.
  – Isn't it all part of the same order?

d – I'm afraid the job isn't going to be ready till Friday.
  – But you said you'd be able to meet the deadline.
  – Yes, I'm sorry …
  – We made it clear that time is critical on this; our instructions seem to have been ignored.
  – We are giving the job absolute priority. The reason for the delay is that the materials were late reaching us – there was a hold up at your end …
  – OK. Er … can you send any of it on Wednesday?
  – Yes, we can batch through about 25%. You can track the order on-line.
  – OK.
  – Just go to our website and click on 'My Order Status'.

3 Listening

a – Hello.
  – Hello Sara. I'm just ringing to confirm that I've spoken to Kelly Mateja at TYH.
  – Yeah.
  – He said that we've got the 23 unit order for the HGF21s. I've checked the stock situation, and we only have 11 units ready. Fortunately, Karl has 12 in the warehouse. So we can do it, just.
  – That's lucky.
  – Yes it is, but I'm expecting another order for ten pieces next month, so we'll have to look at our production schedules.
  – When do they want delivery?
  – The week commencing the 26th.
  – That's OK.
  – Yes, that's fine, but there isn't much cushion.

b – Hello.
  – Hello Donna. Just to let you know what's happening with the Rebal order. Apparently their buyer isn't happy with the initial delivery and is threatening to cancel the whole deal. I've offered to send one of our technical people over tomorrow morning at our expense, and this seemed to calm him down a bit.
  – Do you know what the problem is?
  – Something to do with the weight specifications being wrong. I'm sure that we did what was ordered, but anyway we'll find out tomorrow.
  – Assuming that everything works out OK, is final delivery still set for the end of August?
  – Yes. Let's keep our fingers crossed.

UNIT 21 Customer care

PREPARATION

- It is possible to complete this unit at different speeds, in more or less detail. The fast track takes about 1½ hours, the standard track about 2 hours and the comprehensive track about 3 hours. For more information on the three options, see the notes in the Introduction on pages 10 and 11.
- To check the aims of the unit, look at the Contents box opposite, the Language Notes at the end of the Course Book unit and the Useful Phrases below.
- If available to you, you can use the exercises in the Self-study Guide for extra practice.
- If you have taught the unit before, review the notes you made at the time.

USEFUL PHRASES

I want to make a complaint. Who should I speak to?
Can I take the details?
Are you sure it's plugged in properly?
According to the instructions it's supposed to be silent.
Is this covered by the guarantee?
Leave it with me – I'll get our technical support to call you.
It sounds as if the machine is overheating.
Do you have a service contract?
Call-out time is supposed to be two hours.
This isn't the result of normal wear and tear.
We're very unhappy about the way we're being treated.
I was thinking of sending the buyer at SLX tickets for the Cup Final.
There might be some questions.
It would be better if you took him yourself.
I bought these shoes three days ago – here's the receipt.
They are brand new and the soles are coming away.
It looks as if they've been washed in a machine.
In our view, the wear and tear is due to heavy use, not to a manufacturing fault.
The guarantee doesn't cover defects caused by misuse.
Do you want to exchange them for a new pair, or would you prefer a refund?
Sorry for any inconvenience. Please accept our apologies.
Get back to us if you have any more problems.

LEAD IN (SUGGESTIONS)

- Check how learners have prepared for the lesson. The Preparation section at the start of the unit in the Course Book (page 93) includes some suggestions.
- Have learners looked at the Useful Phrases on page 96 in the Course Book (copied above)?
- Have they brought to class emails or letters relating to a customer care issue? If so, these can be used as a resource later in the lesson.
- Consider leading into the subject by eliciting accounts of the customer care they have received – the best and the worst. As the discussion develops, you can monitor the language needs of the group and the level of interest.

Contents

Expressions
It sounds as if the machine is overheating.
Do you have a service contract?
Call out time is supposed to be two hours.
This isn't the result of normal wear and tear.
We're very unhappy about the way we're being treated.

Language check
Impressions: *seem / look / sound, as if / though,* etc.
Cause and effect: *be caused by, the result of,* etc.
Complaining: *complain about, be unhappy about,* etc.
Vocabulary: *care, concern, support, guarantee, warranty, protection plan, neglect, misuse, wear and tear, refund, replacement, credit note, put customers first, take it back, look into it*

Practice
Practice in giving and receiving customer care
Managers talk about service they receive
Writing a letter of complaint
Case practice: returning goods to a shop

1 CORE PRACTICE

Listening and speaking

- This exercise provides an opportunity to practise a range of situations relating to customer care.
- The exercise is in two parts – listening and speaking. The listening activity (part i) prepares learners for the speaking activity (part ii).
- As you work through the comprehension questions in part i, ask learners to explain how they have arrived at their answers.
- In part ii, encourage learners to adapt the scenarios to their needs. If appropriate, they should introduce the documents they have brought to the class.
- Question a: Point out that *window dressing* = a display designed to impress rather than a reality; *customer-focused* = believing that satisfying the customer is a priority for the company; *retaining* = keeping.
- Question b: This is probably a business-to-business exchange – they are talking about an industrial sorting machine. The male speaker has an Australian accent. Note *It's still under warranty* = the warranty (see Glossary) has not yet expired; *the call-out time* = the maximum amount of time it should take for a technician to come to repair a machine; *I'll get a technician out to you* = I'll send a technician to you.
- Question c: The second speaker, who appears to be the boss, is less enthusiastic because there is no budget for expenditure of this kind. Point

96 UNIT 21

out that *the Cup Final* = the final of a big English football competition; *make a case* = give reasons to support a point of view; *legitimate* = justified / acceptable.
- Question d: The store manager has a non-standard accent. Note *falling apart* = breaking into pieces; *wear and tear* = damage or ageing that occurs due to normal use over a period of time; *I was assured* = I was told confidently (so I would not worry).
- **Further step:** Working in pairs, learners talk through the customer care stories they have brought the class as part of their preparation. Ask them to check they have the vocabulary and language they need to deal with such situations. Supply extra vocabulary as required.

2 LANGUAGE CHECK

- The multiple-choice questions link to the Language Notes at the end of the Course Book unit (page 96), and the related notes in the Business Grammar Guide (see the booklet that accompanies the Course Book).
- The multiple-choice questions enable you to treat the language programme flexibly. Points that are known can be handled briefly. Points that require more remedial attention can be explored in more detail. The Specific Points section below gives you further detailed guidance.
- When working on vocabulary questions, point out the Vocabulary notes in the Language Reference at the end of the unit in the Course Book, and the Glossary on pages 158 – 160. Introduce, as necessary, special terms needed by the class.
- As you work through the questions with the group, you can vary the process in the following ways.
  - Elicit the answer.
  - Discuss why the other options are wrong.
  - Ask learners to prepare examples that relate to their specific needs, e.g.:
    Question 1: *The call-out time is supposed to be one hour. We're very unhappy about the way we're being treated.*
    Amended version: *According to the contract, we are supposed to get a replacement within 24 hours. We are not happy with the service we are receiving.*
- **Further step:** Reinforce customer care vocabulary using a simple word game. Taking the Vocabulary section of the Language Notes in the Course Book as a starting point, learners work in teams: Team 1 chooses a word or phrase; Team 2 scores a point by using it correctly in an example. Team 2 then chooses a word or phrase for Team 1 and so on.

SPECIFIC POINTS

Questions 1, 2 and 7: Complaints
- Go through the examples in the Language Notes.
- Q1: *supposed to* (BGG 20.1) is used to indicate what should happen according to the rules or what one is led to believe. It is often used when the opposite happens in reality (so here the implication is that it was longer than one hour). Note that *with* could also be used after *unhappy*.
- Q2: Point out that *support* would also be acceptable, but *service* is the most natural answer.
- Q7: Review ways of responding to complaints. Elicit examples, e.g.:
  Accepting: *I'm afraid there was a mistake on our side; I am very sorry.*
  Rejecting: *I'm afraid we can't accept your request / demand; I'm afraid I can't help you. According to our records, the product was in perfect working order.*
  Avoiding: *I'm afraid there's nothing I can do; It's not my department / area; I'm afraid my hands are tied.*
  Compromising: *I'll send it to our workshop for analysis; If they say …; It's the best I can do.*

Questions 3 and 4: Verb phrases
- Go through the verbs and verb phrases on page 96. Note *put your complaint in writing* = send it in a letter.
- Q3: Ensure learners understand the meaning of the verb phrases. Ask them to paraphrase, e.g. *we try never to let a customer down* (= we always try to do what the customer expects us to do / provide good service).
- Q4: Point out that *leave it with me* is a phrase often used on the phone to reassure the caller that the problem will be dealt with. Try to elicit other ways of saying *look into* (e.g. investigate) and *get back to you* (e.g. call you again).

Questions 5 and 6: Cause and effect (BGG 18.1)
- Check through the examples in the Language Notes. Elicit examples from class members.

Questions 5, 6 and 8: Vocabulary
- Ensure all the warranty / guarantee terms in the Language Notes have been understood. Note that there is no technical difference between the meaning of these two words. However, there may be some differences in usage (e.g. cars tend to have warranties). Check that all the terms in the Vocabulary section on page 96 are clear: *customer facing* is used to describe jobs which involve direct contact with customers (as opposed to *back office* jobs); *downtime* = the time when a machine is not working and cannot be used; *a defect* (note the stress on the first syllable) = a fault.
- Q5: Try to elicit other possibilities (e.g. *due to, which is the result of*). Note *caused by* is a reduced relative clause (*which is / was / has been* has been omitted – see Unit 7 Language Check Q1, page 37). Ask learners to explain why *leading to* is wrong (*misuse* is not the effect of the *damage*).

- Q6: Check learners know that *because* needs to be followed by *of* before a noun phrase. Note *neglect* = lack of proper care. Point out the use of *under / under the terms of* with warranty, contract, agreement, etc. Ask learners to give examples based on their experience (e.g. *Under the terms of my mobile phone contract, I am entitled to … but …*).
- Q8: Note *misuse* = using something for the wrong purpose or using it excessively.

Questions 9 and 10: Impressions
- Revise the use of the verbs *seem / look / sound / be (as if / though)* in talking about impressions. Go through the examples in the Language Notes. See also BGG 20.2. Elicit examples based on learners' experiences.
- Q9: Note *if* and *though* can be used interchangeably.
- Q10: Note *sounds as if / though* is usually a response to something you have been told.

3 LISTENING
The customer is right
- Before playing the recording, go through the categories in the table on page 94 of the Course Book and ensure the exercise is clear.
- In this authentic recording, Speaker 1 is a Japanese Customer Relations manager; Speaker 2 is the English Sales and Marketing Manager of an international publishing group. Gloss as necessary: *PR (Public Relations)* = maintaining a good public image of the organisation.
- It might be of interest to point out the fillers used by Speaker 2, e.g. *actually; obviously*. These are characteristic of native-speaker speech. There are also two examples of stressed *do* used in affirmative Present Simple utterances (*do have …; do budget for …*).
- **Further step:** In small groups, ask learners to list, in order, the five most important factors which influence customer relations. They may use the factors mentioned in the box and add others. Each group should then should take turns to present its list.

4 WRITING
Letter of complaint
1
- Remind the class that modern business English writing aims to be as clear and brief as possible.
- Go through the letter in the exercise. Elicit views on its clarity, length and level of detail. Gloss as necessary: *the order was two boxes short* = there were two boxes missing; *it (an important opportunity) is now in jeopardy* = there is a danger / strong possibility that we will miss this opportunity.
- Point out that for business purposes the letter is longer and more detailed than necessary – discuss one or two examples, as below.
  Original: *You may recall that when we placed the order, I explained that this was for a new overseas customer. I requested delivery not later than 7 September. You assured me that the goods, modified according to our specifications, would be delivered by 4 September.*
  Revised: *When we placed the order, I requested delivery not later than 7 September. You assured me the goods would be delivered by 4 September.*
- Ask learners, in pairs or groups of three, to amend the letter. Discuss the different versions. Compare them with the version given in the answers.

2
- Ask learners to discuss a time when they complained. You could also ask them to write a letter of complaint relating to this occasion. This can be done, in pairs or for homework.
- If possible, learners should get the context and details from the documents relating to a customer care issue they brought to class as part of their preparation.
- **Further step:** In pairs, learners improvise a phone call that might follow one of the letters they have written – a call from the receiver of the complaining letter to the sender.

5 CASE STUDY
Fair trading
- Cobra is a retail chain of sports shoe shops.

1
- Ask learners to read the Fair Trading Policy leaflet published by Cobra. Gloss vocabulary as necessary: *They have worn badly* = the condition has deteriorated more quickly than one would expect; *not of merchantable quality* = not good enough quality to be offered for sale; *malicious damage* = intentional damage; *Office of Fair Trading* = a Government Office in the UK that protects consumers against unfair or illegal business practices.
- Find out what class members understand by a 'fair trading policy', e.g. It is a policy of treating customers and suppliers justly so that they receive value in line with reasonable expectations.
- Discuss questions **a** and **b** with the class.
- Ask learners to consider question **c** in pairs, and report back.
- There are possible answers to questions **a** to **c** in the answers.

2
- Working in pairs learners practise returning shoes to a Cobra shop.

98 UNIT 21

- Ask learners to prepare for the activity by considering the reasons and possible outcomes listed in the information box, and by looking at the Useful Phrases on page 96.
- You might want to allocate reasons and outcomes to the different pairs to prevent overlap.
- Note that dialogue **d** in Core Practice (page 93 of Course Book) is about returning a product to a shop.
- **Further step:** Video the situations and use the recording for detailed analysis of the communication demonstrated including language used, intonation and body language.

REVIEW
- Go through the Language Notes and the Useful Phrases in the Course Book, if you have not done so already.
- Encourage learners to note down the terms they found useful – especially the ones they need in their work.
- Make a note of this language for your own future reference.
- Encourage learners to practise the new language they have learned.
- They might review it once a day, and identify which new terms they are using and which they need to use more.

Answers

1 Core practice
a i [T] b i [F] c i [T] d i [U]

2 Language check
1 c 2 b 3 a 4 c 5 c
6 a 7 b 8 b 9 a 10 a

3 Listening
Speakers
1 A Japanese maritime engineer
2 An English Sales and Marketing Manager
Speaker 1 speaks as a retail customer. Speaker 2 speaks as a supplier.

Factors affecting customer relations

Speakers:	1	2
Standard of service	✓	
Value for money		
Interest in customer's needs	✓	✓
Credit control procedures		
Frequency of sales calls		
Hospitality / entertainment		✓

4 Writing
(*possible answers*)
1 The letter is clear but possibly too long and detailed – see the version below. The heading might be:
Late delivery – order no. PL 427

> Dear …
> Late delivery – Order No. PL 427
> I am writing to complain about the poor service we have received on our order dated 20 July – I attach a copy.
> 1 When we placed the order, I requested delivery not later than 7 September. You assured me that the goods would be delivered by 4 September.
> 2 On 15 August, T. Larrick told us the job was on schedule.
> 3 When the goods arrived this morning:
> • the order was two boxes short
> • the colour was cream, not white
> • the monogrammed logo was 'DV Hotels', not 'PV Hotels'.
> I am very upset by the way the order has been handled. I would regret ending a business relationship that goes back a long time, but I will make other arrangements if I do not receive acceptable delivery dates before the end of the day.
> Yours sincerely

5 Case study
1 (*possible answers*)
a It is stacked on the counter at retail outlets for customers to help themselves. It is also put in a bag with a purchase.
b The purpose of the document is to reassure potential buyers, and to suggest quality and reliability.
c It clarifies the position by clearly stating the legal position. Cobra hopes this will improve customer relations by reducing misunderstandings.

Audioscripts

1 Core practice
a – We claim to put the customer first, but all it really amounts to is being polite on the telephone and when dealing with clients face to face. The organisation isn't customer focused in the real sense because we don't give customers what they want.
– And what's that?
– They want two things: an efficient service at a competitive price. So the way we can become more customer focused is to listen to what they want and provide it. Dissatisfied customers don't complain; they just go somewhere else. I read that attracting new customers can cost four times as much as retaining them.

b – I've had a lot of trouble getting through to you. Your call centre wouldn't put me through.
– I'm sorry, we've been very busy this morning. If you'll explain the problem, I'll see what I can do.
– OK – well, we are having problems with our C224 sorting machine. It keeps stopping. It makes a funny noise, then cuts out.
– It sounds as if it's overheating. Do you have a service contract?

Customer care 99

- It's still under warranty. According to the contract, the call-out time is supposed to be two hours. We're very unhappy about the way we're being treated.
- I completely understand and I apologise. Leave it with me; I'll get a technician out to you immediately.

c
- I was thinking of giving Marnix Busko tickets for the Cup Final.
- That's a good idea.
- He's an excellent customer. And he recommends us to other people; he brings in a lot of business. I think we need to show our appreciation.
- I agree, but we don't have a budget for entertaining.
- But the company spends a fortune on corporate entertaining. Couldn't we make a case and get the funding?
- We can try, I suppose.
- They want us to build the business – it's a legitimate expense!

d
- I bought this bag a couple of days ago, and look, it's split.
- Have you got the receipt?
- Yes, here it is.
- We can get it fixed for you but …
- Would that be under the guarantee?
- Not really – the guarantee doesn't cover heavy use.
- But it's falling apart. I'd like my money back.
- Well, I can't give you a refund. This isn't the result of normal wear and tear – it's torn.
- Look, when I bought it, I was assured it was a tough, all-purpose bag. I didn't get what I paid for.
- OK, I'll tell you what I'll do … I'll send it to our laboratory for analysis, and if they say it's a design fault or there's something wrong with the material, I'll give you your money back. It's the best I can do.

3 Listening

Speaker 1
In Japan every company makes efforts to provide a better service for customers, so that normally we get very good service in Japan. For example, the working hours – if we go to a Japanese shop just before closing time, they will of course extend their working hours. But in London they don't like to do that; they just close the shop. They say: 'Come back later on, or tomorrow.' This is not good in customer relations. In Japan we believe the customer is always right. And staff in shops and in hotels are very, very polite. There are silent languages between customers and shop staff, you know. And a good sales clerk understands what customers need very quickly because he understands this kind of non-verbal language.

Speaker 2
Occasionally we do have major problems getting our books to the right people at the … at the right time. So we have to have an ongoing programme of good customer relations. Er … this means going out with … major suppliers, talking to them about their problems, seeing what we can do to assist them. Now sometimes we do actually budget for this, we have … what's called an entertainment and travel allowance. And when we go round visiting various people, obviously we take them out to lunch, we take them out to dinner, we occasionally arrange receptions, we occasionally arrange seminars. So there is quite a lot of corporate PR that goes into keeping people happy.

UNIT 22 Home and family

PREPARATION

- There are three possible tracks through the unit: fast (about 1½ hours), standard (about 2 hours) and comprehensive (about 3 hours). For more information on the different tracks, see the notes in the Introduction on pages 10 and 11.
- For details of the aims of the unit, look at the Contents box on this page, the Language Notes at the end of the Course Book unit and the Useful Phrases below.
- If available to you, use the Self-study Guide as a source of supplementary exercises on the key themes of the unit.
- If you have taught the unit before, check the notes you made at the time.

USEFUL PHRASES

In this picture you can see the house where we live.
This was taken at my father's 70th birthday party.
That's my son – he doesn't look like me at all; he resembles his mother.
This is where we lived when I was working in Korea.
That's my mother-in-law in the front there.

We have a freehold property overlooking the river.
We live in a terraced house with a small garden.
It's a quiet neighbourhood / a residential area.
We're surrounded by trees. We have a view of the sea.
There's a local shop just round the corner.

Our place is rented; we have a three-year lease.
We're on two floors.
Upstairs, there are two bedrooms and a bathroom.
We're about 15 minutes from the centre of town.
The apartment is fully serviced.

Since we broke up, I've been on my own.
I have a flatmate who contributes to the rent.
We have a cleaner who comes twice a week.
We share the housework.

The alarm usually goes off just before 6 o'clock.
I get up at about 6.15.
It takes me about 20 minutes to shower and dress.
The children are old enough to get themselves ready.
I drop them off at school on the way to the station.
My commute is about 45 minutes.

LEAD IN (SUGGESTIONS)

- Refer to the Preparation section at the start of the unit in the Course Book (page 97). Check whether learners have brought family photographs and, if possible, messages of congratulations / sympathy to the class. These can be used as a resource through the lesson.
- Check also whether learners have looked at the Useful Phrases on page 100 in the Course Book (copied above). Their comments may indicate which areas of the target language they need to focus on and the level of interest in the topic.
- Consider leading into the subject by discussing homes and families. Be prepared to lead with information about your own home and family.

Contents

Expressions
In this picture you can see the house where we live.
That's my son; he doesn't look like me at all.
We're about 15 minutes from the centre of town.
The alarm usually goes off just before 6 o'clock.
I drop the children off at school on the way to the station.

Language check
Similarities and differences: *similar to*, *the opposite of*, etc.
each / every / all
Possessive *'s*: *a friend of my sister's*, *her parents' house*, etc.
Vocabulary: *single*, *engaged*, *divorced*, *mother / father-in-law*, *half brother / sister*, *a top-floor apartment*, *a terraced house*, *grow up*, *bring up*, *move in / out*

Practice
Taking about your home and family
Listening to people talking about family photos
Writing a request for time off
A feature on couples in business together

1 CORE PRACTICE

Listening and speaking

- This exercise provides an opportunity to practise a range of situations relating to home life.
- The exercise is in two parts – listening and speaking. The listening activity (part i) provides learners with ideas and models for the speaking activity (part ii).
- Ask learners to identify the verbal clues they used when answering the comprehension questions in part i.
- In part ii, encourage learners to adapt the scenarios to their needs. Where possible, they should introduce the realia they have brought to the class.
- Question a: The second woman has a US accent. Point out that *second floor* in UK English = third floor in US English. The floor at ground level = *the ground floor* in UK English, *the first floor* in US English; *lease* (see Glossary).
- Question b: The speaker has a Scottish accent. Point out that *goes off* = rings; *drop the children off at school* = drive them to school and leave them there; *my commute* = my journey to work.
- Question c: The first speaker has a US accent. Note that *step-daughters* = daughters of my wife by a previous marriage; *resemble* = look like / similar to.
- Question d: The female speaker has a non-standard accent. Gloss as necessary: *a place of my own* = a place that belongs to me; *a flat mate* (US English = *roommate*) = someone you share a flat with; *We get along fine* = we have a friendly

Home and family 101

relationship; *we're on our own* = neither of us is married or in a relationship.
- **Further step:** Ask learners individually or in pairs to prepare a further question for each dialogue.

2 LANGUAGE CHECK

- As you go through the multiple-choice questions with the class, point out the Language Notes at the end of the Course Book unit (page 100), and the related notes in the Business Grammar Guide (see the booklet that accompanies the Course Book booklet); there are cross-references from the notes to the BGG.
- The multiple-choice questions provide a starting point for the Language Check. Ensure that the related language points are explored and revised as necessary. The Specific Points section below gives you further detailed guidance.
- Adapt the points to learners' needs. Concentrate on areas where practice is needed.
- When working on vocabulary questions, introduce special terms not covered that learners need. Point out the Glossary on pages 158 – 160.
- For each question consider the following options.
  - Identify the answer.
  - Explore why the other options are wrong.
  - Ask learners to prepare examples that relate to their individual needs, e.g.:
    Question 1: *All three children look very similar to their mother.*
    Amended version: *All my relatives look completely different from each other.*
- **Further step:** Ask learners to put the examples in the questions into exchanges. What might the line before be? What could the next line be?

SPECIFIC POINTS

Questions 1 – 4: Similarities and differences (BGG 15.2) / *each, every, all* (BGG 10.3)
- Go through the Similarities and differences examples in the Language Notes. Ask learners to give personal versions of the examples.
- Discuss the examples of *each, every, all* in the Language Notes. refer to the BGG as necessary (BGG 10.3).
- Q1: *all / all of*, etc. (BGG 10.3) and similarities. Both *all* and *all of the* could be used here; *all the* is also possible. Note *all of* needs to be followed by a determiner (e.g. *the, our, this*) or a pronoun (*them*); it cannot be followed by just a noun. Revise the language of similarities as necessary: *similar to, the same as* and *like*. Elicit an example in one form from a learner, and ask another to transform it, e.g.:
  - A is very similar to B.
  - A and B are very alike.
  - A is very like B.

- Q2: Check that all the vocabulary to describe homes on page 100 is clear: for *leasehold* and *freehold* see Glossary; *terraced house* (US = *row house*) = a house which is attached to other houses either side; *a bungalow* = a house on one level. Revise ways of expressing difference: *aren't like, don't look like, are different from*, etc. Ask learners to use *unlike* in the example (no following preposition). Note that *different to* is a variant in UK English and *different than* in US English. Note also that *very* adds emphasis.
- Q3: Note *each other* is used after a verb and signifies a reciprocal relationship between the two (usually) people or things mentioned in the subject; *one another* could also be used (e.g. *They respected one another*); *each one* refers individually to one of a group (of at least two); *every other* technically means *every second / every alternate*, but it can be used in a looser way to mean *a surprisingly large number of*, especially after *almost* (e.g. *Almost every other person I know seems to be having relationship problems*).
- Q4: Note that *Every* must be followed by a singular countable noun. Note also that *All of my relations* (collective focus) and *Each of my relations* (individual focus) are both possible combinations but *all* needs a plural verb.

Questions 5 and 6: Possessive structures (BGG 11.2, 11.3)
- Review the examples in the Language Notes as necessary.
- Q5: This is a double possessive structure (*a friend of my mother's*). It is used when the first noun refers to one of a group (her mother has not got just one friend). Revise the apostrophe rule – generally *-'s* for singular nouns; *-s'* for regular plural nouns, e.g.:
  my friend's house = the house belongs to one of my friends
  my friends' house = the house belongs to more than one friend.
- Q6: Note that *children* is an irregular plural which does not end in *s*, so the possessive form is *-'s*. Try to elicit *take care of* for *look after*.

Questions 7 and 8: Vocabulary to describe relationships
- Check that learners can understand and use all the items under Relationships on page 100: *mother-in-law* = your husband / wife's mother; *first cousin* = your aunt or uncle's child; *second cousin* = a child of a cousin of your mother or father; *step mother* = your father's current wife (not your real mother); *ex-wife* = former wife; *partner* = someone you are in an established relationship with.
- Q7: If you have *a half brother / sister*, they are the child of only one of your birth parents. A *step brother / sister* is the child of your mother's or father's new husband / wife.
- Q8: Note the use of *get* with *engaged, married, divorced, pregnant* for the event. However, *get* is not used with *separate / split up / break up*.

Question 9: Separable phrasal verbs
- Note *to bring someone up* = to care for someone until they are an adult. It is a separable phrasal verb. Try to elicit *to raise* for *to bring up*. Point out that *to grow up* (= to go through your childhood years to adulthood) cannot have

an object. *I was brought up in* (+ place) is very similar in meaning to *I grew up in* … To practise, your learners could find out where they each grew up. Point out and practise the possessive pronoun in *on … own.* Elicit *by herself / alone* as alternatives.

Question 10: *in / into*
- Note that *into* is needed here, as the verb involves movement and it is followed by a noun or pronoun. Compare the example with the question *When are you moving in?*, which has no following noun. Try to elicit alternatives to *overlooking* (*which has a view of / over …; which overlooks …*). Point out that *our garden is not overlooked* = neighbours cannot see into it.

3 LISTENING

Family background

- The activity involves listening and matching three speakers to photos A, B and C on page 98 of the Course Book. The recordings are authentic.
- Have learners prepare for the exercise by looking at the photos and discussing them.
- Ask them to make notes as they listen to the recordings and then, in pairs, match the speakers to the photographs.
- Speaker 2: *still around* = still alive; Speaker 3: *brother-in-law* = your sister's husband or your husband / wife's brother.
- If appropriate, check that learners also know language such as: *to live together / cohabit* = to live together without being married; *a single parent* = a parent bringing up a child / children alone; *a working mother*; *a same-sex relationship*, etc.
- **Further step:** Ask learners to make a statement similar to the ones recorded about a photo they brought to class.

4 WRITING

A request for time off

- The activity requires learners to prepare a message asking for time off. It can be done as homework.
- Ask learners working in pairs to agree a family event that justifies taking time off.
- Go through the supporting notes on the page with the class. What should they consider before writing? What should they remember while writing? Check whether learners agree with the points. Do they apply in their area?
- Gloss as necessary: *holiday entitlement* = the holiday you have a right to have under the terms of your employment; *time off on compassionate grounds* (compassionate leave) = emergency leave given to someone for personal reasons (e.g. the death of a close relative); *How will your work be covered?* = Who will do your work while you are away?
- Point out that there are Useful Phrases on page 137; gloss as necessary.
- **Further step:** Pass round photocopies of the draft in the answers. Ask learners to compare it with their document and then comment, e.g. *My letter is a little longer but I think it is more persuasive.*

5 FEATURE

Couples in business

1
- This starts as a reading activity. The text is about famous couples who work together in business.
- Working in pairs, ask learners to read the article and the notes alongside it, then decide if the notes cover the main points in the article.
- Gloss terms as necessary: *wary of* = cautious about (because she expected problems); *pull their weight* = work equally hard; *thriving* = very successful; *thrived on the pressures* = the pressures made them function better; *blazing rows* = very heated arguments; *she has the final say* = she makes the final decision; *she defers to him* = she allows him to make the decisions; *taking it literally* = (here probably) focusing on the words (of the criticism) in a negative way; *Relate* = a UK organisation that offers guidance and support to couples who are having problems.
- Ask each pair to join another pair and form a four, then compare their answers. There is a suggested solution in the answers.

2
- Have learners discuss whether they would go into business with their partner. Ask them to prepare for the discussion in pairs.
- Lead a discussion, summarising from time to time.
- **Further step:** Use the discussion as an opportunity to practise summarising. Pass leadership of the discussion to other class members. Encourage the person in the chair to summarise.

REVIEW

- Go through the Language Notes and the Useful Phrases in the Course Book, if you have not done so already.
- Check that the items listed under Vocabulary in the Language Notes in the Course Book have been covered.
- Encourage learners to note down the terms they found useful – particularly the ones they need in their work.
- Make a note of this language for your own future reference.
- Encourage learners to practise the new language they have learned. They might do this by writing key points on a card that they carry with them and refer to through the day.

Home and family   103

Answers

1 Core practice
a i [U] b i [F] c i [U] d i [T]

2 Language check
1 a 2 c 3 b 4 c 5 b
6 a 7 a 8 c 9 b 10 a

3 Listening
Speaker 1 C
Speaker 2 A
Speaker 3 B

4 Writing
(*possible answer*)
Time off
I am writing to ask for time off on 24 – 25 July to attend my daughter's wedding.
I realise this is a busy time but I hope by putting in my request early it will be possible to rearrange the work. I have already spoken to John, who is willing to cover for me. I will make sure that everything is up to date and clear for him. I have already had my full holiday entitlement. So I would like to take this time as unpaid leave.
Regards

5 Feature
1 (*possible answers*)
Revised notes on article.
- Debbie Mole was wary because previous partner was lazy. Set up with husband and it worked.
- Results vary. Works for G & A Roddick and A & R Cheetham, not for J d'Abo or George D (Next). Both ended up divorced.
- Roddicks demonstrate it's important to know each other's strengths and weaknesses. Rows not a problem.
- Zelda West-Meads (Relate) – need a good relationship to start with.

Audioscripts

1 Core practice
a – We live in a modern apartment block; we're on the second floor. It's in a quiet neighbourhood. We have a fine view over the city.
 – Do you own the apartment?
 – No, we're renting because we're not sure how long we're going to be here – we have a three-year lease. But we're very pleased with the area. The facilities are excellent. There's a good golf course, and a swimming pool. And, of course, we're only 20 minutes from the mountains.
 – What about parking?
 – There's parking in the basement.
b We both work. The alarm goes off just before six and I make an effort to get up by about quarter past. I very often get back late, so I try to see the children in the morning. They are all old enough to look after themselves. But I try and have breakfast with them all the same. My wife's mother lives with us, so my wife has to make sure she's OK. We leave the house around 7.30, and drop the children off at school on the way to the station. My commute is about 45 minutes.
c – In this you can see the house where we live. In the front there you can see my wife.
 – Is it a recent picture?
 – Yep, it was taken last year.
 – So your step-daughters are quite young.
 – Yeah, they're five and seven. This picture here is of my father – that was his 63rd birthday party.
 – Is that your mother?
 – Uhmm …
 – You don't resemble them at all, do you?
 – No, but my brothers and sisters are all very similar to each other. It's funny.
d – I'm living in a company apartment at the moment. It's only a temporary arrangement, till I find a place of my own.
 – Do you have a flat mate? I'm actually sharing with a colleague who is in the same situation as me.
 – Did you know each other before?
 – He's a friend of my sister's but I didn't know him before. We get along fine. We don't do much housework, but then the apartment is fully serviced so there's not a lot to do. I'm away on business every other week. It suits us very well because we're both on our own.

3 Listening
Speaker 1
This is a photograph of when we were on holiday a couple of years ago, in South Africa, where I was brought up as a child. And we were staying at this time with my brother and his wife who have a very small cottage. That's my sister-in-law, my brother is just behind her, … she is called Elizabeth, or more correctly, she is called Elizabet because she in fact comes from Denmark.

Speaker 2 (in conversation)
– That is actually my entire family, including my father who died … umm … but otherwise they are all still around who are on this picture.
– How long ago did your father die?
– This was seven years ago, so that picture was taken eight years ago. As you can see … umm … Raffi still is quite young. And Hannah is here … and she must have been at the time about eight … eight years old … nine. And Raffi was … umm … five, four or five.

Speaker 3
I've got four children. I'm there with my husband and all the children, and my brother-in-law is married to a … to a Scottish girl and they have three children. We've just finished the walk and we are coming back down just towards the car.

UNIT 23 Work / life balance

PREPARATION

- It is possible to complete this unit at different speeds, in more or less detail. The fast track takes about 1½ hours, the standard track about 2 hours and the comprehensive track about 3 hours. For more information on the three options, see the notes in the Introduction on pages 10 and 11.
- For details of the aims of the unit, look at the Contents box opposite, the Language Notes at the end of the Course Book unit and the Useful Phrases below.
- If available to you, you can use the exercises in the Self-study Guide for extra practice.
- If you have taught the unit before, review the notes you made at the time.

USEFUL PHRASES

How's your work / life balance?
OK. I'm very keen on golf.
It's fun and I find it helps me unwind.
I take exercise on a regular basis.
We play in a very competitive way.
I go running because it keeps me fit.

At the weekend we have a few friends round for a meal.
For me it's a time to relax and spend time with the family.
We might all go for a walk, if the weather is good.
As a parent, I find it difficult to balance work and domestic commitments.

I much prefer going out to entertaining at home.
It's far more fun and a lot less hassle.
What I like best is meeting up with some friends.
During the week I have to entertain clients.

Saturday is a day for family and shopping.
During the week, my wife has to handle the domestic demands.
Does she accept that?
She agrees with it completely.
She isn't in agreement with it at all.

Do you take work home.
I do from time to time, but I try not to.
I'll work late during the week rather than work over the weekend.

Hey, why don't we get together for a meal or something?
Wow, that would be nice – shall we meet up for lunch on Sunday?
Hmm, OK. Shall we fix a time?

LEAD IN (SUGGESTIONS)

- Consider leading into the subject by asking learners about their work / life balance and how they achieve it. The discussion is likely to indicate the language needs of the class in this area.
- Check how learners have prepared for the lesson (see the Preparation section at the start of the unit in the Course Book, page 101). Have they looked at the Useful Phrases on page 104 in the Course Book (copied above)?
- Check whether they have brought to class printed materials relating to a hobby or interest.

Contents

Expressions
I find it difficult to balance work and domestic commitments.
I'm very keen on golf; it's fun and it helps me unwind.
I take exercise on a regular basis.
I'd much rather eat out than entertain at home.
It's far more relaxing and a lot less hassle.

Language check
More on comparisons: *far more / less interesting than*
Preference: *prefer, would rather, rather than*
Agreement: *agree with, accept, in agreement with*
Alternative adverb forms: *regularly* vs. *on a regular basis*
Non-verbal communication: *Ah, Hey, Oh*
Vocabulary: *get together, meet up, come round, take up, give up, be keen on*

Practice
Talking about leisure time
Interview with a publishing director
A questionnaire on work / life balance
Article and discussion on taking exercise

1 CORE PRACTICE

Listening and speaking

- This exercise provides an opportunity to practise a range of situations relating to work / life balance.
- The exercise is in two parts – listening and speaking. The listening activity (part i) prepares learners for the speaking activity (part ii).
- As you work through the comprehension questions in part i, ask learners to explain how they have arrived at their answers.
- In part ii, encourage learners to adapt the scenarios to their needs. If appropriate, they should introduce the realia they have brought to the class.
- Question a: The female speaker has a non-standard accent. Point out that *I get it wrong* = I do the wrong thing; *the domestic demands* = responsibilities to do with home life; *single-handed* = on her own.
- Question b: The speaker has a US accent. Gloss as necessary: *meeting up with some friends* = meeting some friends; *having them round for dinner* = inviting them to your home for dinner.
- Question c: The female speaker has a non-standard accent. Note *get together for a meal* = meet for a meal.
- Question d: The male speaker has a non-standard accent. Explain that *to unwind* = to relax.
- **Further step:** If possible, video the sketches and use the recordings to analyse wider communication factors such as body language.

Work / life balance

Draw attention to the fact that in different cultures body language may be interpreted in different ways. Are there any local behaviours that might be misunderstood in a global context?

2 LANGUAGE CHECK

- The multiple-choice questions link to the Language Notes at the end of the Course Book unit (page 104) and the related notes in the Business Grammar Guide (see the booklet that accompanies the Course Book).
- The multiple-choice questions enable you to treat the language programme flexibly. Points that are known can be handled briefly. Points that require more remedial attention can be explored in more detail. The Specific Points section below gives you further detailed guidance.
- When working on vocabulary questions, point out the Vocabulary notes in the Language Reference at the end of the unit in the Course Book, and the Glossary on pages 158 – 160. Introduce, as necessary, special terms that learners need.
- For each question consider the following options.
  - Elicit the answer.
  - Discuss why the other options are wrong.
  - If appropriate, ask learners to change the example so the wrong options can be used.
  - Ask learners to prepare examples that relate to their specific needs, e.g.:
    Question 1: *Reading is a lot more relaxing than watching TV.*
    Amended version: *Working full time and bringing up a family is a lot more difficult than I expected.*
- **Further step:** Ask your learners, working in pairs, to choose two language points covered in this exercise that they have problems with. Ask them to produce an example for each with a typical error. Compile a class list, then ask pairs to correct the errors. Finally, discuss as a whole class. You may have to 'doctor' learners' examples so that they include only the error in question.

SPECIFIC POINTS

Questions 1 and 2: Comparisons with modifiers (BGG 15.3)
- Go through the examples in the Language Notes. Point out how modifiers can be used with adjectives (*far less tiring*), or adverbs (*a bit more regularly*) and nouns (*a little more space*). Have your learners create parallel examples that relate to their own lives.
- Q1: Elicit variants of *a lot* (*far, much, considerably*).
- Q2: Note that *many* is the only one of the options that can be used with a countable noun (*places*). Review the modifiers that can be used with countables, uncountables or both (refer to BGG 15.3).

Question 3: Use of multipliers (BGG 15.2), *twice as big as the one we have here*
- Elicit more examples of multipliers and fractions (e.g. *three times as fast as …; half as big as …*). Note that *as … as* must be used after *twice* and fractions, but comparative forms can be used after *… times* (e.g. *three times faster than …*).

Question 4: Expressing preferences (BGG 20.8)
- Point out how a modifier (*far*) is used here to express a preference: *I'd far rather go home.* Elicit *much* as an alternative modifier.

Questions 5 and 6: Expressing agreement / disagreement (BGG 21.2)
- Q5: Draw attention to the prepositions: to agree / disagree *with*, to be *for / against*. Elicit examples and practise as necessary.
- Q6: Note the prepositions: to be *in* agreement *with*. Note *he has a very good point* = he has a strong argument that needs to be considered.

Question 7: Adverbs, alternative forms (BGG 14.7)
- Elicit *regularly* as an alternative. Go through the alternative forms of adverbs listed in the Language Notes. Point out that alternative forms tend to be used when the normal adverb would be too long or unusual, e.g.: *She runs her life in an organised way.* (*organisedly* is not possible.) *They are living apart on a trial basis.* (*trially* is not possible.)

Question 8: Non-verbal communication
- Check examples in the Language Notes. Communication of this kind is very culturally biased. These tend to be UK based. Elicit examples that your learners use. Discuss which can be used in a multi-cultural environment and which would be confusing.

Questions 9 and 10: Verb phrases
- Check the examples listed. Ensure learners can use them.
- Q9: Revise the use of *go / take, come / bring*, e.g. here *come* and *bring* must be used because it involves movement towards the speaker. Compare this with: *Let's go round to visit them and take some flowers*, where the movement is away from the speaker.
- Q10: Note to *give something up* means to stop doing something. It is a separable phrasal verb (*I gave it up*). Explain that *takes up (a lot of time)* = uses / occupies; *up* is optional here but it gives the idea that it might be in an undesirable way. *take up* can be used with other nouns in this sense, e.g. space, money, energy.

3 READING

Exercising the brain

- The activity consists of reading an article, then discussing it in a pair exercise. Partner A supports the case put forward in the article. Partner B argues against it. There is extra information for Partner B on page 137 of the Course Book.

- After learners have read the article, gloss as necessary: *smarter* = more intelligent; *sharp* = clever / quick; *pump(ing) iron* = using weights in the gym; *mental agility* = ability to think quickly and clearly; *the onset* = the start; *couch rats* = rats who do not take exercise (this is a play on the phrase *couch potato* = a person who prefers sitting on a couch to taking exercise); *treadmill* = an exercise wheel (often used for small pets) and also a running machine in the gym; *runaholics* = people who are addicted to running; *fitness fanatics* = people with an extreme liking for exercise.
- Partner B text: *crippled by a wasting disease* = seriously affected by a disease that gradually causes the sufferer to become thin and weak.
- Prepare for the discussion by reviewing the Useful Phrases on page 137 – a list of gambits that can be used in a discussion or argument. Gloss and practise as necessary.
- **Further step:** Below are some possible comprehension questions that can be used here or earlier in the process.
  - *What is the main point of the article?* (Exercise builds the brain.)
  - *What are the grounds for the idea?* (Research on rats indicates that rats that take exercise have higher levels of BDNF, a key growth factor in the brain.)
  - *How does the theory relate to humans?* (The article claims that fitness fanatics like Arnold Schwarzenegger and Jean-Claude Van Damme, both successful from humble origins, prove that the theory applies to humans too.)

4 WRITING
Reading habits

1
- The activity begins with a discussion of book-buying habits, based on statistics presented in the pie charts and bar graphs on the page.
- The statistics refer to habits in the UK. Ask your learners if the picture presented would be different in their countries. Class E referred to in the second bar chart (Hours / week reading for pleasure) includes state pensioners, widows, casual workers, the unemployed and students.
- Ask learners to prepare for the discussion in pairs – there is Useful Language on page 138. Gloss as necessary: *profile* = analysis showing basic characteristics (here presented in a pie chart showing male / female breakdown). Then open the discussion.

2
- Here learners, working in pairs, write a summary of the information contained in charts and graphs.
- You might kick-start the process by discussing approaches and a possible template for the summary – there is a sample draft in the answers.
- Point out that in many business situations, continuous prose is not the best way to communicate. Notice that the sample draft breaks the message down into short paragraphs with clear headings. The information in each paragraph is then broken down into bullet points.
- **Further step:** When learners have written their summaries, circulate the draft from the answers and ask class members to reformat their message for maximum readability.

5 FEATURE
An interview

1
- Note that this listening exercise is based on an authentic recording with Lennie Goodings, a director of Virago Press (a publishing company). She is Canadian.
- Before doing the listening exercise ask learners to read through the questionnaire. Gloss new vocabulary: *come into conflict* = compete against each other (for your time); *workaholism* = the problem of spending too much time working.
- Ask learners to complete the questionnaire on behalf of the speaker. Gloss as necessary: *nanny* = a person who looks after a family's children as a job; *work ethic* = a belief that work is morally good; *switch off* = stop thinking about (work); *an entree* (a French word) = here, an opportunity to meet.

2
- Here learners complete the questionnaire for themselves, then compare results with a partner.
- **Further step:** Ask learners to summarise orally their partner's answers to the questionnaire, e.g.: *I think* (Yahn) *balances work and leisure time very successfully. He makes a rule never to work at weekends or during family holidays. But during the week he puts in very long hours.*

REVIEW
- Go through the Language Notes and the Useful Phrases in the Course Book with the class, if you have not already done so.
- Encourage learners to note down the terms they found useful – especially the ones they need in their work.
- Make a note of this language for your own future reference.

Work / life balance **107**

Answers

1 Core practice
a i [F]   b i [U]   c i [U]   d i [U]

2 Language check
1 b 2 b 3 a 4 a 5 a
6 c 7 c 8 c 9 b 10 c

4 Writing
(*possible answers*)

The four charts give a picture of the interest in books in the UK. The profile indicates who buys books and who reads them.

Who buys books?
- The first pie chart shows the percentage of men and women who buy books – 53% are women, 47% are men.
- The second pie chart breaks the sample down into age groups. The biggest group is between 25 and 34. They represent 22% of the total.
- It is interesting that only 7% of 60 – 64 year-olds buys books. But the figure jumps to 15% in the 65+ group.

Who reads books?
- The first bar chart shows that 70% of the population read at least one book a year, and that nearly 50% read for pleasure.
- The second bar chart gives details of how much time different groups spend reading for pleasure. The average is eight hours per week.
- It is striking that Class E, which includes the poorest and least educated, read for more than 12 hours per week – more than all the other groups.

To sum up, the profile indicates that the level of interest – buying and reading – is high. Men buy fewer books than women and read one hour less per week – seven hours against eight hours.

5 Feature

Do you balance work and leisure successfully?

		TRUE	FALSE
1	Often go through an entire weekend without spending any time on work brought home from the office.	✓	
2	Events at work sometimes force me to miss occasions at home that my family have particularly asked me to get back for.		✓
3	I never dream about work problems.	✓	
4	I have at least three significant leisure interests that have nothing to do with my work.	✓	
5	When I am ill, I tend to take work to bed with me.	(n/a)	
6	I find it easier to talk to work colleagues than to my partner or friends.		✓
7	It is very unusual for me to ring home and say I'm going to be back later than planned.		✓
8	I have had to cancel at least one holiday due to pressure of work.		✓
9	When I'm trying to read a book or magazine, I find my mind keeps wandering back to work problems.		✓
10	I find it a relief to meet new people who have nothing whatever to do with my line of business.		✓

Audioscripts

1 Core practice
a – My job is quite demanding. I try to get home in time to say 'good night' to my children. And when I'm away on business, I always call to keep in contact. To be honest, I find it difficult to get the right balance between my domestic and my work commitments. A lot of the time I get it wrong. But the fact is that I have to provide an income and if I don't do the job properly, they'll get someone else. So my wife has to handle many of the domestic demands single-handed.
 – Does she accept that?
 – Up to a point. She doesn't really agree with it, but it's easier for me to earn on a regular basis.

b – What I like best is meeting up with some friends and going out to a restaurant, or having them round for dinner. Of the two, I'd much rather eat out than entertain at home because it's far more relaxing and it's a lot less hassle. During the week my socialising is really confined to work obligations – entertaining clients, going to official receptions and so on. Sometimes, I get to take a client to the opera. I'd love to go more often but the tickets cost a fortune.

c – Hey, Maria! We must get together for a meal or something.
 – Yes, that would be nice.
 – Well, how about this weekend?
 – That sounds good.
 – Which would suit you better, Friday or Saturday?
 – Er … let me check – Saturday would be better for me.
 – What sort of time?
 – How about 7.30?
 – Right, I'll look forward to that. Shall I see if I can get tickets for the new production at the National Theatre?

d – Saturday is a day for family and shopping – it's mainly a practical day. In the evening we might go to a film.
 – What about babysitting?
 – Our neighbour's daughter usually babysits for us.
 – And Sunday?
 – For me it's a time to relax and spend time with my family. We usually do something together. If the weather's bad, we might watch a film on television. If it's good, we might all go for a walk in the park, which is fun and it helps me unwind.
 – Do you ever take work home?
 – Not if I can avoid it. I'll work late during the week rather than work over the weekend.

108   UNIT 23

5 Feature

- Do you often go through an entire weekend without spending any time on work brought home from the office?
- Not that often. I tend to work on Sunday evenings, after the kids go to bed.
- Do events at work sometimes force you to miss occasions at home that your family have particularly asked you to get back for?
- No, my work tends to be flexible enough. I mean if I have … a sick nanny or something, I can usually get home, so … no I tend not to, I mean.
- Do you ever dream about work problems?
- Oh, all the time. I never not dream about work problems.
- Do you have at least three significant leisure interests that have nothing to do with your work?
- I don't think so. I don't think that I've ever been very good on hobbies, to tell you the truth. I think I've been working … I started working part time when I was 16, and … not that I had to … I didn't come from a terribly poor family or anything. There was kind of just … a work ethic.
- When you are ill, do you take work to bed with you?
- Umm … I'm not ill very often.
- Do you find it easier to talk to work colleagues than to your partner and friends?
- Well it depends what (we're) talking about, you know. Umm … I'm afraid … I mean … my work is very emotional and very intense, so in fact I bring a lot of the conversation home, and go on talking at home, and I am very lucky that … um … John, my partner, is terrifically tolerant and so he allows me to continue the conversation.
- How unusual is it for you to ring home and say that you are going to be back later than you had planned?
- Quite often I do that, I'm afraid. I quite often ring home.
- Have you ever had to cancel a holiday due to pressure of work?
- Very nearly. I never, but very nearly.
- When you are trying to read a book or a magazine for pleasure, do you find that your mind keeps wandering back to work problems?
- I don't think so, no I think I can switch off.
- Do you like to meet new people who have nothing whatever to do with your line of business?
- Not particularly, I mean, yes and no. I mean, I don't, I think, I am incredibly lucky with my business is that … in a sense … everything can fit into the business and … publishing gives one such an entree into so many interesting people, so actually I think I would use my work to meet interesting people rather than … try and avoid them.

UNIT 24 Getting away

PREPARATION

- There are three possible tracks through the unit: fast (about 1½ hours), standard (about 2 hours) and comprehensive (about 3 hours). For more information on the different tracks, see the notes in the Introduction on pages 10 and 11.
- For details of the aims of the unit, look at the Contents box opposite, the Language Notes at the end of the Course Book unit and the Useful Phrases below.
- If you have taught the unit before, check the notes you made at the Review stage.
- There is a Progress Test covering Units 19 – 24 on pages 144 and 145, which can be photocopied and circulated. The answers are on page 148. For the best results, give learners time to prepare.

USEFUL PHRASES

The climate is good, although it can be chilly at night.
The countryside round the city is unspoilt.
The people are warm but fairly reserved.
Do I need a visa?
No, but I advise you to have an anti-tetanus jab.

I'd like to book a mini-break.
Where to? What do you have in mind?
Flights to the Caribbean are fully booked.
Could you let me know if you get a cancellation?
The package includes accommodation at a three-star hotel.
Departing at 14.20 on the 17th and returning on …

The documents are all in this wallet.
Can I see your passport and driving licence?
Could you sign here and here, please?
Which road do I take for Kalinski?
Follow the signs for the coast, and then take Route 27.

What's the best way of getting to the Summer Palace?
It's beyond Fulong, towards Gretik.
It's difficult by public transport; there's no direct service.
It'll take you a long time whichever way you go because it's a very bad road.

I'd like an early check out, please.
I'm afraid you can't use this ticket on a scheduled flight.
If you want to travel tomorrow, you'll have to upgrade to business class.
How much would it cost to upgrade?
I've booked you on to the 12 o'clock flight.

LEAD IN (SUGGESTIONS)

- Refer to the Preparation section at the start of the unit in the Course Book (page 105). Check whether learners have brought to class a postcard and holiday photos relating to a recent break. These can be used as a resource during the lesson.
- Check also whether they have looked at the Useful Phrases on page 108 in the Course Book (copied above). Comments from the class may indicate which areas of the target language they need to focus on and the level of interest in the topic.
- Consider leading into the subject by eliciting stories about a recent holiday. If possible bring pictures from your own holiday.

Contents

Expressions
I want to get away for a few days, preferably somewhere warm.
The climate is good, although it can be chilly at night.
It's best to go before the high season.
I have to get back to my office.
If you want to travel tomorrow, you'll have to upgrade to business class.

Language check
Contrasting ideas: *although*, *even so*, *all the same*
Giving (holiday) advice: *Remember that …*, *I'd advise you to …*
Short form questions: *Where to? How long for?*
whatever, whoever, whenever
Vocabulary: *travel agent, local rep, stand-by passenger, package holiday, high / off season, fully booked, on stand-by, get away, head for, check in / out*

Practice
Organising a holiday
People talking about their holidays
Sending a greetings message back to colleagues
A feature on mini-breaks in New York

1 CORE PRACTICE

Listening and speaking

- This exercise provides an opportunity to practise a range of situations relating to holidays and mini-breaks.
- The exercise is in two parts – listening and speaking. The listening activity (part i) provides learners with ideas and models for the speaking activity (part ii).
- Ask learners to identify the verbal clues they used when answering the comprehension questions in part i.
- In part ii, encourage learners to adapt the scenarios to their needs. Where possible, they should introduce the realia they have brought to the class.
- Question a: The male speaker has a non-standard accent. Gloss as necessary: *get away* = go on holiday; *off-season* = a period of the year when fewer people travel and rates are usually cheaper; *hidden extras* = extra charges such as airport transfers, charges for paying by credit card, etc.
- Question b: The female speaker has an Australian accent. Note *chilly* = cold; *unspoilt* = still in a natural state / not damaged by development; *jabs* = injections (inoculations) to protect you against diseases.
- Question c: The man has a non-standard accent.
- Question d: The woman has a US accent. Gloss as necessary: *upgrade your ticket* = change for a

more expensive one (e.g. economy to club class); *a travel bureau* = a travel agent / agency (UK); *a parade of shops* = a line of shops next to each other in one building.
- **Further step:** In pairs, ask learners to playread the dialogues to the rest of the group (refer them to the audioscript on page 153 of the Course Book).

2 LANGUAGE CHECK

- As you go through the multiple-choice questions with learners, point out the Language Notes at the end of the Course Book unit (page 108), and the related notes in the Business Grammar Guide (see the booklet that accompanies the Course Book); there are cross-references from the notes to the BGG.
- The multiple-choice questions provide a starting point for the Language Check. Ensure that the related language points are explored and revised as necessary. The Specific Points section below gives you further detailed guidance.
- Adapt the points to learners' needs. Concentrate on areas where practice is needed.
- When working on vocabulary questions, introduce special terms not covered that learners need. Point out the Glossary on pages 158 – 160 of the Course Book.
- For each question consider the following options.
  - Identify the answer.
  - Explore why the other options are wrong.
  - Ask learners to prepare examples that relate to their specific needs, e.g.:
    Question 1: *The special package is very good value in spite of the fact that it is slightly more expensive.* Amended version: *The three-day mini-break is very tempting in spite of the fact that I can't really afford it.*
- **Further step:** Ask learners, working in pairs or small groups, to prepare a dialogue using all ten examples in the multiple-choice questions.

SPECIFIC POINTS

Questions 1 and 2: Contrast clauses (BGG 18.2)
- Go through the examples in the Language Notes.
- Q1: Only *in spite of* and *despite* are followed by *the fact that*. Elicit why *the fact that* is needed (it turns a verb phrase – *it is slightly more expensive* – into a noun phrase, which is required after *in spite of / despite*). Ask learners to use *however* in the example (without *the fact that*). Point out that when writing, *however* usually begins a new sentence (it can follow a semi-colon) but *despite / the fact that* do not. A *mini-break* = a short holiday (e.g. a weekend), often taken in addition to longer annual holidays.

- Q2: Both *Even so* and *All the same* could be used here. Try to elicit other possibilities: *Nevertheless*; *Despite this*; *However*; *but*. Ask learners to transform the example so that *Even though* could be used (*Even though I put a label … the airline still managed to lose it*). Note the use of *still* to reinforce the meaning. Point out that *in* needs to be stressed in *checked in*; *check in / out* are also used for arriving and leaving a hotel. Note how *check through* is used: *I've checked my luggage through from London to Bangkok* (*so I don't need to check it in again in Dubai*). Note *tagged* = put an airline luggage label on.

Question 3: Holiday travel tips, giving advice (BGG 21.1)
- Check through the examples in the Language Notes.
- Note *You don't need / You don't require* could both be used here (both can be followed by a noun). Ensure your learners understand that they mean that something isn't necessary. Elicit also *You don't have to* (*get / have …*). Practise giving the advice in other ways (*I'd advise you to get*, etc.). Point out that *in my opinion* is not used with *advise / suggest*. Extend this exercise by asking your learners to give other useful travel trips.

Questions 4 and 5: Some prepositions
- Q4: Point out that *beside* the beach = *on / next to* the beach; *among* my friends = *with* my friends. Ask learners to change the example so that the other prepositions listed can be used, e.g.:
  We're staying in a small hotel beyond the village. It's a long journey for my friends.
  We are staying in a small hotel beneath the mountains. It is very popular with my friends.
  If appropriate, extend the exercise by introducing more prepositions.
- Q5: *I'm heading for the coast* = the coast is my destination (could also be said as *I'm making for the coast*; *I'm heading towards the coast*; *I'm heading up / down the coast*; *I'm going along the coast*). Note that one meaning of *get off* is to leave work at the end of the day (e.g. *I get off early on Fridays*). Also *to get out* can mean to go out and socialise (e.g. *We don't get out much now we have a baby*).

Question 6: Short questions
- Practise by exchanging short form questions round the class, e.g.:
  - *I'm off on a mini- break.*
  - *Where to? / Who with? / How long for?*
- Point out that: *What for?* = For what purpose / why?

Question 7: *whatever, wherever, whoever*, etc.
- Go through the examples listed in the Language Notes. Point out that ___*ever* usually means *It doesn't matter* or *No matter which / who / what,* etc. Note that *No matter … can only be used at the beginning of a sentence. Here, *whichever* refers back to two options (*bus* or *train*).

Questions 8 to 10: Vocabulary related to travelling
- Check through the Vocabulary section on page 108. Gloss as necessary: *local rep* = the representative of the holiday

Getting away 111

company in the holiday place; *self-catering* = with facilities for preparing your own food (e.g. an apartment with cooking facilities).

- Q8: Establish the situation here (it's a hotel). Note *bill* = an itemised request for payment (usually on paper); note also *phone / electricity bill*, etc. Point out that in the UK *bill* is also used in a restaurant (= *check* in the US).
- Q9: Note *package* is usually used with *holiday* to indicate that the flight and accommodation are included in the cost. Often this involves a *charter flight* (where the plane is leased by a tour operator). A *scheduled flight* is one that follows a regular timetable organised by the company that owns the aircraft (e.g. Gulf Air).
- Q10: Note *fully booked* = full (no seats available). If a flight is *overbooked*, too many tickets have been sold (anticipating some *no-shows*). Explain that *to be put on stand-by* = to be put on a list for any tickets that become available on a fully booked flight; *waiting list* would be possible but needs a definite article.

---

3 LISTENING
Holiday destinations

- Three speakers talk about what they like doing when they are on holiday. The recordings are authentic. Speaker 1 is Australian, Speaker 2 from the US, Speaker 3 from Goa in India.
- Gloss as necessary. Speaker 3: *idyllic* = very beautiful, peaceful, relaxing.
- Have learners go through the table of activities and say how they like to spend their holidays. Are there other ideas they would like to add to the list?
- Learners listen in pairs and make notes, then complete the table.
- **Further step:** Ask learners to talk about their favourite holiday destinations. What makes a holiday destination or particular type of holiday special?

4 WRITING
Greetings to colleagues

- The activity involves learners sending a message back to the office while they are on holiday.
- Using the photos they have brought to class as a guide, in pairs learners decide the broad details of the holiday or mini-break they are 'on'.
- Have the pairs check the list of bullet points that might be covered in a message of this sort, and the Useful Language on page 138.
- Ask pairs to form groups of four and review the messages they have written. There is a sample in the answers.
- **Further step:** Each pair exchanges messages with another pair. Then, writing as the person / people who 'received' the message, each pair writes a reply.

5 FEATURE
New York

1
- This is a pairwork activity, which would work well as a phone call. Partner B advises Partner A on what to do on a mini-break in New York. Partner A reads the article on page 107. Partner B reads the text on page 138.

2
- As an introduction to this task, check which big cities learners have visited. What were the highlights?
- As this is an information-gap exercise, it would be better to deal with the vocabulary in detail after the activity. If help is needed before the activity, you could either gloss in two groups or hand out vocabulary notes.
- Partner A's text page 107: *The Apple of Temptations* is a play on words: it is a reference to Adam and Eve and New York's nickname, The Big Apple; *irresistible* = impossible to refuse; *a taster* = a small introductory experience; *legions of* = large numbers of; *skirt* = go round the edge of.
- Partner B's text page 138: *slip down into* = go to; *psychedelic* = with bright patterns and colours, like you might see if you took a mind-altering drug; *awnings* = fabric or plastic covers attached to a building to protect people from the weather; *the first time round* = in this text it refers to the 1960s (the hippy era); *gracious* = elegant; *zig-zag* = shaped like a z; *gallery* = place for showing works of art; *browse* = look around (but not intending to buy); *exquisite* = beautiful / wonderful; *deli* = delicatessen – (a specialist shop selling cooked or prepared foods (e.g. cold meats, cheese, sandwiches), often from other countries.
- After the activity, ask learners to find words and phrases in the text on page 107 that mean the same as: walk slowly = *stroll*; paths for horses = *bridleways*; lift = *elevator*; jump on = *hop aboard*; return journey = *round-trip*; try something you like = *sample what you fancy*.
- Note that prepositions are missing at the start of the second paragraph: *Stroll (in) Central Park early (in the) morning*.
- **Further step:** Partner A calls Partner B on returning from the trip to New York. They talk about the places in the texts, e.g.:
  Did you …?
  Was it …?
  Did you manage to get to …?
  What was / were … like?

REVIEW

- Go through the Language Notes and the Useful Phrases in the Course Book, if you have not done so already.
- Check the items listed under Vocabulary in the Language Notes in the Course Book have been covered.
- Encourage learners to note down the terms they found particularly useful – especially the ones they need in their working lives.
- Make a note of this language for your own future reference.
- Encourage learners to practise the new language they have learned, to bring it into their communication.

Answers

1 Core practice
a i [U]   b i [F]   c i [T]   d i [U]

2 Language check
1 c   2 a   3 b   4 c   5 b
6 a   7 b   8 c   9 b   10 c

3 Listening
When on holiday

Speakers:	1	2	3
I like to relax and forget work.	✓		✓
I like to be somewhere hot.	✓		✓
I like to visit the sea.	✓	✓	✓
I like sightseeing /experiencing a different culture.	✓		
I like to try the local food.			✓
I spend time with my children / family.			
I enjoy taking exercise.	✓		
I like reading.	✓		
I take work with me.		✓	

4 Writing
(*possible email message*)

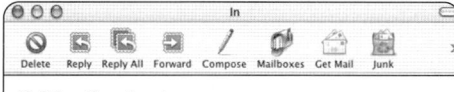

Holiday Greetings!

Hi everyone!

We got here yesterday, and I'm still pretty tired – it was a six-hour flight. We came for the sun and sand and both are fantastic. The hotel is right on the beach. Tomorrow we are going shark fishing. This means an early start, so I'll be in contact later in the day. I think I'm six hours behind you. Normally, I'll log on twice a day. In an emergency, try my mobile or leave a message with the hotel (00366 7194 0355). Say 'Hi' to Ulf if you see him, and thank him for recommending this beautiful place.

I hope you are having fun without me!

Best regards

Audioscripts

1 Core practice

a – I want to get away for a few days, preferably somewhere warm.
  – Where to?
  – I don't mind really. I'll take whatever you've got.
  – Well, what about Rhodes? I have a special off-season break which includes flight and accommodation.
  – Are there any hidden extras?
  – Well, airport tax is extra, of course. In spite of that, it's very good value.

b – I was there last summer.
  – How long for?
  – Two weeks. The climate is great, although it can be chilly at night. They've got some wonderful unspoilt beaches. It's best to go in April before the high season.
  – Where were you?
  – Near Wichuchu, on the south island.
  – What are the people like?
  – They're a bit reserved. Even so, it's a good place to unwind. The lifestyle is very easy going.
  – What about formalities? Do you need a visa?
  – Yes, you do. And you need various jabs. Whatever you do, don't drink the water. My partner was ill …

c – I want to get to the Imperial Palace. According to this guide it's just outside Fulong.
  – Yes, it's slightly beyond Fulong. It's on the road towards Gretik. The best way to get there is by car.
  – Is it possible to go by public transport?
  – Yes, but it involves a few changes.
  – Could you write down the directions for me?
  – Yes, of course. I'd advise you not to use an unlicensed taxi.

d – I have to get back to my office.
  – When by?
  – Well, as soon as possible really. Where can I change my travel arrangements?
  – Are you booked on a regular flight?
  – No, it's a special package.
  – I think you'll have to upgrade your ticket. You really need to go to a travel bureau.
  – Is there one within walking distance?
  – There's one in the parade of shops just under the hotel.

3 Listening

Speaker 1
I like some time to sort of unwind and relax and laze around, and think about things. I like some time to read and I like something good to be able to go and look at, something kind of cultural if possible. I also like to get some kind of physical exercise like swimming or riding or something like that. I think my favourite place to go on holiday, of course, is Australia, because that combines all these things … usually if you go round Christmas time it is the summer, so it is nice and warm.

Speaker 2
I like to go to the seaside, especially the Mediterranean seaside of France and Italy. And … one of the things that I like to do when I'm on holiday, believe it or not, is I work. I bring my work along with me, I sit on the beach and read the things that I have to do. I like my work so I don't like to be away from it. I like to keep thinking about it, so I typically work in the morning and then in the afternoon I will usually have fun.

Speaker 3
My favourite place is Goa where it is … where it is so relaxed. I mean, even though I originate from Goa, the people are so relaxed and so friendly. The main thing is … it has sand, sea and sun. And that … with the traditional food … makes Goa an idyllic place to unwind.

Getting away 113

UNIT 25 Politics and business

PREPARATION

- It is possible to complete this unit at different speeds, in more or less detail. The fast track takes about 1½ hours, the standard track about 2 hours, and the comprehensive track about 3 hours. For more information on the three options, see the notes in the Introduction on pages 10 and 11.
- For details of the aims of the unit, look at the Contents box on this page, the Language Notes at the end of the Course Book unit and the Useful Phrases below.
- If available to you, use the exercises in the Self-study Guide as extra practice.

USEFUL PHRASES

The government is a coalition between parties of the left and centre.
It has been in power for five years.
It is difficult to predict who will win the next election.
It's almost impossible to forecast the result.
The social democrats are ahead in the opinion polls.
Nevertheless, the right have a good chance.
There has been a strong swing to the right.
However, the left are still ahead.
We don't think the electorate will elect a right-wing government.
Relations with our neighbours are good.
They announced a new trade agreement on the news.
A spokesperson informed us that they would take a vote tomorrow.
There are pressure groups who are against the agreement.
They say the government should ban imports from the area.
What's your position on rail privatisation?
I'm for it – I'm in favour.
I'm very much against it.
The evidence against privatisation is very clear.
In most cases, prices have risen.
Experience shows that service deteriorates.
I don't agree at all.
Statistics show that passenger numbers go up.
Investment increases faster than it does under state control.
The fact is that privatisation increases efficiency.
In my view, the government should hold a referendum.

LEAD IN (SUGGESTIONS)

- Check how learners have prepared for the lesson – see the Preparation section at the start of the unit in the Course Book (page 109). Have they looked at the Useful Phrases on page 112 in the Course Book (copied above)?
- Check whether they have brought to the class newspaper articles on issues that are relevant to their work. These can be used as a resource later in the lesson.
- Consider leading into the subject by eliciting stories from the news and discussing how they impact work. As the discussion develops, monitor the language needs of the group and the level of interest.

Contents

Expressions
The government is a coalition of the left and centre.
It is difficult to predict who will win the next election.
However, the right have a good chance.
They announced a new trade agreement on the news.
The evidence against privatisation is very clear.

Language check
Verbs of reporting: *say*, *announce*, *warn*, etc.
Contrasts and alternatives: *however*, *whereas*, etc.
Vocabulary: *local / state / federal government*, *balance of payments*, *imports*, *exports*, *vote for / against*, *hold a referendum*

Practice
Talking about government policies
Discussing political / economic issues
Considering election possibilities
Writing a political / economic briefing on an area

1 CORE PRACTICE

Listening and speaking

- This exercise gives the class an opportunity to practise a range of situations relating to politics and business.
- The exercise is in two parts – listening and speaking. The listening activity (part i) prepares learners for the speaking activity (part ii).
- As you work through the comprehension questions in part i, ask learners to explain how they have arrived at their answers.
- In part ii, encourage learners to adapt the scenarios to their needs. If appropriate, they should introduce the articles they have brought to class.
- Question a: The male speaker has a North European accent. The information is that the zone is not being respected. This does not mean that it has been rejected. Note *issue* = an important topic or problem (usually social or political) that people often have different opinions about.
- Question b: The male speaker has a US accent. Gloss as necessary: *policies* = actions (laws, plans, etc.); *logistics* = moving materials and products from business to business and to customers; *pressure groups* = groups of people who work together to try to influence the government; *hold a referendum* = have a national vote on a specific issue.
- Question c: Both speakers have South African accents. The woman is against changing the voting system – she doesn't say which party she supports. A *coalition* = a temporary joining together of two or more groups (e.g. political

114 UNIT 25

parties) for a specific purpose (e.g. to form a government).
- Question d: If appropriate, explain that in a European context, *Social Democrat* = centre left, *National Democrat* = centre right, *Christian Democrat* = right; *a swing* = a movement (due to an increase in voter support).
- **Further step:** Video the sketches and use the recordings to analyse wider communication factors such as body language. Draw attention to the fact that in different cultures body language may be interpreted in different ways.

2 LANGUAGE CHECK

- The multiple-choice questions link to the Language Notes at the end of the Course Book unit (page 112), and the related notes in the Business Grammar Guide (see the booklet that accompanies the Course Book).
- These questions enable you to treat the language programme flexibly. Points that are known can be handled briefly. Points that require more remedial attention can be explored in more detail. The Specific Points section below gives you further detailed guidance.
- When working on vocabulary questions, point out the Vocabulary notes in the Language Reference at the end of the unit in the Course Book, and the Glossary on pages 158 – 160. Introduce, as necessary, special terms that learners need.
- For each question, consider the following options.
  - Elicit the answer.
  - Discuss why the other options are wrong.
  - If appropriate, ask learners to change the example so that the wrong options can be used.
  - Ask learners to prepare a version of each example that relates to their specific needs, e.g.: Question 1: *The minister denied receiving the money.* Amended version: *A government spokesperson denied that the donations were illegal. He refused to say how much money was involved.*
- **Further step:** Using any newspaper articles your learners have brought to class, ask them to identify quotations which can then be changed into reported speech and invite them to forecast how stories in the news will develop.

SPECIFIC POINTS

Questions 1 and 2: Verbs of reporting (BGG 5.1)
- Go through the examples in the Language Notes.
- Q1: Ask your learners to transform this example into direct speech (e.g. *'I didn't receive the money'*). Note that after *deny* a *that* clause can be used (*He denied that he had received the money*).

- Q2: Note *warn* is followed by an object + infinitive when it involves advice about what someone should or should not do (e.g. *They warned her not to say anything*). In other situations it can be followed by a *that* clause (e.g. *The union warned that another strike was likely*). Ask your learners to transform the example so the verbs in the wrong options can be used, e.g. *suggested (that) we shouldn't go out; said (that) we shouldn't go out.*

Questions 3 and 4: Forecasting
- Go through the examples that follow. See also BGG 2.2 and 2.5.
  What do you think is going to happen in the election? The Republican Party is sure / certain / bound / likely / unlikely to win.
  I think / don't think the electorate will support the Government.
  I reckon / believe the Prime Minster will have to resign.
  It is difficult to guess / predict / forecast how the unions will react.
  I anticipate / don't anticipate many changes.
  I am sure the issue will be resolved soon.
- Q3: Point out that after a construction *It is easy / difficult …* an infinitive is used. Also note the indirect question word order in the second clause (not *what will the outcome be*). In predictions both *will* and *going to* are used.
- Q4: Degrees of likelihood. All three options are grammatically correct but only option **c** makes sense.

Questions 5 to 7 and 10: Vocabulary related to economics and politics
- Go through the items listed in the Language Notes. Check the Glossary for some of the political and economic terms. Also: *federal government* = relating to the central government and not the individual governments of the smaller regions or states that have joined together to form a larger union (e.g. the USA or Australia); *a monopoly* = a situation in which one company has complete control of an area of business or industry, not allowing others to have a share; *is ahead* = is in front / is the leader.
- Q5: Explain that, in some political systems, *the opposition* = the largest party that is not elected to government; *a joint venture* = a new business activity where two or more companies join together to share risks, profits, expertise, etc.
- Q6: Note *better off* is the comparative form of *well off* = to have enough money to live comfortably. For *the standard of living* (= the level of wealth and comfort of people in a particular society) we could also say *living standards*. Explain that *the cost of living* = the amount of money spent on basic necessities (food, clothing, housing, etc.). For *rate of inflation / inflation rate*, see Glossary.
- Q7: *Public sector borrowing* = money borrowed by the government for the parts of a nation's activities controlled by the state, e.g. health, defence (US defense) (c.f. *the private sector*).

- Q10: Note the use of *hold* with *vote / election / referendum*. Note also the use of prepositions with *vote* (*on* an issue; *for* = support; *against* = not support).

Questions 8 and 9: Contrasts and alternatives (BGG 18.2, 18.3)
- Review the examples in the Language Notes.
- Q8: This relationship is one of alternatives. Ask learners to suggest another way of expressing this relationship using the same example – *or* (*else*) ….
- Q9: This is an area of much confusion. Stress to your learners that *on the other hand* and *whereas* cannot be used for all contrast relationships (unlike *however*, which is a useful all-purpose contrast marker). *On the other hand* is used when we are looking at two sides of an argument (e.g. *Raising taxes for motorists might alienate voters. On the other hand, people will recognise that the government is being environmentally responsible*). *Whereas* is used where two ideas differ in the same respect (e.g. *I usually vote Labour, whereas my husband votes Conservative*). In the example in Q9 the relationship is one of the second idea being unexpected in light of the first idea.

3 LISTENING

Politically correct

- Begin by finding out what learners understand by the term *politically correct*. Ask them to agree a definition. Possible answer: *demonstrating correct behaviour and language in sensitive areas like gender balance, colour, sexual orientation*, etc. The phrase is often shortened to *PC* (the noun is *political correctness*).
- The recording is based on an interview with Kathleen Kelly Reardon, author of *It's All Politics: Winning in a World Where Hard Work and Talent Aren't Enough*. The part of Ms Reardon is spoken by an actor. Both speakers have US accents.
- Ask learners to check questions a, b and c in the exercise before they listen.
- Learners then answer these questions and discuss Ms Reardon's views. Do they agree with her?
- Ask learners to find phrases in the audioscript that mean the same as: keeping mobile and alert = *staying on your toes*; confuse and disorientate others = *keep others off balance*; say something very stupid or inappropriate = *put your foot in your mouth*; admit (to a mistake) = *own up*. Gloss other terms, as necessary: *contradictions* = situations or ideas that are very different from each other and seem to oppose each other; *what's supposedly going on* = what seems to be happening; *overdo the apology* = apologise too strongly.

- **Further step:** Learners discuss and agree their own list of the three worst moves to make politically in an office.

4 WRITING

Country profile

- This activity involves reading a country profile, then producing one themselves.
- Ask learners to read the briefing on Venezuela. Gloss as necessary: *stilts* = long pieces of wood that are used to support a house and raise its level (to protect it against flood damage, etc.); *petroleum* = dark, thick oil produced in rock from which fuels such as petrol and diesel are produced; *bauxite* = a type of rock from which aluminium (US aluminum) is produced; *radical reform* = extreme social and political change; *ties* = links / close friendly relationships.
- In pairs, learners then categorise points **a** to **i**: economic, geographical, historical, etc. This might lead to discussion because some points span more than one category.
- The pairs then prepare a briefing document for their country / area. This might involve some research. You might want to give the task for homework.
- **Further step:** Learners deliver the information in their written work as a presentation and take questions from the rest of the group.

5 CASE STUDY

Rail privatisation

- This is a role-play discussion of the issues involved in rail privatisation. Partner A is in favour of privatisation. Partner B is against.
- Check that learners understand the term *privatisation* = selling a nationalised industry to private owners.
- There is a newspaper article on page 111 of the Course Book and extra notes on page 138 – arguments in favour for Partner A and against for Partner B.
- Go through the article, glossing as necessary: *in line with* = following / similar to; *freight* = the transportation of goods; *split* = divide; *the track* = the rail (parallel metal bars) that trains run on; *is not unique to Europe* = is not happening only in Europe; *The debate … is brought into sharp focus by accidents* = when there is an accident, the discussion receives more attention; *regulators* = the official body that makes sure that the companies that operate in an area of public interest are run fairly and efficiently.
- Ask the pairs to study the notes on page 138 and prepare for the role play. Gloss as necessary.

- Partner A text: *neglect* = lack of care; *allocating* = distributing / sharing out.
- Partner B text: *deteriorates* = gets worse; *safety is compromised* = safety standards become lower; *exploit* = treat unfairly (for their advantage); *have no teeth* = have no power.
• As the exercise progresses, make a note of political and economic terms that need to be introduced.
• **Further step:** Have a vote on the issue of rail privatisation. Each class member makes a statement summarising his / her position before the vote. Ensure that correct terms are used: *All those in favour / against; The motion is carried*, etc.

REVIEW

• Go through the Language Notes and the Useful Phrases in the Course Book, if you have not done so already.
• Ask learners to note down the terms they found useful – especially the ones they need in their work.
• Make a note of this language for your own future reference.
• Encourage learners to practise the new language they have learned. They might do this by setting targets, e.g. to use a particular structure or vocabulary item three times today.

Answers

1 Core practice
a i [F]   b i [F]   c i [U]   d i [T]

2 Language check
1 b   2 c   3 a   4 c   5 a
6 b   7 b   8 b   9 a   10 a

3 Listening
(*possible answers*)
a According to Ms Reardon, the skills you need to win in office politics are learning to observe, looking for contradictions, asking questions, using a range of options to manage problems.
b Send a brief memo describing what you actually meant to say.
c Trusting your assumptions. Being predictable. Winning at all costs.

4 Writing
a [H]   b [G]   c [G] / [S]   d [P]
e [E]   f [E]   g [E]   h [P]   i [E] / [P]

Audioscripts

1 Core practice
a – We have very good relations with our neighbours most of the time. The one problematic area at the moment concerns fishing rights. Our government has set a ten-mile zone round the coast but this zone is not being respected.
– But you say relations are still good.
– They are. I am sure the fishing issue will be resolved. Otherwise things run very smoothly. They announced on the news recently that we are even considering a new trade agreement.
b – Government policies are having a disastrous effect on our business. We're a logistics company and a large part of our business is transporting livestock. The government has recently imposed strict restrictions on the distances that we can take the animals by road and some of our customers are thinking of using rail transport instead.
– What is the reason for the government policy?
– No good reason. There are a lot of pressure groups who have been trying to stop the trade in animals. They say it's cruel and propose that it's banned. I think they should hold a referendum on the issue.
c – The current government is a coalition between parties of the left and centre. It's actually a minority government and it could fall at any time.
– What's the alternative?
– Good question. We have so many parties and so many interests that I don't think we will ever have a strong government. I reckon that if this government is defeated, we will simply get another weak coalition. At the same time, I'm not in favour of changing the voting system.
– Why not?
d – It's very difficult to predict who will win the next election. Nevertheless, I would say the National Democrats have a good chance. There's been a strong swing to the right, especially since the scandal involving the socialist defence minister.
– Yes, I suppose that might make a difference. Alternatively people may just forget about it. I really don't think the country will elect a right-wing government this time.

3 Listening

An interview with Kathleen Kelly Reardon (KKR)
Int: What skills are necessary to win at office politics?
KKR: Learning to observe. Make a science of observing people who do well in your organisation. Look for contradictions between what's supposedly going on and what actually is. Train yourself to generate options when confronted by a problem. By staying on your toes, you keep others off balance. When in doubt about anything, ask some questions.
Int: If you put your foot in your mouth in a meeting with your boss, what's the best first step toward repairing relations?
KKR: Send a brief memo describing what you actually meant to say. While you don't want to overdo the apology, it's better to acknowledge your mistake than to leave the impression that you didn't even notice it. Everyone makes mistakes. It takes class to own up to them.
Int: What three actions top your list for the worst moves to make politically?
KKR: Trusting your assumptions. Being predictable. Winning at all costs.
(From *American Airlines* magazine; the part of Ms Reardon is spoken by an actor.)

UNIT 26 Taxation

PREPARATION

- There are three possible tracks through the unit: fast (about 1½ hours), standard (about 2 hours) and comprehensive (about 3 hours). For more information on the different tracks, see the notes in the Introduction on pages 10 and 11.
- For details of the aims of the unit, look at the Contents box opposite, the Language Notes at the end of the Course Book unit and the Useful Phrases below.
- If available to you, you can use the Self-study Guide as a source of supplementary exercises on the key themes of the unit.
- If you have taught the unit before, check the notes you made at the time.

USEFUL PHRASES

How much did we pay in tax last year?
Companies are taxed at a rate of 25%.
Three years ago the government announced it would cut the rate to 15% the following year.
As far as I know, it didn't happen.

Our tax bill was $500,000.
I pay tax at 40% on an income of £50,000 per year.

The tax authorities informed us that we had to pay a late filing penalty.
We were late filing our tax return.
Our accountant promised she'd file the return the next day.
The tax office claim it arrived late.

As far as I know, you can reclaim the tax.
You have to fill in a special form.
You take the form to the refunds office at the airport.

The tax rate / burden is very high.
How much does a middle manager pay in tax?
About 30% of my salary goes in tax.
We're not taxed on the first $5,000 we earn.

You can set against tax the money you pay into a pension scheme.
A capital gain on the sale of a private house is tax free.
It's very tax efficient.

Is there much tax evasion in your country?
I'm not an expert, but my accountant claims most companies are above board.

LEAD IN (SUGGESTIONS)

- Consider leading into the subject by asking learns to talk about the tax system in their country / area, if possible eliciting stories that are in the news.
- Refer to the Preparation section at the start of the unit in the Course Book (page 113). Check whether learners have brought correspondence relating to tax. This can be used as a resource throughout the lesson.
- Check also whether they have looked at the Useful Phrases on page 116 in the Course Book (copied above). Comments from the group may indicate which areas of the target language they need to focus on and the level of interest in the topic.

Expressions
How much did we pay in tax last year?
Companies are taxed at a rate of 25%.
They announced they would cut the rate to 15%.
As far as I know, you can reclaim the tax.
Our accountant promised she'd file the return the next day.

Language check
Reported speech: *asked us if*, *announced that*
Reported speech timeframes: *following day*, *previous year*, etc.
Terms used to qualify statements: *as far as I know*, *I'm not an expert but*, etc.
Vocabulary: *income tax*, *corporation tax*, *sales tax*, *tax liability*, *tax allowance*, *tax assessment*, *tax exempt*, *tax refund*, *tax free*, *go in tax*, *go up / down*, *fill in a return*

Practice
Talking about personal and company tax
Dealing with tax queries – examples from a specialist site
Tax case studies – reading and listening
'Death and taxes' – an article

1 CORE PRACTICE

Listening and speaking

- This exercise provides an opportunity to practise a range of situations relating to taxation matters.
- The exercise is in two parts – listening and speaking. The listening activity (part i) provides learners with ideas and models for the speaking activity (part ii).
- Ask learners to identify the verbal clues they used when answering the comprehension questions in part i.
- In part ii, encourage learners to adapt the scenarios to their needs. As you work through the situations, look for opportunities to add relevance by bringing in and applying the tax correspondence learners have brought to class.
- Question a: The male speaker has a US accent. Gloss as necessary: *fill in a form* = complete a form. The speaker seems to know a lot about tax regulations, but he suggests he is not a tax expert by starting with: *As far as I know* … But this might be modesty.
- Question b: The male speaker has a non-standard accent. Note in this instance that *allowances* = amounts of money that you are allowed to earn free of tax. The government was going to cut corporation tax, but *it didn't happen*.
- Question c: The female speaker has a non-standard accent. Gloss as necessary: *share schemes* = plans which allow employees to

118 UNIT 26

acquire shares in their company – either by being given them or having the option to buy them; *avoiding tax* = paying as little tax as possible; *set ... against tax* = deduct from your taxable income; *tax efficient* = an arrangement that results in a low tax liability; *property* = buildings (e.g. a house) or land; *capital gains tax* = tax on profits from selling something you own (e.g. property or investments); *tax relief* (see Glossary).
- Question d: The man has a Latin American accent. Note *tax evasion* = illegally trying not to pay tax; *above board* = correct and legal; *I don't believe all companies are angels* = not all companies are morally perfect.
- **Further step:** When learners have completed their individual practice in part ii, ask them to prepare it as a sketch and perform it to the rest of the group.

2 LANGUAGE CHECK

- As you go through the multiple-choice questions with learners, point out the Language Notes at the end of the Course Book unit (page 116) and the related notes in the Business Grammar Guide (see the booklet that accompanies the Course Book); there are cross-references from the notes to the BGG.
- The multiple-choice questions provide a starting point for the Language Check. Ensure that the related language points are explored and revised, as necessary. The Specific Points section below gives you further detailed guidance.
- Adapt the points to learners' needs. Concentrate on areas where practice is needed.
- When working on vocabulary questions, introduce special terms not covered that learners need. Point out the Glossary on pages 158 – 160 of the Course Book.
- For each question, consider the following options.
  - Identify the answer.
  - Explore why the other options are wrong.
  - Ask learners to prepare examples that relate to their individual needs, e.g.:
    Question 1: *The tax return needs to be completed by the end of the month.*
    Amended version: *The tax rebate they owe us should reach our account by the end of the week.*
- **Further step:** Ask learners, working in pairs or threes, to identify a number of examples (maybe three or four) of the core language points explored above in the documents they have brought to class.

SPECIFIC POINTS

Questions 1 and 2: Tax vocabulary (see also Questions 9 and 10)
- Go through the tax terms listed in the Language Notes – see also the Glossary. Note *tax rebate / refund* = an amount of money returned to you from the government when you have paid too much tax; *a tax holiday* = a temporary reduction or exemption from tax – governments might offer tax holidays as an incentive for business investment; *tax arrears* = money that is owed to the government in tax and should have been paid; *corporation tax* = tax on companies' profits. Ask learners to use the vocabulary in examples that relate to their circumstances (e.g. *My company is exempt from fuel tax because 25% of our vans are electric*).
- Q1: Explain that *tax liability* = the amount of tax owed; for *tax relief* and *tax return*, see Glossary.
- Q2: Only *deductible* collocates with *expense*. A *tax-deductible expense* is one that can be taken off your taxable income. If something is *tax exempt* it means you don't have to pay tax on it (e.g. children's clothing in the UK). A person can also be *exempt from paying* certain taxes (e.g. if you are disabled, you might be exempt from paying car tax).

Questions 3 and 4: Qualifying statements
- Go through the list of phrases in the Language Notes.
- Q3: *Don't quote me* is used when you are not 100% sure about the truth of the following statement; *discrepancies* = differences between, for example, figures that should be the same.
- Q4: *As far as I know* is followed by something you believe to be true. *Off the top of my head* is used when someone asks you a factual question and you answer from memory or by guessing. Practise further by asking each learner to make a guess about something related to their work (e.g. *Off the top of my head, I'd say we sold about 5,000 of that model last year*).

Questions 5 to 8: Reported speech (BGG 5)
- Consider the examples listed in the Language Notes. For all the examples, ask learners to transform the reported speech into direct speech.
- Q5: Reported questions (BGG 5.4) and tense changes (BGG 5.2). Note the shift back of the tense in the reported sentence *Do you know → If I knew*.
- Q6: Changes in time references (BGG 5.3). Analyse the differences between direct and reported speech ('*We will be in touch with you next week*'). Note *will → would* and *next week → the following week*. Point out that the time reference (*next week*) would not change if the reporting takes place in the same week. Also the tense change (*will → would*) would be optional in this case.
- Q7: Direct speech = '*You will have to pay ...* '. Note that *that* is optional after *warn*. A *late filing penalty* is a fine for sending in your tax return late.

Taxation **119**

- Q8: All three verbs would fit into the example, as they can all be used with personal objects and thus can be used in the passive. Note that *advised* here has a similar meaning to *told*. This is quite formal usage. The time phrase (*a few days ago*) has not been transformed here into *a few days before*.

Questions 9 and 10: Tax vocabulary (see also Questions 1 and 2) and verb phrases

- Q9: Note *bracket* here collocates best with *tax*. Note the informal usage *goes in / on tax*. It means *is spent on*.
- Q10: Note *Get the money together* = obtain (often from different sources); *pay off* = pay the whole amount of a debt.

3 LISTENING

Tax liabilities

- The activity involves reading mini-case scenarios and matching them with recorded comments by the people involved.
- Ask learners to discuss printed cases in pairs. Gloss as necessary.
  Case 1: *Inland Revenue* = the UK tax ministry.
  Case 2: *VAT* = value added tax (UK sales tax); *Customs and Excise* = the UK body responsible for collecting tax on imports; *waived* = dropped, given up.
  Case 3: *set up* = create, organise; *self-administered* = organised and run (by the directors themselves); *innovative* = using new methods or ideas.
  Case 4: *restructured* = reorganised (to benefit the people involved); *net proceeds* = the amount of money received from the sale after tax has been deducted; *financing arrangements* = borrowing arrangements.
  Case 5: *inheritance tax* = tax payable on property left to someone in a will; *smooth* = easy / without problems; *virtually nil* = almost nothing.
- Play the recording. Speaker 1 has a non-standard accent; Speaker 2 an Indian accent; Speaker 3 an Australian accent; Speaker 4 a South African accent. For Speaker 2, point out *they went through the accounts with a fine toothcomb* = they examined them in great detail; *capitulated* = (here) agreed they had been wrong. Speaker 5, *appealed against* = asked for [the assessment] to be changed.
- **Further step:** Ask learners either to reproduce one of the scenarios and the related comments as an anecdote, or to relate an anecdote of their own, about tax saved.

4 WRITING

Tax queries

- The activity involves responding to tax queries in writing, using whatever knowledge learners have. Make clear here they are not supposed to be experts.
- Ask learners, working in pairs or threes, to consider queries **a** and **b** and to modify the advice given to fit the local regulations (as they understand them). Gloss as necessary: *withhold* = keep back; *tips* = extra money (e.g. 10% of the cost) given for good service.
- Ask the pairs or threes to discuss query **c**, write their advice, and compare it with the opinion on page 138. Note *bequest* = money or property left in a will.
- Learners then consider queries **d** to **f**. Note *lodging* = accommodation.
- **Further step:** Ask learners to present queries arising from the correspondence they brought to class. Ask the class to choose one, discuss it and write a response.

5 FEATURE

Death and taxes

- This is a reading exercise linked to comprehension questions.
- If necessary explain: the *Grim Reaper* = a symbol of death who wears a hood and carries a scythe; *Benjamin Franklin* (1706–1790) = one of the founding fathers of the USA, a statesman, inventor and printer. Point out if necessary that the title is a play on words: *taxing* also means difficult / needing a lot of thought or effort.
- Ask learners, working in pairs, to read the text and answer the questions.
- Check detailed understanding by asking learners to find phrases in the text that mean the same as: avoid = *dodge*; located for official purposes = *domiciled*; a place where most tax can be avoided = *a tax haven*; to make two things equal, to give two things equal status = *to put ... on an equal footing*; to compensate for = *to make up for*.
- Gloss other vocabulary as necessary: *It's devoid of meaning* = it doesn't have any meaning; *a kayak* = a small light boat; *detected* = discovered; *demand* = a request (for payment); *claims ... against his tax bill* = deducts from his taxable income; *mortality* = the fact that we do not live forever; *powers of execution* = perhaps another play on words, as *execution* can mean carrying out / doing something or putting someone to death; *well into* = a long way into; *shortfall* = what they should have paid (in taxes).

- **Further step:** Organise a class quiz. Each learner prepares a question on the text. It can be a text or a content question. Learners then put their questions to the group and everyone answers.

REVIEW

- Go through the Language Notes and Useful Phrases in the Course Book, if you have not done so already.
- Check that the items listed under Vocabulary in the Language Notes in the Course Book have been covered.
- Encourage learners to note down the terms they found useful – particularly the ones they need in their working lives.
- Make a note of this language for your own future reference.
- Remind learners that practice is the key to progress. It is important that they motivate themselves to practise.

Answers

1 Core practice
a i [T]   b i [F]   c i [T]   d i [T]

2 Language check
1 c   2 b   3 a   4 b   5 b
6 c   7 a   8 c   9 b   10 a

3 Listening
Case 1 – Speaker 2
Case 2 – Speaker 5
Case 3 – Speaker 4
Case 4 – Speaker 3
Case 5 – Speaker 1

5 Feature
(*possible answers*)
a Tax avoidance is not paying tax you are not liable for, not paying too much tax.
b Tax evasion is not paying tax you should pay. It is illegal.
c Concern about taxes is always with us – in the same way, we are always aware that one day we will die.
d You can avoid and evade taxes – they are uncertain. You can avoid death but you can't evade it – it is certain.

Audioscripts

1 Core practice
a – As far as I know, to reclaim sales tax you have to show your passport when you buy goods and fill in a form. You take the form to the airport where they have an office which refunds the sales tax. As an alternative, you can buy things in the duty free shops. Is that the same system in your country?
 – More or less, I think. It's not really my area.
b – I think the income tax system in this country is pretty fair. Twenty years ago the top rates were high. Now they're down to between 35% and 45%, depending on what allowances you're entitled to.
 – What about company taxes?
 – Basic corporation tax is currently 25%, and on top of that local taxes are high in this area. Three years ago the government announced it was going to cut the rate to 15%, but it didn't happen.
 – So how much does a middle manager on an average salary pay in tax?
c – There are a number of share schemes that are an efficient way of avoiding tax. If you keep money in these schemes for a number of years, you can take your profits tax free. Then, of course, pension schemes are also a good investment. You can set the total value of the money you pay into a pension scheme against tax. It's very tax efficient.
 – What about investment in property?
 – It depends on the way the property market is going. You have to pay capital gains tax on any substantial profits. Generally, we get tax relief on gains under £30,000; that's about $52,000.
d – Tax evasion is a problem, but companies have to be above board. Everything must be properly accounted for; invoices must be produced, documentation checked, etc.
 – Look, I'm not an expert but I don't believe all companies are angels. An accountant was telling me about a client of hers who claimed that some huge oil tanks were full. The following day she checked and there was nothing in them. The client insisted it was just a misunderstanding, but a couple of days later he admitted he'd sold the oil and banked the money – tax free.

3 Listening

Speaker 1
We didn't see why we should pass so much over to the taxman after our father died. There's no justice in that.

Speaker 2
We couldn't believe it. We were expecting a routine tax inspection, but they went through the accounts with a fine toothcomb – then presented us with a colossal bill. Obviously there'd been some gross misunderstanding, because they soon capitulated – after our accountants had sorted it out.

Speaker 3
I bought some shares, paying far less than I had expected to pay, yet my partner didn't lose anything. I'm not quite sure how the accountants sorted it out, but I was very happy about it.

Speaker 4
Basically, what they did was to provide us with an excellent new pension and bonus scheme with drastically reduced tax liability.

Speaker 5
We appealed against the assessment, and to our amazement we didn't have to pay anything.

UNIT 27 Legal matters

PREPARATION

- It is possible to complete this unit at different speeds, in more or less detail. The fast track takes about 1½ hours, the standard track about 2 hours, and the comprehensive track about 3 hours. For more information on the three options, see the notes in the Introduction on pages 10 and 11.
- For details of the aims of the unit, look at the Contents box opposite, the Language Notes at the end of the Course Book unit and the Useful Phrases below.
- If available to you, you can use the exercises in the Self-study Guide as extra practice.
- If you have taught the unit before, review the notes you made at the time.

USEFUL PHRASES

Our lawyers have warned us it wouldn't be worth going to court.
We hope to settle out of court.
We are prepared to consider arbitration.
We would like to avoid a lengthy court case.

We took legal advice.
We were advised that we had a strong case.
We decided to sue for breach of contract.
We took them to court.
They contested the claim.
How did it turn out?
The court awarded us compensation.
The judge ordered them to pay our costs.
The company went bankrupt last week.

The receivers have been called in.
Their finance director was convicted of fraud.
Why weren't we notified?
I thought it was required by law.
By law I'm entitled to three weeks' annual holiday.
That doesn't mean I get it.

This layout is a mess.
The logo needs to go in the top, left-hand corner.
We need to add another bullet point.
It shouldn't be in bold – it should be in italics.
Shall we take out the third point?
That should be a comma, not a semi-colon.
Did you run it through the spellcheck?

LEAD IN (SUGGESTIONS)

- Consider leading into the subject by eliciting stories from learners relating to legal matters. As the discussion develops, you can monitor the language needs of the group.
- Check how learners have prepared for the lesson; see the Preparation section at the start of the unit in the Course Book (page 117). Have they looked at the Useful Phrases on page 120 in the Course Book (copied above)?
- Check whether they have brought a document they consider is poorly laid out; this can be used later in the class.

Contents

Expressions
Our lawyers warned us it wouldn't be worth going to court.
Their finance director was convicted of fraud.
Why weren't we notified? I thought it was required by law.
This document is a mess.
We need to add another bullet point.

Language check
More on reported speech: advice, commands, questions
Making reference: *concerning, with regard to*, etc.
Terms related to text layout: *underlined, in brackets*, etc.
Vocabulary: *laws, legislation, regulations, a case, a trial, a legal decision, a judge, a jury, a verdict, to go to court, to sue for, to settle out of court*

Practice
Talking about legal matters
Listening – a journalist talking about medical liability
Summarising legal advice
Case study – a document on customers' rights

1 CORE PRACTICE
Listening and speaking

- This exercise provides an opportunity to practise a range of situations relating to legal matters.
- The exercise is in two parts – listening and speaking. The listening activity (part i) prepares learners for the speaking activity (part ii).
- In part ii, encourage learners to adapt the scenarios to their needs. If appropriate, they should introduce the documents they have brought to the class.
- Question a: Gloss vocabulary as required: *a patent issue* = a disagreement over a patent (*a patent* = an official document which shows that a company has an exclusive right to make and sell an invention); *an exact replica* = an exact copy; *moulding machine* = either a machine that makes moulds or a machine that puts fluid substances into a mould (note, in US English spelling would be *molding*); *How did it turn out?* = What was the result?; *seized* = taken away (with legal authority); *give various undertakings* = make various promises (a formal expression).
- Question b: The male speaker has a Spanish US accent. See Glossary for *arbitration*; *pay up* = pay; *a final demand notice* = a final letter asking for payment (before further action is taken); *take a firm line* = act in a forceful way.
- Question c: The second speaker has a US accent. Note *call the receivers in* = call in the official receivers who take charge when a company goes bankrupt; *notified* = told (officially); *a creditor* = someone who is owed money.

- Question d: The woman has an Indian accent. If necessary, indicate the difference between 'single' and "double" inverted commas. Note *logo* = a design or a symbol used to promote a company; *a hard copy* = a print-out.
- **Further step:** Ask learners to talk about a time when they were involved with the law or legal matters. Ask them to identify the main language you need to handle the experience in English.

2 LANGUAGE CHECK

- The multiple-choice questions link to the Language Notes at the end of the Course Book unit (page 120), and the related notes in the Business Grammar Guide (see the booklet that accompanies the Course Book).
- The Specific Points section below gives you further detailed guidance.
- When working on vocabulary questions, point out the Vocabulary notes in the Language Reference at the end of the unit in the Course Book and the Glossary on pages 158 – 160. Introduce, as necessary, special terms that learners need.
- With each question, consider the following options.
  - Identify the answer.
  - Explore why the other alternatives are wrong.
  - Ask learners to prepare examples that relate to their personal or working needs, e.g.:
    Question 1: *Once it has been signed, the agreement will be binding on both parties.*
    Amended version: *If either side break the agreement, the other side can sue for damages.*
- **Further step:** If possible, bring some newspapers to the class. Ask learners to look through articles on legal matters (court cases, etc.) and identify a number of examples (maybe three or four) of the core language points explored above.

SPECIFIC POINTS

Questions 1 to 3 and 8: Vocabulary
- Go through the terms listed in the Language Notes. Legal matters can involve a lot of specialised vocabulary. Covered here are the core terms that most advanced speakers should know. Consider giving the terms listed in the vocabulary notes for homework, and then testing. Note: *to be in breach of contract* = to be breaking a contract; *to appeal against a decision* = to ask a higher court to look again at a decision made by a lower court; *the verdict* = the decision given at the end of a trial; *to contest* (a claim, etc.) = to say formally it is wrong and try to get it changed (note the stress is on the second syllable of *contest*); *to file for* (bankruptcy, divorce) = to make an official request for.

- Q1: Gloss as necessary: *binding* = cannot legally be broken; *parties* = people forming different sides in a legal matter. Elicit *when* for *once*.
- Q2: Point out that *to start legal proceedings* = to start legal action; *prosecution* = the trial of someone in a court of law to try to prove they are guilty of having committed a crime (note *the prosecution* is also a term for the lawyers who are trying to prove the guilt of the accused person); *damages* = money paid in compensation for loss or injury. Point out the phrases *to sue for / claim / be awarded damages*.
- Q3: Point out the phrases *to be found guilty / not guilty of* + *a crime*. To have *previous convictions* = to have been found guilty of particular crimes in the past. See glossary for *fraud*; *to be let off* = to not be punished for having committed a crime or to be given a less strong punishment than would be expected.
- Q8: Note *the defendant* = the person who has been accused of a crime; *to be convicted of* (a crime) = to be found guilty in a court of law; *to impose* = to officially force something (e.g. *a fine* or *a ban*) to be obeyed. It is used to describe the act of introducing the punishment, etc.; *enforce* is usually used with *a law / regulation*, etc. and means to ensure something is being complied with.

Questions 4 and 5: Making reference
- Discuss the examples in the Language Notes.
- Q4: This is a way of introducing a topic, then making a comment on it or asking a question about it. Ask your learners to suggest alternatives, e.g. *Concerning …*; *With regard to …*
- Q5: Practise also question forms, e.g.:
  - *The boss wants to see us.*
  - *What's it about / concerning / regarding / in connection with?*

Questions 6 and 7: Referring to text and layout
- Refer to the examples in the Language Notes.
- Q6: Point out preposition usage (*at* and *in*). The *small print* (US *fine print*) – see Glossary – is often regarded with suspicion as it may contain information that is disadvantageous to the person signing the document. Point out the use of the adjectival form *left / right-hand* before a noun. Elicit other examples, e.g. *on the left-hand side; a right-hand drive car.*
- Q7: Point out the use of *in* with *bold*; also note *in italics, in capitals*, etc. Note *add* = put in; *delete* = take out.

Questions 9 and 10: Reported speech
- Look through the examples in the notes with learners. Explain that in a legal context verbs of reporting are used that need to be used with care in other circumstances, e.g.:
  The court ordered us to pay the fine immediately.
  The police demanded to know the name of our insurers.
- Q9: Ask learners to correct option **a** (= *I warned them not to sue*). Elicit another structure that could be used with *advise / warn* in the example (*I advised / warned them that they should not sue …*). Note *to sue* = to take legal

action against someone (usually for compensation). Point out the use of the preposition *for*. It can either mean *in order to obtain* (e.g. *to sue for damages*) or it can introduce the reason why someone is suing (e.g. *to sue for malpractice*). Ensure learners have understood *unless* by asking them to rephrase the sentence (e.g. *I advised them to sue only if they had a good case*).

- Q10: A *tribunal* = a group of people who have been appointed, usually by the government, to examine legal issues; an *industrial tribunal* makes judgements in disputes between companies and their workers. Explain that *to instruct someone to do something* = to order or tell someone to do something (formal usage); *to caution* = to warn (officially, if it is by the police).

3 LISTENING
Medical malpractice

- Learners match a recorded text of a journalist talking about medical malpractice in the USA with a written summary.
- The journalist is Doug Wojcieszak of the *Boston Globe*. His words are spoken by an actor (US accent).
- Before reading, ask learners to read the three possible summaries. Gloss as necessary: *medical malpractice* = the incorrect treatment of a patient by a medical practitioner resulting in injury or loss; *to drop* = stop / discontinue; *defensive posture* = defensive strategy, strategy that aims to protect the hospital; *cases are settled* = an agreement is reached without the case having to go to court.
- As learners listen to the recording you may need to explain: *playing into the hands of* = making yourself vulnerable to; *greedy* = wanting to make as much money as possible; *Conventional wisdom would suggest as much* = this is what most people would think / this would be the common sense view; *lawsuits* = a court case between two private parties; *implement* = do / put into practice; *stung by* = penalised by.
- **Further step:** Discuss the following questions as a group.
  What are the essential features of the new policy? (Dropping the defensive posture, saying sorry and offering reasonable compensation.)
  Why does it work? (People feel heard, fairly treated and therefore inclined to cooperate.)
  Would it work in your learners' business or area?

4 READING
Legal advice

- This is a reading comprehension exercise. The text advises on how to deal with unsolicited goods.

- Prepare for the exercise by dividing learners into threes and asking them to think through how to protect themselves and their business from unsolicited goods. Have them present their recommendations to the rest of the class.
- With everyone in the group, try to reach agreement on key recommendations and write them down.
- The working groups now read the document and answer the questions. Gloss as necessary: *an offence* = a crime; *intimidated* = frightened / nervous; *a bluff* = an attempt to deceive you by making you think something is going to happen when it is not; *virtually impossible* = almost impossible; *exercise any control* = do anything (to solve the problem); *recovery of* = getting back.
- **Further step:** Ask learners to modify their key recommendations in the light of the advice they have just read.

5 FEATURE
Customers' rights

- The main aim here is to practise referring to a document – a requirement in legal situations. The document is published by a manufacturer of retail goods. It explains the company's policy on goods returned by customers.
- Gloss terms as required: *fit for the purpose* = able to satisfy the purpose; *redress* = compensation; *constitute* = be considered to be; *the Sale of Goods Act* = a UK law covering rights and responsibilities of retail buyers and sellers; *seconds* = goods that are not in perfect condition; *shop soiled* = dirty from having been in the shop for some time; *flood-salvage stock* = goods that have been saved from being water-damaged in a flood.

1
- Learners begin by identifying sections in the text, as required in instructions **a** to **e**.
- To further practise working with a document, ask learners to suggest changes to the document that would make it clearer or more readable, e.g.:
  The font is quite light, it would be easier to read if it was darker.
  It needs a heading. What about …?
  It should be centred.

2
- Learners discuss the content as indicated by the questions listed.
- Ask learners to explain the purpose of the document and to suggest why the company produced it. Possible answer: *To discourage frivolous returns and related disagreements. Alternatively, the company might have changed its policy on returns and retailers need help with putting the new policy across.*

- **Further step:** In pairs or threes learners consider one of the documents brought to class as part of the preparation, and make changes with a view to improving the layout and clarity.

REVIEW

- Go through the Language Notes and the Useful Phrases in the Course Book, if you have not done so already.
- Encourage learners to note down the terms they found useful – especially the ones they need in their work.
- Encourage learners to practise the new language they have learned. They might remind themselves by putting key points on their laptops so they come up on the screen from time to time.

Answers

1 Core practice
a i [F] b i [T] c i [U] d i [F]

2 Language check
1 c   2 b   3 a   4 c   5 a
6 b   7 c   8 a   9 b   10 b

3 Listening
The summary that is most accurate is **c**.

4 Reading
1 Question a
- Do not open them.
- Respond quickly.
- If you do open them, return them to the original packaging.

Question b
- That you do not intend to pay.
- That they should collect by a certain date.
- That they should not send any more.

Question c
- Because people who send unsolicited goods might say they did not receive your response.

Question d
- If you use them.
- If you decide you want to keep them.

2 *deemed* = seen, thought of
thereby = therefore
unsolicited = not requested, not ordered
prohibitively = very (so expensive that it prohibits action)

5 Feature
1 a 'If the goods are found to be faulty …', etc.
  b '… will not be able to seek … '
  c 'If the fault was pointed out to the buyer …', etc.
  d 'If the goods are found to be cheaper elsewhere.'
  e 'buying'

Audioscripts

1 Core practice
a – We had to go to court over a patent issue.
  – What happened?
  – One of our salesmen was at an exhibition and he saw an exact replica of our BJI moulding machine. We put the matter in the hands of our agent in the country concerned and he took legal action against the firm.
  – How did it turn out?
  – Very well. We won the case. Their stock was seized and we were awarded substantial compensation. The court ordered them to give various undertakings and to sign guarantees for the future.
b – Are you prepared to consider arbitration?
  – Look, the last thing we want is a lengthy court case. Our lawyers have advised us it wouldn't be worth going to court in this case.
  – So why are you threatening them with legal proceedings if they don't pay up within seven days?
  – Because that's the way we always handle matters like this. Sending a final demand notice is standard procedure for us. They'll pay up, but not until the last minute – you have to take a firm line.
c – I got a call regarding T2 Chemicals.
  – The company that owes us for the shipment to Nigeria?
  – Yes – apparently they had to call the receivers in.
  – Oh … I knew they were having problems but I didn't realise it was that serious.
  – Why haven't we been notified – we're a creditor?
  – I thought it was required by law.
  – By law I'm entitled to four weeks' annual holiday. That doesn't mean I get it.
d – I don't think this document is very clear.
  – You're right – the layout is a bit of a mess. First the heading needs to be in bold, and I suggest that we delete the third line of the second paragraph. That's the sentence beginning 'Receipts make it clear'.
  – Why is the word 'faulty' in inverted commas, three lines further down?
  – I don't know. Let's take them out. And the logo needs to go in the top left-hand corner.
  – Yes, did you run it through the spellcheck?
  – Not yet. I'll do that now.
  – Could you let me have a hard copy?

3 Listening
Many people will have been amazed that Harvard Medical School is actually encouraging doctors to apologise for medical errors. Are they mad? Surely that will just play into the hands of greedy trial lawyers? Conventional wisdom would suggest as much, but a policy of saying sorry has in fact been shown to reduce lawsuits and liability costs in hospitals across America. The first hospital formally to implement it was the Lexington VA in Kentucky. The hospital had been stung by two multi-million-dollar lawsuits, but after introducing the apology policy, its average malpractice payouts fell to $16,000. Other hospitals have likewise reported positive results from adopting this approach with people. They have all found that when doctors apologised for errors and offer a fair compensation, cases are settled quickly and reasonably. What's more, they have found that dropping their defensive posture also leads less people to bring unjustified malpractice cases against doctors.
(From *The Week*; Doug Wojcieszak's words are spoken by an actor.)

UNIT 28 Planning

PREPARATION

- There are three possible tracks through the unit: fast (about 1½ hours), standard (about 2 hours) and comprehensive (about 3 hours). For more information on the different tracks, see the notes in the Introduction on pages 10 and 11.
- For details of the aims of the unit, look at the Contents box on this page, the Language Notes at the end of the Course Book unit and the Useful Phrases below.
- If available to you, you can use the Self-study Guide as a source of supplementary exercises on the key themes of the unit.
- If you have taught the unit before, check the notes you made at the time.

USEFUL PHRASES

The scheme was planned in three phases.
My role was to liaise with the other participants.
It was mainly a trouble-shooting role, wasn't it?
Yes, it was; I had to keep the work on track.

There were a number of unforeseen hold-ups.
We didn't allow enough time for research.
We missed a key milestone.
We had to reschedule the live testing.
The end date had to be put back a month.

A key member of the project team has had to drop out.
They have some family problems.
So we are a little behind schedule.
This could seriously affect the timetable.
We didn't anticipate this in our contingency plan.

These papers relate to a court case we're involved in.
There's no action required at the moment.
This is junk mail which I want to look through.
It's low priority, so I keep putting it off.
The deadline for this is the 24th.
I need to chase them – I'd better do that today.

In the first place, I need to make an action plan.
Then I need to prioritise.
There are a number of factors that have to be taken into account.
It's sometimes difficult to keep to the plan.
My main obstacle is lack of time.
At the moment I am on schedule.

LEAD IN (SUGGESTIONS)

- Refer to the Preparation section at the start of the unit in the Course Book (page 121). Check whether learners have brought examples of action plans and 'to do' lists to the class. These can be used as a resource through the lesson.
- Check also whether they have looked at the Useful Phrases on page 124 in the Course Book (copied above).
- Project managers say that failing to plan is planning to fail. Consider leading into the class by talking about plans that have worked and plans that have gone wrong. Be prepared to give examples of your own.

Contents

Expressions
The scheme was planned in three phases.
My role is to liaise with the other participants.
To start with, I need to make an action plan.
There are a number of factors to be taken into account.
At the moment we are on schedule.

Language check
Indicating sequence: *to start with, in the second stage,* etc.
Terms related to structuring ideas / arguments: *for one thing, in addition to that* Gender-free reference: *he or she, they*
Tag questions: *You do, don't you?*
Vocabulary: *schedule, timetable, deadline, phase, stage, milestone, feasibility study, contingency plan, on target, on schedule, on track, take into account, put forward / back*

Practice
Talking about plans and commitments
Listening to a project update
Writing an outline plan
Reading about a major project and assessing it

---

1 CORE PRACTICE

Listening and speaking

- This exercise provides an opportunity to practise a range of situations relating to planning.
- The exercise is in two parts – listening and speaking. The listening activity (part i) provides learners with ideas and models for the speaking activity (part ii).
- Ask learners to identify the verbal clues they used when answering the comprehension questions in part i.
- In part ii, encourage learners to adapt the scenarios to their needs. Where possible they should introduce the realia they have brought to the class.
- Question a: The second man has a non-standard accent (perhaps Irish). Explain new vocabulary as necessary: *a pilot (scheme)* = a test to discover and solve problems before something is introduced; *setbacks* = problems / delays; *withdrew* = decided not to take part in; *put back* = changed to a later date / postponed.
- Question b: The man has a US accent. Note *the state of the art* = the most advanced developments in the field; *assembled* = put together; *prototype* = first model (of a machine) which forms the basis of later models; *site-tested in a field study* = tested and researched among possible consumers; *trouble-shooting* = problem solving.

- Question c: The speaker has an Australian accent. Gloss as necessary: *abandoned* = stopped / given up; *feasibility studies* = preliminary studies to see whether a project is likely to be possible and successful, and to estimate its cost; *contingency plans* (see Glossary); *hold-ups* = delays, *a plan 'b'* = an alternative plan / a contingency plan.
- Question d: The speaker is going through papers on her desk. Note *the ball's in their court* = they have to make the next move.
- **Further step:** Ask learners individually or in pairs to prepare a further question for each dialogue.

2 LANGUAGE CHECK

- As you go through the multiple-choice questions with the class, point out the Language Notes at the end of the Course Book unit (page 124), and the related notes in the Business Grammar Guide (see the booklet that accompanies the Course Book); there are cross-references from the notes to the BGG.
- The multiple-choice questions provide a starting point for the Language Check. Ensure that the related language points are explored and revised, as necessary. The Specific Points section below gives you further detailed guidance.
- Adapt the points to learners' needs. Concentrate on the areas where practice is needed.
- When working on vocabulary questions, introduce special terms not covered that learners need. Point out the Glossary on pages 158 – 160 of the Course Book.
- For each question consider the following options.
  - Identify the answer.
  - Explore why the other alternatives are wrong.
  - Ask learners to prepare examples that relate to their working needs, e.g.:
    Question 1: *The first step is to call a meeting of the interested parties, to make an action plan and then prioritise.*
    Amended version: *For us, the first step is to ensure we know exactly what the customer wants, that we are doing the right thing. Then we start the planning process.*
- **Further step:** Reinforce customer planning vocabulary using a simple word game. Taking the Vocabulary section of the Language Notes in the Course Book as a starting point, learners works in teams: Team 1 chooses a word or phrase; Team 2 scores a point by using it correctly in an example. Team 2 then chooses a word or phrase for Team 1 and so on.

SPECIFIC POINTS

Questions 1 to 4: Indicating sequence
- Take learners through the examples in the Language Notes. Discuss and elicit examples.
- Q1: To *prioritise* (also *prioritize*) means to rank things in order of importance.
- Q2: Elicit alternatives to *to start with*, e.g.: *First of all …; Firstly …; In the first place ….*
- Q3: *On completion of* needs to be followed by a noun (e.g. *On completion of the project*). Note also *It is nearing completion* (= nearly finished) and *completion date*. Only *at the same time as* can be used with the Past Continuous in the following clause. It indicates two things going on consecutively. Explain that *field-study* = research carried out in a real location (outside the laboratory).
- Q4: Explain that *in the end* and *eventually* are typically used when problems are resolved after there have been some difficulties. Note that *finally* would not be appropriate here.

Question 5: Structuring ideas
- Check the examples in the Language Notes. Only *All the same* has the correct meaning here as the relationship between the two clauses is one of contrast. Elicit alternatives from the class (e.g. *Nevertheless; Despite this; However*). *For another thing* (often following *For one thing …*) and *besides* introduce another supporting argument or reason to justify an action or opinion, e.g. *I don't think we should modify the prototype at this stage. (For one thing), it would delay the completion date. For another thing, / Besides, it would be very costly.*

Questions 6 and 7: Gender-free reference (BGG 12.3)
- Go through the examples in the Language Notes.
- Q6: Point out that although *they / their* does not strictly agree grammatically with the singular *any member*, it is an increasingly common way of making a non gender-specific reference and avoids the rather heavy *he or she (his or her); he / she (his / her)*. Using just *he* is now considered to be old-fashioned. Elicit other noun gender-specific nouns (e.g. *employee, worker, participant, student, speaker*).
- Q7: The feminine form (*spokeswoman*) is correct here because the sex is specified (<u>her</u> *view*). Note that masculine forms ending in *-man* may have a gender-free form ending in *-person / -people*. Ironically, in modern usage the *-or / -er* masculine form has replaced the feminine *-ess* form as the gender-free form for some words: a female might describe herself as *an actor; a landlord*, etc.

Question 8: Tag questions
- Review the examples in the Language Notes. Point out the use of *no* to agree with a negative statement in a tag question. This often causes problems so give further practice by asking your learners to respond truthfully to positive and negative tag questions, e.g.:

Planning   **127**

- *You don't work weekends, do you?*
- *No, I don't.*
- Point out that *that's right* often follows *yes* or *no* when agreeing with a tag question. Also, if we are denying the truth of a statement we often add *actually*, e.g.:
  - *You understand, don't you?*
  - *No, I don't actually.*
  The above comments also apply to statements that function as questions.
- Point out the difference between *to plan something* (organise it) and *to plan for something* (prepare what will happen when / if it occurs).

Questions 9 and 10: Vocabulary related to planning
- Demonstrate and discuss the terms listed in the Language Notes. Note *goes live* = to become operational / start working; *roll out* = to make a new product, system, etc. available for the first time.
- Q9: Explain that *take into account* = consider (when making a judgement).
- Q10: Both *allow for* and *make allowance(s) for* could be used here (= take something into consideration when making a plan or decision). To *put something right* = to correct it.

3 LISTENING

A project

- The project is based on an interview with the head of GEOSA, a German project management company.
- Note that the speaker does not refer to costing in the recording although it is an important part of project management. Questions of costing and finance are crucial to the viability of a project as a whole, and are the main focus in the early stages. This recording was made after the decision to go ahead had been taken. It focuses on the technical and organisational side of the project management.
- Go through the text on the page. Discuss points **a** to **i**. Are some more important than others? Are any key considerations missing from the list? Gloss as required: *on a time-phased basis* = so that they are available to be used at the right time; *liaising with* = communicating and working together with.
- Gloss terms in the audioscript as necessary: *a consortium* = a group of companies that have joined together for a particular purpose; *the EU* = the European Union; *milestone meetings* = meetings at important points in the schedule.
- **Further step:** In pairs, learners list the steps required before the project can begin. Here is a list of possible solutions.
  1. Create a consortium.
  2. Put in an application for EU funds.
  3. Organise a special workshop for interested companies.
  4. Break the project down into single workable packages.
  5. Break the work packages into sub-tasks.
  6. Decide who is responsible for each package and who participants pass results to.
  7. Establish a timetable and plan milestone meetings.
  8. The project is then ready to start.

4 CASE STDY

A start-up

- The activity involves reading a briefing document, deciding an outline plan, and putting the plan in writing.
1 • Ask learners to read the briefing text on page 122 of the Course Book. Gloss where necessary: *thriving careers* = careers that are going well; *give them up* = leave them; *a hunch* = an intuitive guess; *committing* = putting in / investing; *perception* = idea.
2 • In groups, learners discuss how the two women can achieve their goals. They should then put their recommendations in writing. There is a sample in the Answer Key.
  - **Further step:** Ask learners to role-play a scene in which Sally-Anne Duke and Carola Sutton ask the project planning team about the plan. Decide who will play the parts of the two women.

5 READING

Case study

- The text describes plans for a tunnel to the USA and Russia. You might lead into the exercise by discussing other large-scale projects.
1 • The vocabulary exercise can be done in pairs. In addition to the targeted language (in a box), the following may need glossing: *boost* = stimulate; *far-fetched* = unrealistic; *undeterred* = not discouraged; *lobbying* = trying to influence (politicians); *the cabinet* = a group of senior ministers; *forging ahead* = making significant progress; *burrowing* = tunnelling; *raised* (money) = collected together; *put paid to the plans* = stopped / destroyed the plans.
2 • Ask learners in pairs or as one body to conduct a simple project assessment, using the questions on the page as a guide. Possible answers are given in brackets.
  - *How feasible is the project?* (Probably not very. It is a very big undertaking and the environment is not easy. It would be difficult to build, costs would be high. The

project would depend on a stable relationship between the States and Russia. This is not guaranteed.)
- *What are the main obstacles?* (The cost and the fact that thousands of kilometres of track would have to be laid to link the tunnel with existing rail networks. Also, there might be resistance from the environmental lobby.)
- *What will the benefits be?* (The tunnel would revolutionise world trade – deliveries from China would reach the States in half the time.)
- *Do you think it will go ahead?* (Difficult to say. The drilling conditions are more favourable than the conditions between France and England for the Channel Tunnel, and that got built – after many delays.)

- **Further step:** Learners present their project assessment to the Interhemispheric Bering Strait Tunnel and Railroad Group Board, and answer questions. Half the group acts for the Board and prepare questions. The other half makes the presentation.

REVIEW

- Check the items listed under Vocabulary in the Language Notes in the Course Book have been covered.
- Encourage learners to note down the terms they found useful – particularly the ones they need in their work.
- Make a note of this language for your own future reference.
- Remind learners that practice is the key to progress and that they need to use new language so it becomes part of their skill.

Answers

1 Core practice
a i [F]   b i [T]   c i [T]   d i [U]

2 Language check
1 c   2 c   3 b   4 a   5 b
6 c   7 c   8 b   9 c   10 a

3 Listening
Planning is an essential part of managing a project and is a means of:
a deciding who does what, when, how and why ✓
b determining the resources required ✓
c allocating these resources on a time-phased basis
d allocating and defining responsibility
e integrating the work of all the organisations involved ✓
f liaising with all those involved in the projects ✓
g controlling progress ✓
h estimating time to completion ✓
i handling unexpected events and changes.

4 Case study
1 (*possible answer*)
Outline plan for the project
- The first step is to assess the market – check whether there is sufficient demand and explore the sources of supply. If possible, attend a course in antiques at an adult education institute. By the end of this phase, the women should know whether the idea is feasible.
- The next step is to learn about running a business. Again, this might involve attending a course – possibly run by the local Chamber of Commerce. At the same time, get legal advice and talk to an accountant about starting a business.
- Decide on the action steps that need to be completed before trading can begin.
- If finance is needed, prepare a business plan – here again an accountant would be needed.
- Think of a name for the organisation.
- Find premises.
- Decide on a start date.
- Design and prepare publicity literature.
- Once the outline plan has been agreed, the women will have to decide who does what, and agree timeframes.

5 Reading
a consortium   b drawing
c venture   d project
e realised   f vision
g fulfil   h obstacle
i feasibility   j members
k study   l research
m counterparts n techniques
o conditions

Audioscripts

1 Core practice

a – It was a pilot, wasn't it?
   – Yes. The purpose of the project was to organise a pilot scheme to test a new cash card. This was organised in three phases. Stage one was preparing the cards and making them look right. Stage two was signing up local suppliers and retailers in the area. The next stage was the promotion of the scheme in the local community. The first phases went pretty well; everything went according to plan. But then we had a couple of setbacks – there were problems with the technology, so the card was late. And some of the suppliers withdrew from the programme. So the start date had to be put back.
   – That led to other problems, didn't it?
   – Yes, it did – and a lot of confusion.
   – You haven't started yet, have you?
   – No.

b – At the moment we are involved in background analysis of the market, and research into the state of the art – which will help to show us which direction we should go in. Then we will develop the individual components for the system. After that, the components will be assembled and we will build a laboratory prototype. This will then be site-tested in a field study. And our role at every stage in the process is to coordinate the work …
   – It's mainly a trouble-shooting role isn't it?
   – Yes.

c – In the end the project was abandoned. It's a pity, really, because the feasibility studies were very encouraging. Looking back, I think the biggest mistake was not having proper contingency plans. There are often hold-ups with this kind of project. You have to be ready for them. You need a plan 'b'.

d – There's some junk mail which I want to look through before I throw it out. Most of it isn't urgent. Er, these documents relate to a court case I'm involved in. At the moment the ball's in their court – so no action is required from me. And this is a tax return – I'm waiting for information from my accountant. That's quite important. What's this? Oh, I'd forgotten about that.
   I'd better make a 'to do' list, and promise …

3 Listening

We started with the concept of an automatic waste-sorting system. At the moment we have semi-automated systems – where workers identify objects on a screen and mark them on a touch-screen for sorting, and a robot then collects them, or removes them. And the aim of this project is to create a fully automated system, where the recognition and identification functions, which are manual at the moment, are done automatically. So, the first step was to create a consortium of different companies who are interested in the idea and can work together on the project. At the same time, we put in an application to the EU for funds for research and development. We talked to a number of companies who we thought might be interested, and the companies that were interested were invited to a special workshop. The main purpose of this event was to break the project down into a number of single-work packages, and then to define those packages so that the end result of each package is the starting point for the next package. And we also broke the packages down into sub-tasks. We planned the whole project in such a way that when all the work packages have been completed, the end result will be an automatic sorting system. The next step in the planning process was to decide who was responsible for each package, and who the participants have to pass results to. And finally, we established a timetable, and planned milestone meetings. We defined what should be achieved by each point. And then the project was ready to start.

UNIT 29 Work in progress

PREPARATION

- It is possible to complete this unit in more or less detail. The fast track takes about 1½ hours, the standard track about 2 hours and the comprehensive track is about 3 hours. For more information on the three options, see the notes in the Introduction on pages 10 and 11.
- For details of the aims of the unit, look at the Contents box on this page, the Language Notes at the end of the unit in the Course Book and the Useful Phrases below.
- If available to you, use the exercises in the Self-study Guide for extra practice.
- If you have taught the unit before, review the notes you made at the time.

USEFUL PHRASES

What's the position with regard to this project?
I need an update on the state of play.
The project has fallen behind schedule.
Do we have a contingency plan?

We are in the process of revising our estimate.
It should be completed in good time.
The work is ahead of schedule.
We expect to finish on time.
We are supposed to go live on the 27th.

Progress is being held up by the weather.
Our supplier let us down with the delivery.
How long has this been going on?
Could you chase them up?

I'll begin by saying a few words about the delays.
I'll say more about them in a moment.
In my view, the next step is to establish the facts.

This table shows the current position.
The dotted line indicates costs.
Current orders are worth $10 million.
That's a 12% increase on last year.
At the moment we're spending too much.
So the budget has been cut back slightly.

Does everyone follow that?
Before I summarise the key points, are there any questions?

LEAD IN (SUGGESTIONS)

- Consider leading into the subject by eliciting stories from learners about their current work. Is it on schedule? If not, what is causing the delays? As the discussion develops, you can monitor the language needs of the group.
- Check how learners have prepared for the lesson; see the Preparation section at the start of the unit in the Course Book (page 125). Have they looked at the Useful Phrases on page 128 in the Course Book (copied above)?
- Check whether they have brought to class graphs and tables that relate to their work. These can be used as a resource in the lesson.

Contents

Expressions
I need an update on the state of play.
The project has fallen behind schedule.
Do we have a contingency plan?
This table shows … / The dotted line indicates …
Before I summarise the key points, are there any questions?

Language check
Reporting on the state of play: *go according to plan, on / behind schedule*
Terms used in presentations
Referring to graphs / tables:
This table shows …, As you can see from the dotted line …
Vocabulary: *update, progress check, overview, contingency plan, alternative, plan B, improvement, increase, rise, deduction, decrease, fall, be held up, be let down, chase up*

Practice
Giving project updates, discussing progress
Listening to reports by project managers
Writing a project update
Reviewing a company's performance
Presenting conclusions

---

1 CORE PRACTICE

Listening and speaking

- This exercise provides an opportunity to practise situations and language relating to work in progress.
- The exercise is in two parts – listening and speaking. The listening activity (part i) prepares learners for the speaking activity (part ii).
- As you work through the comprehension questions in part i, ask learners to explain how they have arrived at their answers.
- In part ii, encourage learners to adapt the scenarios to their needs. If appropriate, they should introduce the realia they have brought to the class.
- Question a: The second woman has a US accent. Gloss as necessary: *There was a lot of resistance from retailers* = they did not want to accept the changes; point out the phrase *fallen (badly) behind schedule* and contrast it with *be on schedule* and *be ahead of schedule*.
- Question b: The second man has a non-standard accent. *The current state of play* = the current position / situation; *the subcontractor* = a person or company employed to do the job on behalf of (and employed by) the primary contractor.
- Question c: The first woman has a non-standard accent. Note *planned for* = taken into consideration / allowed for (at the planning stage); *modifications* = changes.

- Question d: Note *to outsell* = sell more than; *substantial* = fast / big; *maintaining our market share* = keeping our share of the market / selling the same amount as before; *knock-on effects* = effects that an action has on other situations.
- **Further step:** Lead a discussion in which learners talk about the cultural differences they have observed or experienced in the areas of planning and time. Do all nationalities behave the same? Do some plan more than others? Is it good manners / practice to arrive early? Or is it normal to be a little late?

2 LANGUAGE CHECK

- The multiple-choice questions link to the Language Notes at the end of the Course Book unit (page 128), and the related notes in the Business Grammar Guide (see the booklet that accompanies the Course Book).
- The multiple-choice questions enable you to treat the language programme flexibly. Points that learners know can be handled briefly. Points that require more remedial attention can be explored in more detail. The Specific Points section below gives you further detailed guidance.
- When working on vocabulary questions, point out the Vocabulary notes in the Language Reference at the end of the unit in the Course Book, and the Glossary on pages 158 – 160. Introduce, as necessary, special terms that learners need.
- For each question, consider the following options.
  - Elicit the answer.
  - Discuss why the other alternatives are wrong.
  - If appropriate, ask learners to change the example so the wrong options can be used.
  - Ask learners to prepare examples that relate to their specific needs, e.g.:
    Question 1: *We are in the process of refurbishing your head office.*
    Amended version: *The client has changed the specification – we are in the process of revising the project plan.*
- **Further step:** From the points reviewed above, each learner identifies one that he / she gets wrong, prepares an example and offers it to the group. Remaining class members say whether it is correct or not.

SPECIFIC POINTS

Questions 1 and 2: Reporting on the state of play
- Go through the examples in the Language Notes.
- Q1: Point out the prepositions involved: *in progress, in the process of, on the point of.*
- Q2: Note these expressions with *time*: *in good time / with time to spare* mean ahead of schedule; *on time* = on schedule; *in time* (often with *for*) = early enough, e.g. *We noticed the problem just in time (to prevent a problem); We got there in time for the start of the presentation.*

Questions 3 and 4: Terms used in presentations
- Review the examples in the Language Notes. As one large group or smaller groups, ask learners to identify the stages of a presentation, e.g. introduction, overview, main themes, summary, questions, close. Then ask them to link the stages with the examples listed in the Language Notes. Elicit further examples as necessary.
- Q4: Point out that only *overview* (= summary) can be used as a noun. It is not used as a verb. To *overlook* = to fail to notice / have a view over; to *oversee* = to supervise.

Questions 5 and 6: Referring to graphs and tables (see also Questions 7 and 8)
- Using the examples learners have brought to class, ask them to demonstrate the expressions in the Language Notes, where possible. Get them to produce simple graphs to illustrate the wrong option.
- Q5: Ensure your learners understand that *units completed* means *units that have been completed*. Draw attention to the use of the Present Simple for permanent facts (e.g. *This line shows …; The solid line represents …*).
- Q6: Elicit other ways of expressing the ideas in the example, e.g. a big drop = *a significant fall*; small increase = *slight rise*, etc. Point out that *gradual* collocates well with *decline* as it emphasises the slow rate of change.

Questions 7 and 8: Referring to graphs and tables, and describing trends
- Go through the examples in the Language notes. Revise the basic vocabulary for describing trends, e.g.: *go up / rise / increase; go down / fall / drop / decline; remain level / stay constant; slight(ly) / considerable(bly); gradual(ly) / sharp(ly).*
- Q7: Note the use of the Present Continuous passive here. Point out that the Present Continuous is often used for present trends. Elicit other ways of expressing the ideas in the example: are being (considerably) increased (considerably) = *raised moderately*; (slightly) reduced (slightly) = *cut back a little*; kept / held constant = *maintained at the same level*.
- Q8: Point out the use of the Present Continuous with *currently*. Note *represents* is often used when expressing a number as a percentage. Explain that *a rise of 100%* is an alternative to *a 100% rise*. Practise the noun forms for movement (note that *go up / down* do not have noun equivalents).

Questions 9 and 10: Vocabulary
- Go through the words and phrases in the Language Notes.
- Q9: Elicit *delaying* for *holding up*.
- Q10: Try to elicit *progressing* for *coming along* and *How far have you got? / Where are you up to with it?* for *Where have you got to …?*

3 LISTENING

Progress reports

- The exercise features authentic recordings. Details of the speakers are given on the recording and in the audioscript. Speaker 1 is Irish: *to have a slight overrun* = to just miss the deadline. Speaker 2 is English.
- Ask learners to listen and make notes, then prepare progress reports using the template in the exercise.
- **Further step:** Ask learners who are currently involved in projects to comment on the state of play of these projects.

4 WRITING

Progress chasing

- The activity starts as a pairwork exercise: Partner A has to check with Partner B on the progress of an office refurbishment project in a phone call.
- Check that the roles are clear. Information for Partner B is on page 139 of the Course Book.
- Gloss vocabulary as necessary: *refurbishment* = bringing back to a new condition / making brighter; *cloakrooms* = (UK) places where coats can be left; also *cloakroom* (US *restroom*) = a polite word for toilet in a public building.
- Note that the preparation should include agreeing dates and time lines. For example, assuming today's date is 21 June, and the project end date is 30 June, the time line might be as follows:
  Wed 21 June – today's date
  Fri 23 June – new fire escape completed ahead of schedule
  Wed 28 June – new washbasins delivered
  Thur 29 June – new office furniture delivered on time
  Fri 30 June – project end date
  Fri 7 July – cloakrooms and washrooms completed
  Fri 21 July – kitchen facilities, earliest likely completion date
- After the phone call, pairs work together to write a project report. Point out there is a possible draft in the answers. Note the expansion of Partner B's information, which is in note form, into complete sentences with subjects and full forms of the verb *be*.
- Discuss layout and headings. Ensure that pre-experience learners understand that a report of this kind is not an academic essay. It needs to be as concise and as accessible as possible.
- **Further step:** Pairs combine into fours and compare their reports. Ask them to identify the characteristics in each document that add to readability (clear headings, consistent spacing, short sentences, etc.).

5 CASE STUDY

People Tree: a company review

- The activity involves reading information about People Tree, a pioneer in fair trade and ecology fashion, and reviewing the company's progress and performance.
- Ask learners to work in pairs or threes. Go through the documents – the web page printout on page 127 and the newspaper article on page 139. Gloss as necessary: *fair trade* = a way of doing business which is fair to suppliers and customers; *marginalized* = not treated equally or fairly (by more dominant social groups); *get the business off the ground* = start the business; *a difficult nut to crack* = a difficult thing to do; *like-minded* = with similar views / ideals; *Selfridges* = a big, upmarket department store in London; *showcased* = allowed them to present (to attract the public's attention); *flagship store* = the store on which the reputation of the company depends; *What sets People Tree apart* = what makes People Tree different from other companies; *livelihoods* = ways of making money to pay for the basic necessities of life; *an artisan* = a person who does skilled work with their hands; *rife* = very common.
- In Step 1: lead a discussion based on the questions listed in the rubric.
- In Step 2: in small groups, learners prepare a review of the company and present it to everyone else. Below are some notes.

Progress

- At first it was difficult to get the business off the ground in the UK because people didn't understand the differences between People Tree and other clothing firms.
- Then they began working through like-minded shops like Aveda. Their early catalogues, printed on 100% recycled paper, were well received. The company grew 50% in 12 months. Selfridges showcased the People Tree collection.
- The company's products are now available through Europe, particularly in the UK and Italy. The People Tree in-house design team has grown to 8 in the UK, 40 in Tokyo. People Tree are looking for partners to open their first shop in Europe.

Performance against Mission

1. Trading Partners: People Tree supports partners by helping them revive their livelihoods and develop their communities. It pays producers a fair price, provides assistance with product design and quality control, and commits to ordering regularly.
2. Environment: There is no direct information in the article on People Tree's efforts to protect the

Work in progress 133

environment in production, packaging and transportation of products. But they work with 20 producer groups in 20 developing countries, and the support includes help to meet environmental standards.

3 Customers: As sales increase, the company offers a growing number of customers an opportunity to participate in a trading partnership that supports people and the environment. There are no figures for global sales in the article but in the UK alone they grew 50% in 12 months.

4 Us: The aim to allow people to use their ability in an environment that is nurturing seems to be working well. The in-house team is growing and round the world 10,000 people are working for People Tree.

5 Wider: The facts and fixtures clearly show that the company is creating a business based on mutual respect and that Fair Trade can work.

- **Further step:** Learners role-play a face-to-face review between a review team and a team representing the management of the company. The review team:
  - ask questions about the performance areas indicated by the Mission Statement, and acknowledge successes
  - discuss plans for the future (learners might access the People Tree website for up-to-date information)
  - consider possible areas for improvement (e.g. spreading the message to other companies more quickly).

REVIEW

- Go through the Language Notes and the Useful Phrases in the Course Book, if you have not done so already.
- Have learners note down the terms they found useful – especially the ones they need in their work.
- Make a note of this language for your own future reference.

Answers

1 Core practice
a i [U]   b i [F]   c i [T]   d i [T]

2 Language check
1 b   2 a   3 c   4 b   5 b
6 c   7 c   8 b   9 a   10 c

3 Listening

PROGRESS REPORT		
Report by	Project description	Progress /Comments
Martin Doyle, Managing Director of Software Systems Solutions, Dublin	Putting in computer systems for the in-flight entertainment systems of the Aer Lingus Airbus	There was a danger of an overrun because the monitor didn't arrive on time. They sorted out the problem and the job will be completed on time.
Joanna Van Heynigen, a partner in an architectural practice	A new building in Oxford	The work is late because the specification for one of the roofing materials was changed. The building will probably open two weeks late.

4 Writing
(*possible answer*)

Offices in Dublin, Ireland – Project Update

- Installation of new telephone and IT circuits
  This work is on schedule and should finish on time.
- Refurbishment of cloakroom and washrooms
  This is behind schedule because the new washbasins have not been delivered. They are now expected next week. The work should be completed ten days after that.
- Kitchen facilities upgrade – including flooring and wall tiling
  This work is behind schedule. The supervisor has had flu and key materials have not been delivered on time. We now expect to complete three weeks late.
- Installation of new office furniture
  The furniture is in the warehouse waiting to be delivered. There should be no problems.
- Construction of a new fire escape
  Good news here – this job is progressing well and should be finished by the end of this week, ahead of schedule.

Audioscripts

1 Core practice

a
- What's the position on OK Cosmetics?
- My information is that they've achieved most of their targets for the current period. They've had one or two problems in connection with their plans to reduce the amount of packaging they use. There was a lot of resistance from retailers, who like beauty products to be expensively packaged. I gather the scheme has fallen badly behind schedule.
- Do you know when it'll be completed?
- No, I don't have a date for that.

b
- The project involves installing a voice recognition security system on all the main entrances. It's going fairly smoothly. The current state of play is that the new doors are in place, all the wiring and the equipment have been fitted – at the moment the subcontractor is in the process of testing the computer program. The only hold up is that they're having trouble making appointments with staff members to record the voice samples. They're about a week behind schedule, so the change-over may be delayed a little.
- Do you have a contingency plan for that?

c
- When do you think you'll finish? There's a lot of pressure at this end.
- Well, the fire officer wants automatic time switches fitted on the emergency lighting. That's something we hadn't planned for.
- How long is that going to take?
- It shouldn't take more than a couple of days.
- And what's the position with regard to the fire escape?
- That's now OK. We made the modifications and the inspector approved them.

d This table shows sales over the last five years, and you can see that although we're maintaining our market share, there isn't much growth. That's on the dotted line there. Now compare that with the red line here which indicates sales of electronic products. As you can see, the rate of increase is very substantial indeed. It's clearly an important growth area. If we put more resources into this market, there'll be a number of knock-on effects. I'll say more about those in a moment. Did you all get a copy of the overview I circulated? If you didn't, there's one in the folder in front of you.

3 Listening

Speaker 1: Martin Doyle, Managing Director of Software Systems Solutions, Dublin, talks about putting in-flight entertainment systems on board an Aer Lingus Airbus.

The project has … thankfully finished on time. There was a danger where we were going to have a slight overrun when the monitor for the computer system on board the aeroplane … didn't arrive on time. They sent in the wrong piece of software, and the monitor and the software just wouldn't talk to one another. But thankfully we sorted that one out. And we have spent extra hours working on the project, and … it will now be completed on time.

Speaker 2: Joanna Van Heynigen, a partner in Van Heynigen and Haward, an architectural practice, comments on progress with a new building in Oxford.

It's going well on site because the builder is good and really does want to get the building finished on time. But it … it is late – part of it's late and that'll probably mean that the whole job is late. The reason it's late is that there was a change in the specification of one of the roofing materials so he had to order it and the whole of the rest of the roof depends on this particular material arriving in time. So it's not really his fault … even though we'd quite like to think it was. It's the fact that we changed the specification. This will mean that the building will probably open two weeks late. And we've talked to the client about this and they're reasonably calm about it. If it was very much later than that, they would begin to panic, and then we'd have to … start letting the builder work at weekends and evenings.

UNIT 30 Feedback and review

PREPARATION

- It is possible to complete this unit at different speeds, in more or less detail. The fast track takes about 1½ hours, the standard track about 2 hours and the comprehensive track about 3 hours. For more information on the three options, see the notes in the Introduction on pages 10 and 11.
- For details of the aims of the unit, look at the Contents box opposite, the Language Notes at the end of the Course Book unit and the Useful Phrases below.
- If available to you, you can use the exercises in the Self-study Guide as extra practice.
- If you have taught the unit before, review the notes you made at the time.
- There is a Progress Test covering Units 25 – 30 on pages 146 and 147, which can be photocopied and circulated. The answers are on page 148. For the best results, give learners time to prepare.

USEFUL PHRASES

How would you evaluate the course?
What's your overall assessment?
On a scale of one 1 to 10, how would you rate your performance?
I'd give it 8 out of 10.
In my view it was really excellent.
Parts were OK, but overall I thought it was below standard.
Frankly, it was absolutely awful.
Bearing in mind the circumstances, I reckon you did really well.
Speaking as someone who finds studying quite difficult, I found the instruction first class.
We didn't do too badly, considering the circumstances.
I'm inclined to think the products were rather second rate.
As far as I'm concerned, it was on the right lines.
I have absolutely no doubt her performance can improve.
On the whole, I felt the content was extremely well-planned.
Generally, the feedback suggests the material is more or less OK.
My overall conclusion is that we made good progress.
But I'm disappointed I didn't meet my targets.
To sum up, I'd say you did a good job.
What are your next steps?

LEAD IN (SUGGESTIONS)

- Check how learners have prepared for the lesson; see the Preparation section at the start of the unit in the Course Book (page 129). Have they looked at the Useful Phrases on page 132 in the Course Book (copied above)?
- Check whether they have come prepared to talk about a review process they have been involved in. This experience can become a resource later in the lesson.
- Consider leading into the subject by talking about reviews that learners have been involved in. The discussion will indicate the language needs of the group.

Contents

Expressions
What's your overall assessment?
Bearing in mind the circumstances, I thought we did really well.
I'm disappointed I didn't meet my targets.
To sum up, I'd say you did a good job.

Language check
More on giving opinions: *am positive, consider, guess*
Terms used in evaluating: *really outstanding, quite disappointing*
Summarising: *My overall view ..., On the whole ...*
Indicating context: *Bearing in mind ..., Considering ...*
Vocabulary: *assessment, evaluation, feedback, aim, target, objective, meet targets, put into practice, make progress*

Practice
Performance review (self and others)
Work style questionnaire
Discussing next steps

1 CORE PRACTICE

Listening and speaking

- This exercise provides an opportunity to practise situations relating to feedback and review.
- The exercise is in two parts – listening and speaking. The listening activity (part i) prepares learners for the speaking activity (part ii).
- As you work through the comprehension questions in part i, ask learners to explain how they have arrived at their answers.
- In part ii, encourage learners to adapt the scenarios to their needs. If appropriate, they should introduce the realia they have brought to the class.
- Question a: The woman has a Spanish accent. Gloss language as necessary: *clearly laid out* = clearly presented / organised. If appropriate, point out the noun *layout*.
- Question b: The man has a US accent; the woman a South African accent. Explain *get through the (Grade 3) test* = pass the test. Compare *get through / pass the test* with *take the test*.
- Question c: The female speaker has a non-standard accent; the male speaker has a slight UK West Country accent. Note *on the right lines* = right / correct.
- Question d: The man has a non-standard accent. Explain that *put ... into practice* = apply.
- **Further step:** When learners have completed their individual practice in part ii, ask them to prepare it as a sketch and perform it to the rest of the group.

2 LANGUAGE CHECK

- The multiple-choice questions link to the Language Notes at the end of the Course Book unit (page 132), and the related notes in the Business Grammar Guide (see the booklet that accompanies the Course Book).
- These questions enable you to treat the language programme flexibly. Points that are known can be handled briefly. Points that require more remedial attention can be explored in more detail. The Specific Points section below gives you further detailed guidance.
- When working on vocabulary questions, point out the Vocabulary notes in the Language Reference at the end of the unit in the Course Book, and the Glossary on pages 158 – 160. Introduce, as necessary, special terms needed by learners.
- Think about the following options for each question.
    - Elicit the answer.
    - Discuss why the other options are wrong.
    - Ask learners to prepare examples that relate to their specific needs, e.g.:
      Question 1: *In my view his performance was rather second-rate.*
      Amended version: *I thought the first part of your presentation was a bit boring – too many figures, not enough interpretation.*
- **Further step:** Learners give opinions on / discuss experience they have had of feedback and review, incorporating at least two of the language points covered in the ten questions.

SPECIFIC POINTS

Questions 1 to 4, and 7 and 8: Giving opinions and evaluating (BGG 21.3), and Modifying adverbs (BGG 14.4)
- Go through the examples in the Language Notes.
- Q1: Point out the use of *rather* to modify the adjective *second-rate* = not very good. Note *rather* is often used with words that have a negative meaning (e.g. *I'm inclined to think they're rather unreliable*). When used with words that have a positive meaning, it conveys the idea that something was unexpected (e.g. *I thought the meeting went rather well*). Note that *quite, fairly, a bit* can also be used to weaken the meaning of an adjective (e.g. *As I see it, she's a bit young for the* job). Explain that *absolutely* is used with strong (non-gradable) adjectives to strengthen the meaning (e.g. *It was absolutely brilliant*).
- Q2: Point out the use of adverbs to support strong views (e.g. *I'm absolutely sure…; I definitely think that …; I really don't think …*).
- Q3: Both *really* and *highly* can be used to intensify meaning; *really* collocates with *outstanding*, but *highly* does not. Point out that *really* (which is more common in informal usage) is a useful 'all-purpose' intensifier, as it can be used with a wide range of adjectives; *highly* does not collocate with all adjectives, so advise learners to make a note of collocations they come across. Some examples are: *highly paid; highly successful; highly significant; highly unlikely*. It can also be used to modify a verb (e.g. *I can highly recommend it; She speaks highly of you* = has a high opinion of you). Try to elicit more collocations.
- Q4: Note that *wasn't too bad* is closer in meaning to *good* than *bad*.

Questions 5 and 6: Summarising
- Start by looking through the examples in the Language Notes. Point out that summarising often involves reported speech, e.g.:
  Generally staff felt (said) there was too much interference from management.
  Overall people (said they) wanted more time to prepare.
- Draw attention to the verbs often used to express 'say' in a summary: *feel, indicate, suggest, show*, etc.
- Q5: Elicit other ways of saying *on the whole*, e.g. *generally (speaking)*. Both *suggest* and *indicate* could be used here but *maintain* would not be appropriate as the verb needs a human subject.
- Q6: You might want to teach *in / with hindsight* for *looking back*. Both *clear* and *obvious* could also be used after *fairly*. Note *fairly*, when used with these adjectives in this context, has more the meaning of *very*.

Questions 7 and 8: Indicating context
- Go through the examples in the Language Notes to get across the concept. To practise, invite learners to respond to a central statement, using phrases that indicate context, e.g. *Multinational companies are good for the world*.
    - *From a Western point of view, this might be true.*
    - *In environmental terms, I feel this is completely wrong.*
    - *Bearing in mind the number of jobs they provide, it would be difficult to ban them.*
- Q7: *Bearing in mind / considering / taking into consideration* are used to introduce a fact (here = the lack of time) that needs to be thought about when considering something else. Try to elicit other examples (e.g. *Bearing in mind the extra costs involved, I don't think it would be wise to upgrade our computer network at this stage*).
- Q8: Here *Speaking as someone who (doesn't like …)* has a similar meaning to: *Considering (I don't like …)*.

Questions 9 and 10: Vocabulary related to feedback
- Go through the terms listed in the Vocabulary section on page 132: *peer review* = review done by colleagues (at the same level seniority); *quick wins* = easily achievable early successes which can build confidence in individuals or kick-start a programme of action.

Feedback and review

- Q10: Note the collocation *to draw a conclusion* = to make a judgment on something after considering all the relevant facts of the situation. Note also *to draw a comparison between* ... Elicit *to come to a conclusion*. Both *survey* and *research* are appropriate in this example.

---

3 APPLICATION
Self-assessment

- Learners undertake a self-assessment, then discuss their conclusions in pairs.
- Ask learners to conduct a simple review of their progress and performance in their English studies, using the questions listed on page 130 of the Course Book as a guide.
- In pairs compare conclusions, again using the questions listed as a structure. Below are some examples.
  Partner A: *So what were your aims at the beginning of the course?*
  And how do you feel you've done?
  How did you achieve that?
  What strengths did you show?
  Partner B: *What about you?*
- **Further step:** Each learner writes a summary of the assessment on behalf of their partner, e.g.:
  – *Nina feels she has made good progress during the course. Her vocabulary has increased and she makes fewer grammar mistakes. She attended class regularly and kept clear notes.*
  – *Her main problem is that she is very busy and doesn't have enough time to practise outside class. She didn't do all the homework.*
  – *She knows one or two native speakers and plans to see if she can meet one of them regularly for conversation practice, possibly in a conversation exchange – English for Spanish.*

4 QUESTIONNAIRE
Work styles

- This is a reading and discussion activity involving a questionnaire.
- In pairs, learners answer questions designed to test if they are workaholics. The analysis is after the questions.
- Gloss vocabulary as necessary: *wimps* = weak and pathetic people; *dread* = have a great fear of (something in the future); *motoring along in a low gear* = moving slowly (when you could be going faster); *making the most of your career* = optimising your career opportunities.
- Lead a class discussion in which learners compare scores. Do they agree with the analysis?

- The piece is about stress and pressure. Encourage learners to use the language demonstrated: *extreme stress, work pressure, reasonable balance, internally driven, highly pressurised, high-pressure job, reassess your priorities*.
- **Further step:** Having identified their work style, learners might discuss ways of improving. Those who already have a very good balance might act as advisers to their stressed colleagues.

5 LISTENING
Performance review

- This is a listening activity, involving listening to a review meeting and completing the related form. The manager in the review has a Dutch accent.
- Check that learners understand *appraisal*. Point out that generally appraisals are annual and formally recorded; *reviews* are less formal and typically take place monthly or bi-monthly; *feedback* is the content or evaluation that is given to an employee in an appraisal or review.
- Note that this interview takes place after the first four months of employment. It is probably an end-of-probation review.
- Ask learners working in pairs to prepare for the listening exercise by going through the form. Gloss as necessary: *exceeded* = did better than; *telemarketing* = selling or promoting goods by telephone; *leads* = information on potential customers; *in the field* = while out travelling and meeting customers, etc.; *hectic* = very busy; *telephone manner* = way of dealing with people on the telephone; *exposure to* = contact with; *itineraries* = travel plans and schedules; *aspirations* = hopes / ambitions.
- Listening in pairs, learners then make notes and write answers to questions 1, 3 and 4. On the basis of the rest of the feedback, each pair writes an answer to question 2.
  – Excerpt 1: *on the road* = while travelling.
  – Excerpt 3: *approach* = way of dealing with things.
- **Further step:** Using the review form and the audioscript as guides, and working in pairs, ask learners to practise an interview of this kind.

REVIEW

- Go through the Language Notes and the Useful Phrases in the Course Book, if you have not done so already.
- Check the items listed under Vocabulary in the Language Notes in the Course Book have been covered.
- Encourage learners to note down the terms they found particularly useful – particularly the ones they need in their working lives.
- Make a note of this language for your own future reference.
- Encourage learners to use the new language they have learned. For example, they might put key points into a presentation or report.

Answers

1 Core practice
a i [T]   b i [T]   c i [T]   d i [T]

2 Language check
1 b   2 c   3 a   4 b   5 c   6 b   7 a   8 c   9 a   10 b

5 Listening
(*possible answers*)

1 B+ Theo needs to plan appointments more carefully in order to maximise his effectiveness. His reports need to be more concise.
2 Theo needs to improve his time management. His visiting schedules need to be planned more realistically. The paperwork and follow up when back in the office needs to be done more quickly. His reports should be shorter and need to focus more on key information.
3 Theo is keen to work in our export markets, especially the Netherlands and Germany, where he could use his language skills.
4 I'm enjoying the job very much. It has taken me a little time to get used to the size of my area. I find writing the customer reports takes a lot of time. If I could have the use of a laptop, I could complete the paperwork at the time when it's fresh, which will save time.

Audioscripts

1 Core practice

a – What's your overall feedback?
 – Well, speaking as someone who isn't used to studying, I thought the programme was very well planned and easy to use. I like the way the material was clearly laid out in the workbooks.
 – So on a scale of one to ten how would you rate the programme?
 – Oh I'd say it was definitely eight, maybe more.
 – Do you have any comments that would help with planning future courses? Any areas for improvement?
 – Yes, I think the briefing before the course was below the general standard.
 – So, you had some disappointments. What were your main achievements?

b – Are you satisfied with the progress you've made?
 – Well, yes and no; I'm disappointed I didn't meet my targets, but perhaps they were a bit unrealistic. I'd hoped to get through the Grade 3 test. The trouble is I had a lot of conflicting commitments at the time, so I missed quite a few of the classes, which in turn meant I wasn't ready to take the test. But they said I should pass next time – so I didn't do too badly bearing in mind all the distractions and so on. I did make some progress.

c – How was your course?
 – OK. Some people thought the content was a bit difficult. As far as I'm concerned, it was more or less on the right lines. The content was relevant and I thought the teaching was really first class. My only criticism is that it was too classroom-based. I wanted to do extra work in my own time. To my mind we weren't given enough to do on our own.
 – What about the administration?
 – Basically everything was fine – except the accommodation, which frankly was absolutely awful.

d – Have you decided on your next steps?
 – Well, the first thing I need is a break. After that I think my next step will be to put what I've learned into practice, and use it, especially in work. I have a long list of action points.

 – Looking ahead, are you planning to do any other courses?
 – Yes, I'd like to attend a course on sales documentation, maybe sometime next year.

5 Listening

SM = Sales Manager
SR = Sales Rep

Excerpt 1
SM: I'd like to talk you through the points I've made in this appraisal form to make sure that everything is clear. We can discuss my comments as we go through. OK?
SR: Yes, that's fine.
SM: So, your first area of responsibility – I think you did well here, but of course there's room for improvement. The rating I've given you is B+. And the comment I've made is that you 'need to plan your appointments more carefully'. I think that's an important point, 'in order to maximise your effectiveness on the road'. And something we've talked about quite a bit – I've put that your 'reports should be more concise'. Does that seem fair to you?

Excerpt 2
SM: In the fourth area here, under 'additional comments' and 'areas of future interest', I made a note of the fact that you're keen to work in our export markets. That's true, isn't it?
SR: Yes, I'd very much like to be able to use my language skills in my work. It's one of my strong points. I'm fluent in Dutch and German, and I know we do a lot of business in those markets.
SM: Yes, that's certainly something for the future.

Excerpt 3
SM: So, now we come to the section for your comments …
SR: Well, I'm enjoying the job very much. It's true, it's taken me a little time to get used to the size of my area. I'm not used to handling so many accounts. So, I've had to change my approach to cope with the workload. The thing I've found most difficult is the report writing – there never seems to be enough time. As I said earlier, it would help a lot if I could have the use of a laptop, because then I could write on the road while the details are still fresh in my mind.

Progress checks

Progress tests (Units 1 – 6)

Complete the sentences by choosing the option (a – d) that fits best.

1 It's a company that really looks .... its people. .... is very low.
   a at / Absenteeism
   b for / Head count
   c into / Time lost
   d after / Staff turnover

2 As you may know, we .... our logistics operation. While we .... for Kim Zehrer, who .... that side of things, I'll say a bit about the current changes.
   a reorganise / wait / runs
   b are reorganising / are waiting / runs
   c reorganise / are waiting / is running
   d reorganise / are waiting / runs

3 I .... working in Siberia. I .... cold climates.
   a didn't use to / am not used to
   b can't get used to / am used to
   c am used to / used to
   d can't get used to / am not used to

4 As far as .... , the cost of complying with the new regulations is far too high. We do not .... that they are necessary.
   a we believe / think
   b we would have thought / agree
   c we are concerned / accept
   d our view is / go along with

5 – There aren't .... people here in August; it's holiday time.
  – Will .... of the core team be around?
  – Yes, but ....
   a many / any / very few
   b a lot of / much / little
   c any / a few of / very little
   d lots of / some / a few

6 We are .... up of two companies. Marco will .... through the corporate values we share. Then I'll .... you round the plant.
   a set / go / take
   b done / talk / go
   c put / walk / get
   d made / run / show

7 The company was set .... in 1999. After the .... , the processing plant was sold .... and the processing operation was .... to Semco.
   a down / restructuring / out / offshored
   b forward / bankruptcy / to / relocated
   c up / reorganisation / off / outsourced
   d out / rationalisation / back / taken over

8 100% recycling is now .... feasible, but it is still .... expensive.
   a technically / extremely
   b highly / politically
   c environmentally / completely
   d reasonably / theoretically

9 There are .... couple of alterations to your programme. Hernan Canto will be taking .... workshop after lunch. Hernan is .... actuary and works in .... Finance.
   a a / a / a / –
   b a / the / the / the
   c – / the / an / the
   d a / the / an / –

10 We are located .... the north of Grapevine County. It's a heavily populated urban area. Our site is .... the outskirts of Lewes Town. We can send a car to pick ....
   a in / on / you up
   b to / in / up you
   c at / at / you out
   d on / though / on you

11 They .... a lot of problems. The system .... ; it .... wrong.
   a have / is being upgraded / is keeping going
   b are having / is being upgraded / is always going
   c have got / is upgrading / always goes wrong
   d experience / is upgraded / keeps going

12 In 2005 the new CEO .... after she .... with the company for only six months.
   a was replaced / has been
   b has been replaced / was
   c was replaced / had been
   d had been replaced / was being

13 The staff were skilled but very .... motivated. We were .... paid and .... worked.
   a dis- / badly / highly
   b un- / under- / over
   c de- / low- / too
   d non- / poorly / low

14 The old reactors are being .... out because it is very difficult to get .... nuclear waste.
   a shut / away from
   b cleared / out of
   c phased / rid of
   d run / down to

140 PROGRESS CHECKS

15 We spent .... year preparing. Then the monsoons came early and it rained .... time. .... people warned us this might happen but we didn't listen.
a the whole / all the / A number of
b whole of / all / A number
c all / the whole / An amount of
d the whole of / all of the / An amount

16 I .... the day was .... disappointing – apart from the audiovisual demo, which everyone says was .... great.
a am gathering / a bit / really
b think / quite / extremely
c am thinking / slightly / highly
d gather / pretty / absolutely

17 I .... as a manager for several years before I .... on a leadership course.
a had been working / went
b have been working / was going
c was working / have gone
d had worked / have been going

18 We need to follow .... the C47 project. Could you find .... how things are going and get .... to me?
a up / out about / through
b through / time for / round
c up on / out / back
d through with / – / over

Progress tests (Units 7 – 12)

Complete the sentences by choosing the option (a – d) that fits best.

1 It is very cold this evening. We are sure it .... Therefore we .... to close the exhibition early.
a is snowing / will plan
b snows / plan
c is going to snow / are planning
d will snow / are going to plan

2 The police .... their investigation before we .... They .... email their report. We need it for the insurance claim.
a won't complete / will leave / will
b won't be completing / are leaving / will be
c won't be completed / are going to leave / have to
d won't have completed / leave / will have to

3 I'm afraid we can't .... your demands in .... We are prepared to meet you half way. We have in .... something in the region of 3.5%.
a accept / total / preparation
b agree / cash / thought
c meet / full / mind
d pay / time / hand

4 Today we will be interviewing five school leavers, ... have applied for an internship with us. That is the programme .... I was telling you .... earlier.
a all of who / that / the details of
b all of whom / – / about
c who / about which / about
d that / which / –

5 When we lost the Syrex account, we .... off 400 people. We had to .... them go because there wasn't enough work. We lost another 100 through natural ....
a laid / let / wastage   b sent / make / loss
c let / get / redundancy   d put / allow / reduction

6 Can I give you a .... of advice? It's a good .... to learn a few words of Arabic. But whatever you do, don't .... religion.
a piece / planning / criticise
b guideline / suggestion / small talk
c rule / preparation / mention
d word / idea / discuss

7 The hotel provides .... access but there was something wrong .... the connection in my room. I think the cable was ....
a Internet free high-speed / about / fused
b free high-speed Internet / with / faulty
c high-speed Internet free / in / broken
d free Internet high-speed / for / jammed

8 I'm thinking of .... early retirement. I don't want to keep .... till I'm made redundant.
a take / work
b having / to work
c taking / working
d to have / to working

9 We are supposed .... in contact with all our customers and .... relationships with new prospects, but .... takes time.
   a to be / to create / circulate
   b to stay / making / to mix
   c working / explore / socialising
   d to keep / to build / networking

10 .... the small print, my colleagues had some questions. But .... the document yet, I can't comment.
   a After reading / not having seen
   b After they had read / I have not seen
   c When they had read / since having not seen
   d Having read / as not having seen

11 I was very sorry .... that you are planning .... We'll miss .... you around.
   a to hear / retiring / to have
   b to hear / to retire / having
   c to hear / to retire / have
   d hearing / to retire / to having

12 I .... follow up on the contacts I made this afternoon. Last time I left it too late. I am .... make the same mistake again.
   a am planning / not determined to
   b was going / intending to not
   c was planning to / determined not to
   d am going to / intended not to

13 I .... in the application form incorrectly so they .... me down. I wasn't even ....
   a wrote / put / listed
   b completed / set / shortlisted
   c filled / turned / interviewed
   d updated / sent / called

14 The .... on Internet selling is .... to start. Why don't you come .... and visit our .... afterwards?
   a session / about / over / stand
   b workshop / due / off / stall
   c presentation / certain / off / display area
   d seminar / going / round / place

15 I'm sorry, there have been some delays caused by an .... Your baggage .... on carousel 5 in about three minutes.
   a security earlier alert / will arrive
   b security alert earlier / is arriving
   c earlier security alert / will be arriving
   d alert security earlier / is going to arrive

16 We need to work out a reward .... that includes enough .... benefits to attract quality staff, and shows that we are not out of .... with modern trends.
   a recognition / side / step
   b bonus / special / time
   c strategy / extra / understanding
   d package / fringe / touch

17 The conference .... in Dubai next year. If you .... there, we can meet ....
   a will be / are / out
   b is going to be / are going to be / up
   c is / are going / together
   d is going / will be / there

18 May I introduce Pete Beringer, ... you will be reporting .... Pete has organised an induction programme .... explains the company background and culture for all the staff .... have just joined.
   a who / to / that / who
   b to whom / to / which / that
   c that / for / – / who
   d – / on / which / that

Progress tests (Units 13 – 18)

Complete the sentences by choosing the option (a – d) that fits best.

1. Time management in most offices is not good. Staff spend about 50% of their time .... The course helps people to organise .... more effectively.
   a. problem solving / yourself
   b. trouble shooting / oneself
   c. firefighting / themselves
   d. prioritising / ourselves

2. Do they have a quality certificate? If .... , we can't .... them tendering for the contract.
   a. not / allow
   b. only / stop
   c. true / avoid
   d. so / prevent

3. The management committee .... to consider a pay demand that isn't linked to a productivity agreement. In my opinion they are almost .... to turn your claim ....
   a. definitely won't / sure / out
   b. is very unlikely / bound / down
   c. is not likely / definitely / in
   d. will not be willing / likely / up

4. .... you call our fraud line as soon as possible. You are covered for any losses .... you report the details immediately.
   a. I suggest / as long as
   b. I advise / as well as
   c. I recommend / as far as
   d. You must / provided

5. We .... delivered better quality if we .... spent more time and money on training. If I had a free hand, I .... change the current system.
   a. would / have / –
   b. have / – / would have
   c. – / would have / will
   d. would have / had / would

6. The regulator does .... checks every .... Very seldom .... any advance warning.
   a. site / often / we get
   b. spot / so often / do we get
   c. sudden / time to time / don't we get
   d. quick / now and then / we don't get

7. They .... waiting to be paid since January. They .... complained before now.
   a. can't have / would be
   b. couldn't be / would have been
   c. couldn't have been / would
   d. can't have been / would have

8. I cover .... my colleague when she is under pressure and .... That way we can keep .... the workload.
   a. up / pro rata / outside of
   b. with / versus / next to
   c. for / vice versa / on top of
   d. to / pros and cons / in front of

9. We normally receive a .... at New Year. It's usually 10% of your .... We also get a 12.5% discount on all company products. It's a .... that goes with the job.
   a. fee / gross earnings / non-financial benefit
   b. bonus / gross salary / perk
   c. commission / take-home pay / reward
   d. overtime payment / total package / remuneration

10. .... that some of our sales people were making a very bad impression, I .... out what the problem was and sorted it out.
    a. Had I known / would have found
    b. If I had known / would find
    c. If I knew / have found
    d. If had I known / had found

11. It was a disaster. I wish it .... happened. But the situation won't improve, ... we make changes.
    a. didn't / without
    b. wouldn't / providing
    c. wasn't / otherwise
    d. hadn't / unless

12. There is an .... of US$30 on accounts that exceed the ....
    a. over budget cost / credit status
    b. overdue fee / credit rating
    c. overlimit fee / credit limit
    d. overtime charge / credit record

13. I think good work should .... The management might .... to pay performance-related commission. We ought .... in a request.
    a. recognised / willing / put
    b. be recognised / be willing / to put
    c. recognise / to be willing / to make
    d. to be recognised / be prepared / putting

14. We are not yet in compliance .... the new regulations, and .... our competitors. We are not required .... law to apply them till next year.
    a. with / neither are / by
    b. to / nor are / in
    c. for / as are / for
    d. by / so are / at

15 We have been finding it difficult to keep our .... expenses .... Our .... costs are .... by $9 million.
  a day to day / back / working / bigger
  b day-to-day / down / running / up
  c day to-day / in / outgoing / out
  d day-today / out / overhead / more

16 You .... to have kept us informed about the situation. We could .... the due date. I'm afraid there is nothing we can do now.
  a should / have been extended
  b might / extend
  c ought / have extended
  d need / be extending

17 Over the last year we performed well in respect of our core .... increased significantly. Our .... problem was that .... from the Middle East were down by 11%.
  a activitys / Turn-over / biggest / reciepts
  b activeties / Turn over / biggest / receits
  c activetys / Turnover / bigest / reciets
  d activities / Turnover / biggest / receipts

18 To succeed we have to offer value .... money. Our people have to take pride .... their work. Any shoddy work will come .... light through our quality check procedures.
  a with / by / in   b for / in / to
  c in / with / into   d by / at / on

Progress tests (Units 19 – 24)

Complete the sentences by choosing the option (a – d) that fits best.

1 My favourite place for .... is Italy. I feel very at home there – .... the fact that the way of life is very different. I find it easy .... there.
  a an off-season holiday / although / unwind
  b a mini-break / in spite of / to unwind
  c a package / even so / unwinding
  d getting away / while / to be unwinding

2 We are renting a .... apartment with a .... of the sea. There's parking in the basement. We have a three-year ....
  a top / sight / mortgage
  b first-floor / overlooking / contract
  c attic / access / agreement
  d top-floor / view / lease

3 I fully .... Musa's point. As parents, I think we all find it difficult to .... work and social commitments. My guess is that we are all .... agreement on this.
  a accept / balance / in
  b agree / run / with
  c disagree / make / on
  d take / handle / by

4 .... the data from the market research, we recommend a TV campaign. .... properly, we believe this would work. But .... the client, you have the final say.
  a After assessing / If handled / because
  b Being assessed / Handling / being
  c Having assessed / Handled / as
  d Assessing / By handling / since

5 If a .... fault has .... this problem, the company should repair the goods free of change, ... the warranty.
  a misuse / resulted / by
  b wear and tear / due to / from
  c neglect / led to / with
  d manufacturing / caused / under

6 These fuel tanks are on special .... They .... about 3,000 .... when they are full. And we have them .... stock.
  a offer / hold / litres / in
  b discount / weigh / kilos / by
  c price / measure / cubic metres / on
  d deal / carry / gallons / by

7 .... you do, don't drink the water. It's very easy to get tummy trouble. In fact, ... to eat in the hotel whenever possible and to get a cholera .... before you go.
  a Whichever / I suggest / injection
  b Wherever / it's best / insurance
  c Whatever / my advice is / jab
  d Whenever / it's a good idea / inoculation

8 It .... the machine has been cleaned with the wrong solvents. Your maintenance staff .... ignored the operating instructions.
  a sounds as / seem to
  b looks like / seemed
  c sounds as though / seem to be
  d looks as if / seem to have

144 PROGRESS CHECKS

9 – I thought the presentation by the .... manager was really excellent.
   – I agree; she .... put the message .... more clearly.
   a account / couldn't have / across
   b advertising / couldn't / through
   c customer / can't have / down
   d sales / can't / over

10 .... son, Ragi, has just got engaged to my .... sister. My parents are delighted – they are old ....
   a Mohammed and Anjnas' / youngest / friends
   b Mohammed's and Anjna's / step / friend's
   c Mohammed and Anjna's / half / friends
   d Mohammed and Anjnas' / first / friends'

11 The new fitness centre has .... more facilities but it's .... more expensive. It's worth the extra money because I find working out a lot more relaxing than .... TV.
   a a bit / a little / to be watching
   b far / a bit / watching
   c a little / a few / to watch
   d a lot of / no / watch

12 We are behind with this order .... a supplier let us .... – that's the only ....
   a as / up / why
   b so that / out / truth
   c since / through / explanation
   d because / down / reason

13 I go running on a regular .... , usually with a group of friends. We don't do it .... a competitive way, just to .... fit.
   a way / on / make   b manner / with / become
   c basis / in / keep   d time / for / stay

14 – He's going away .... of the fact that we have to meet this deadline.
   – .... ?
   a though / Whereabouts   b regardless / How long for
   c despite / What for   d in spite / Who to

15 When we bought it, we were .... that it would work in our system. It is .... to work without an adapter. We are not happy .... it. We'd like our money ....
   a assured / supposed / with / back
   b convinced / guaranteed / about / refund
   c sold / promised / for / paid
   d told / intended / in / discounted

16 The campaign is .... at young parents and is based on posters. But the .... groups don't like the colours – they say the posters should .... redesigned.
   a on target / customer / been
   b targeting / research / have been
   c being targeted / study / to be
   d targeted / focus / be

17 .... my relatives live in Lebanon. We are very different .... , but we keep in close contact. We have a big family reunion .... year.
   a All of / with / every other / each
   b Every one of / to / each one / all
   c All / from / each other / every
   d Each of / for / everyone / every other

18 We .... a minimum of US$55 a ton – it's too much. And the suppliers insist on .... in ....
   a are being charged / being paid / advance
   b are charged / be paid / cash
   c charge / payment / time
   d are changing / pay / arrears

Progress tests (Units 25 – 30)

Complete the sentences by choosing the option (a – d) that fits best.

1 The .... was .... guilty of fraud; he wasn't sent to prison but he was .... heavily. He may appeal .... the conviction.
   a accused / judged / charged / for
   b criminal / agreed / penalised / about
   c convicted / made / punished / on
   d defendant / found / fined / against

2 On a scale of 1 to 10, how would you .... her performance?
   I'd say round 6. I .... to think she achieved her .... aim but some of her work was .... messy.
   a score / inclined / general / completely
   b rate / tend / overall / quite
   c number / seem / main / highly
   d measure / have / whole / more or less

3 Two years ago the government .... it would cut the .... of .... tax to 20% the .... year.
   a outlined / level / earnings / next
   b told / speed / personal / after
   c announced / rate / income / following
   d informed / volume / individual / later

4 That .... me to my next point – call-out times. The dotted line on this .... shows a sharp drop .... our performance in June.
   a brings / graph / in   b takes / bar chart / on
   c tells / pie chart / of   d introduces / curve / by

5 I think my boss is quite right wing, ... I'm a Democrat. But she .... being a member of the Republican Party.
   a otherwise / refuses
   b alternatively / rejects
   c however / maintains
   d whereas / denies

6 With .... to the court case, our lawyers have .... us it's not worth suing for .... – the company has gone ....
   a regarding / instructed / compensation / bankruptcy
   b concerning / written / repayment / bust
   c regard / advised / damages / bankrupt
   d connection / notified / costs / receivership

7 You can .... the money you pay .... a pension scheme against tax. It's very tax ....
   a set / into / efficient   b put / for / friendly
   c get / with / cheap   d charge / through / saving

8 The basic concept is extremely simple .... being very commercial. If everyone does .... job properly, the project should finish .... target.
   a in other words / his / in
   b apart from / his/her / inside
   c as well as / their / on
   d on the whole / his or her / within

9 The Social Democrats are .... in the opinion .... many people are not convinced they will win the ....
   a in front / surveys / At the same time, / choice
   b first / tests / But / vote
   c above / research / All the same, / poll
   d ahead / polls / Nevertheless, / election

10 The heading needs to be in .... , not in italics – and the logo should be .... the top, left-hand corner. And I suggest we .... out the final bullet point.
   a font / at / put   b bold / in / take
   c underlined / on / delete d red / by / push

11 In business .... , we have .... no doubt that the time and money invested in training was well spent and will help us to .... our targets.
   a view / quite / achieve
   b point / slightly / reach
   c terms / absolutely / meet
   d position / extremely / pass

12 – We didn't anticipate so many .... in our .... plan, did we?
   – .... (Agree)
   a setbacks / contingency / No, we didn't.
   b hold-ups / feasibility / Yes we didn't.
   c milestones / timetable / Yes we did.
   d obstacles / deadline / No we did.

13 – Is there much tax .... in your country?
   – I'm not .... but my accountant .... most companies are above ....
   a fraud / an inspector / urges / honest
   b evasion / an expert / claims / board
   c crime / a lawyer / mentions / the law
   d avoidance / a specialist / assures / suspicion

146 PROGRESS CHECKS

14 First, an .... on the state of play. In spite of the recession, demand has .... steady. Current orders are worth €8m – that's a 1% increase .... last year.
   a report / stayed / of
   b summary / been / from
   c update / remained / on
   d overview / maintained / above

15 – To start .... , we need to make a project plan.
   – No, ... to that we should do a .... study. On .... of the study, we will be able to start planning.
   a out / before / site / finishing
   b first / advance / field / completing
   c phase / previous / research / outcome
   d with / prior / feasibility / completion

16 The papers predict that the .... of inflation will rise over the next 12 months. Public .... borrowing is too high and this is having an impact on the .... of living.
   a cost / area / price
   b rate / sector / cost
   c speed / party / charge
   d level / department / standard

17 The performance .... came to the .... that she has made good progress. Her next .... is to put what she has learned .... practice.
   a review / conclusion / step / into
   b evaluation / summary / action / in
   c assessment / feedback / point / at
   d measurement / view / plan / for

18 Things are going according .... plan. We expect .... testing next week – two days .... of schedule. We are supposed to .... live on the 14th.
   a with / finish / behind / be
   b on / finishing / on / start
   c by / to finishing / in front / work
   d to / to finish / ahead / go

Progress checks: answers

The related unit is indicated in brackets.

Units 1 – 6

1 d (5)	7 c (4)	13 b (5)
2 b (2)	8 a (6)	14 c (6)
3 d (4)	9 d (2)	15 a (1)
4 c (6)	10 a (1)	16 d (3)
5 a (1)	11 b (3)	17 a (5)
6 d (2)	12 c (4)	18 c (3)

Units 7 – 12

1 c (10)	7 b (12)	13 c (7)
2 d (12)	8 c (9)	14 a (10)
3 c (8)	9 d (11)	15 c (12)
4 b (7)	10 a (8)	16 d (8)
5 a (9)	11 b (9)	17 b (10)
6 d (11)	12 c (11)	18 a (7)

Units 13 – 18

1 c (16)	7 d (14)	13 b (13)
2 d (17)	8 c (16)	14 a (18)
3 b (13)	9 b (13)	15 b (14)
4 a (15)	10 a (18)	16 c (15)
5 d (17)	11 d (16)	17 d (14)
6 b (18)	12 c (15)	18 b (17)

Units 19 – 24

1 b (24)	7 c (24)	13 c (23)
2 d (22)	8 d (21)	14 b (24)
3 a (23)	9 a (19)	15 a (21)
4 c (19)	10 c (22)	16 d (19)
5 d (21)	11 b (23)	17 c (22)
6 a (20)	12 d (20)	18 a (20)

Units 25 – 30

1 d (27)	7 a (26)	13 b (26)
2 b (30)	8 c (28)	14 c (29)
3 c (26)	9 d (25)	15 d (28)
4 a (29)	10 b (27)	16 b (25)
5 d (25)	11 c (30)	17 a (30)
6 c (27)	12 a (28)	18 d (29)

Glossary of business-related terms

absenteeism: being absent from work; this can include staying away from work for no good reason
actuary: person employed to calculate risk, usually for an insurance company
advertising agency: office that plans, prepares and manages advertising for companies
advertising campaign: campaign designed to promote a product, service or company
allowance: part of an income which is not taxed
APAC: abbreviation for the Asia and Pacific area
appraisal: a review of a staff member by his / her manager, usually done once a year
appropriation: act of putting money aside for a special purpose, e.g. appropriation of funds to the reserve
arbitration: settling of a dispute by an outside person, chosen by both sides
asset(s): thing(s) that belongs to a company or person, and that has a value
audit: n examination of the books and accounts of a company; **v** to examine the books and accounts of a company
back office: clerical personnel who provide support services for customer-facing front office staff
backlog: work that is waiting to be done
balance: sum remaining (on an account)
balance of payments: comparison between total receipts and payments arising from a country's international trade in goods, services and financial transactions
balance sheet: statement of the financial position of a company at a particular time
bankrupt: to be unable to pay your creditors and to have your assets managed by the Court; to go bankrupt (idiomatic: to go broke / bust)
benchmark: a measure of performance that can be used to assess other performances
black economy: goods and services which are paid for in cash and therefore not declared for tax
bonus: special payment to workers for good work or extra productivity
boom: time when business activity is increasing rapidly
bottom line: last line on a profit-and-loss account indicating the total profit or loss
boycott: n refusal to buy or to deal in certain products; **v** to refuse to buy or to deal in certain products
brand: the symbolic embodiment of all the information connected with a product or service, including the name and logo
brochure: a publicity booklet
bulk: large quantity of goods
bullet points: a list of points usually identified with dots or asterisks
business unit (BU): part of an organisation, often treated as a separate entity within the parent organisation
buy in: to purchase externally
capital costs: money spent on fixed assets (property, etc.)
cartel: group of companies that try to fix the price or to regulate the supply of a product for their own profit
cashflow: cash which comes into a company from sales, or the money which goes out in purchases or overhead expenditure
casting vote: deciding vote usually by the chairperson
classified ads / advertisements: advertisers listed in a newspaper under special headings, e.g. jobs wanted

closed shop: system where a company agrees to employ only union members in certain jobs
commission: 1 money paid to a salesperson or agent, usually a percentage of the sales made; **2** group of people officially appointed to examine a specific problem
compliance: fully meeting the requirements of the laws, rules and regulations that apply
consignment: (generally) a delivery of goods, (technically) goods sent to someone who will sell them for you
consortium: group of companies which work together on a particular project
consumer research: research into why customers buy goods and what goods they really want to buy
contingency plan: alternative plan that can be put into action if something goes wrong with the other plan
contract staff: staff employed to do a particular job for a company; these staff are not usually permanent
cost effective: producing the best results in relation to the costs incurred
cost of living: money spent on food, heating, rent, etc.
credit control: check that customers pay on time and do not owe more than their credit limit
credit limit: fixed amount which is the most a customer can owe on credit
credit rating: amount which a credit agency feels a customer should be allowed to borrow
current liabilities: debts that may be repayable within 12 months, e.g. bank overdraft
customer relationship management (CRM): covers all aspects of the relationship a company has with its customers, related to sales or service
customer services: a department that provides support to customers by answering enquiries, handling complaints, etc.
cutting-edge: technically very advanced, at the front edge of development
deadline: date by which something has to be done
deadlock: the two sides can't agree
delegation: 1 group of people who represent others at a meeting; **2** act of passing authority or responsibility to someone else
depreciation: reduction in the value of an asset; provision to write off the cost of a fixed asset, e.g. a machine
direct taxation: tax, such as income tax, which is paid direct to the government
discount: reduction, reduced charge
dividend: percentage of profits paid to shareholders
dotted line: indicates a second (usually lesser) reporting responsibility, e.g. *I have a dotted line to ...*
downsizing: reducing the number of people employed in a company to make it more profitable
dress codes: rules or guidelines that specify how an employee should dress, e.g. formal, smart, casual
earnings: money earned / total earnings
EMEA: abbreviation for Europe, Middle East, Africa
equal opportunities: strategies to ensure different sexes and races receive equal opportunities at work
exchange rate: price at which one currency is exchanged for another
expenditure: any money spent
feasibility study: e.g. to carry out a feasibility study = to carry out an examination of costs and profits to see if the project should be started

fixed assets: property or machinery which a company uses, but which it does not buy and sell as part of its regular trade
fixed costs: costs that do not vary with sales, e.g. rent
(a) flat: UK English, an apartment
flat rate: charge which always stays the same
flexitime: system where workers can start or stop work at different hours, provided that they work a certain number of hours per day or week
flier: brief, one-sheet, low-cost advertisement, often put through doors, left on car windscreens, or handed out in the street to passers-by
focus group: small group of target customers employed to give their views on products / services
franchise: licence to trade using a brand name and paying a royalty for it
fraud: making money by making people believe something that is not true
freehold property: property which the owner holds permanently and does not pay rent for
front office: the customer-facing operations of a company such as customer service, customer support, call centres and sales
global: referring to the world economy and world markets
golden handshake: large, usually tax free, sum of money given to a senior employee who resigns from a company before the end of his / her contract
gross: total or with no deductions, e.g. gross earnings = total earnings before tax and other deductions
gross profit: sales less direct cost of sales, e.g. manufacturing costs
guideline: suggestion as to how something should be done
handout: information in the form of a document that is handed out during a lecture
hard currency: currency of a country which has a strong economy and which can easily be changed into other currencies
head-hunter: person or company which finds senior staff and offers them jobs in other companies
human resources (HR): workers which a company has available (seen from the point of view of their skills and experience)
incentives: e.g. staff incentives = pay and better conditions offered to workers to make them work better
indirect taxation: tax, such as sales tax, which is paid to someone who then pays it to the government
industrial relations: relations between management and workers
inflation rate: percentage increase in prices over a 12-month period
infrastructure: e.g. a country's infrastructure = the road and rail systems of a country
in-house: done within a company by its own staff
insert: a sheet of advertising information that is put in something, usually a magazine
investment: placing of money so that it will increase in value and produce interest
invoice: n note asking for payment for goods or services supplied; v to send an invoice to someone
job sharing: situation where two people share a job, each working part-time
junk mail: unsolicited advertising material sent through the post
lay-off: action of dismissing a worker for a time
leaflet: sheet of paper giving information that is used to advertise something
lease: written contract for letting or renting a building, land or equipment against the payment of rent
leasehold property: property held on a lease
liabilities: debts of a business or person; anything that is owed to someone else (see current liabilities)

liability: legal responsibility for damage or loss, etc.
liquidation: closing of a company and selling of its assets
live testing: testing a product or system in real conditions
logistics: the management of materials, parts, supplies and finished goods moving into and out of the business
mail order catalogue: catalogue from which a customer can order items, which are then sent by mail
mail shot: leaflets sent by mail to possible customers
mark-up: amount added to cost price to give the selling price
merger: joining together of two or more companies
message (advertising message): key idea that an advertisement aims to communicate
middle office: responsible for financial reporting, internal auditing, risk management; in smaller organisations the role is performed by the back office
milestone: a significant marker or point, e.g. *We have reached our milestone, so now we need a new target*
moonlighting: doing a second job for cash as well as a regular job
mortgage: agreement where someone borrows money to buy a property using the property as security, and repays by regular mortgage payments
natural wastage: loss of workers because they resign or retire, not through redundancy or dismissals
net: after all deductions have been made; e.g. net income
offset: to balance one thing against another so that they balance each other out
offshore: transfer parts of the business to a different country where costs are lower
outgoings: any money spent
outsource: obtain goods or services from an outside supplier; to contract work out; not sourcing internally
overheads: costs not directly related to producing goods / services, e.g. directors' salaries
overrun: to go beyond a limit, e.g. *We have overrun our time allocation, so will need to end this meeting now*
oversee: to supervise other workers
pay differentials: differences in pay between workers
payroll: 1 list of people employed and paid by a company; 2 money paid by a company in salaries
PDA: personal digital assistant, a hand-held digital organiser
PDP: personal development plan
perks: extra items given by a company to workers in addition to their salary
picket: n striking worker who stands at the gates of a factory to try to persuade other workers not to go to work; v to put pickets at the gate of a factory
piloting stage: stage at which a project is tested on a small number of people to see if it will work in practice
plant: machinery or large factory
poster: large advertisement designed to be stuck on a wall
premium: 1 e.g. insurance premium = annual payment made by a person or a company to an insurance company; 2 e.g. to pay a premium = to pay extra
private enterprise: businesses which are owned by private shareholders, not by the state
privatisation: selling a nationalised company to private owners
procurement: action of buying equipment, materials or services for a company
productivity: rate of output per worker or per machine in a factory
profile: brief description giving the basic characteristics of, e.g., a particular market

profit and loss account: statement of a company's expenditure and income over a period of time, almost always one calendar year, showing whether the company has made a profit or loss

profit margin: percentage difference between sales income and the cost of sales

promote: to improve the image of a product by a sales campaign, advertising, etc.

purchase order: official order made out by a purchasing department

quality standard certificate: certificate awarded after inspection showing that a company and its products are of a sufficiently high standard

quantity discount: reduction given to customers who buy large quantities

receipts: any money received

receiver: government official who is appointed to run a company which is in financial difficulties, to pay off its debts as far as possible and to close it down

receivership: the state of being in the hands of a receiver

redundancy: the state of being no longer employed, because the job is no longer necessary

redundancy package: various benefits and payments given to a worker who is being made redundant

reimbursement: paying back money

relocate: to move to a different place

rep: representative, e.g. sales representative

retail: n sale of goods to the general public;
v to sell goods direct to the public

return on investment (ROI): actual or perceived future value of an expense or investment

revenue(s): 1 money received as sales, commission, etc.;
2 money received by a government in tax

running costs: money spent on the day-to-day cost of keeping a business going

sale or return: the retailer pays only for the goods he / she sells, the rest are returned to the supplier

sales forecast: estimate of future sales

sales ledger: book in which sales to each customer are recorded

screen (to screen calls): to check or filter calls and then connect only the most important

service company: company which does not make products, but offers a service

shares in a company: documents that show the owner is a shareholder and entitled to a share of the profits (dividend)

shareholder: person who owns shares in a company

shift system / shift work: a system where one group of workers works for a period and is then replaced by another group

shop steward: elected trade union representative who reports workers' complaints to the management

slogan: words that can be remembered easily, often used in publicity for a product

slump: period of economic collapse and high unemployment

small print: the conditions of a contract, often printed in a very small typeface

sponsor: n person who pays money to help a business venture in return for advertising rights;
v to pay money to help research or business development

stakeholder: anyone who has an interest in the project

statutory: fixed by law and therefore cannot be changed, e.g. a statutory holiday

subcontract: to employ another company to do work on a particular project

subordinate: member of staff who is directed by someone in a more senior position

subsidiary: company which is owned by a parent company

subsidy: 1 money given to help something which is not profitable;
2 money given by a government to make something cheaper

surcharge: extra charge

surplus: income less all deductions

tax avoidance: legally avoiding tax

tax bracket: tax category

tax deductible: items that can be deducted from income before tax is calculated

tax efficient: an arrangement that results in only a small liability for tax

tax evasion: trying illegally not to pay tax

tax exempt: free from tax

tax rebate: money paid in tax which is returned

tax relief: allowing someone not to pay tax on certain parts of his / her income

tax return: completed tax form, with details of income and allowances

time management: the organisation of time so that it is spent in the most efficient way

to-do list: a list of things that you have to do

TQM: total quality management; a management approach that focuses on customer satisfaction

trade agreement: agreement between countries on general items of trade

trade customers: customers who buy not for their personal use but for use in their business or for resale

trade fair: large exhibition organised for related companies to advertise and sell their products

transfer: 1 to move money from one place to another;
2 to move people or products to a new place

trouble-shooting: problem solving

turnover: total sales of a company, including goods and services

unsocial hours: working hours when most people are not at work, e.g. evenings and public holidays

user-friendly: which a user finds easy to use

variable costs: costs that rise and fall with sales, e.g. materials

warranty: a legal document which promises that a machine will work properly, e.g. *the 12-month warranty covers spare parts but not labour costs*

wholesale: buying goods from manufacturers and selling in large quantities to traders

workflow: the process by which tasks pass from one person or department to the next

workload: amount of work that a person has to do

work to rule: to work strictly according to rules agreed between the company and the trade union, and therefore to work slowly

write off: reduce the book value of an asset to zero because it is lost or damaged

Grammar / language index

	UNIT
Accord (*and so does*, etc.)	18
Adjectives	
comparative	23
nouns used as ... (*hotel guest*, etc.)	12
opposites (prefixes, etc.)	5
order of	12
Adverbs and advert phrases	
alternative forms (*with care, on a ... basis*, etc.)	23
contrasting (*however*, etc.)	25
frequency	18
modifying meaning (*environmentally friendly*, etc.)	6
modifying strength (*far, extremely*, etc.)	6, 30
really, quite, pretty, etc.	3, 30
time markers	4, 10
Advice / suggestions	11, 15, 24
Agreement / disagreement	6, 23
all (the) / the whole	1
Alternative sentence structures	17
It is a mystery what he does vs. *What he does is a mystery*, etc.	
although, even so, in spite of, etc.	24
Articles (*a / an / the / –*)	2
As / since I have (not) vs. *Having (not)*	8
bound to / likely / unlikely to	13, 25
Cause and effect	8, 21
Comparison	22, 23
Complaints	21
concerning, with regard to, etc.	27
Conditionals	
if only	16
inversions	18
if vs. *in case*	18
second and third (*if I knew, if I had known*)	17
without *if*	15, 16, 17
Contrasting ideas (*however, alternatively*, etc.)	25
Countability	
few / a few	1
little / a little	1
much / many	1
no / not any	1
Demands, making and countering	8
Drawing conclusions / summarising	30
due to	10, 21
cause (*due to the weather*)	21
forecast (*due to start*)	10
each, every, all	22
Evaluating	30
few / a few vs. *little / a little*	1
Forecasting, likelihood	13, 25
Fractions, ratios	13
Frequency	18
Future	
going to	10
will	10
Continuous (*will be + -ing*)	12

	UNIT
Perfect (*will have*)	12
Present Continuous	10
Simple Present	10
Gender-free reference (*he, she, they*)	28
Gerund / infinitive (verb + ...)	9
Graphs, tables, charts	29
however, alternatively, etc.	25
Hyphens	14
Imperatives (warnings)	2
Imperfections, describing:	
dusty, cracked, etc.	12
in order to, so as to, etc.	20
concerning, with regard to	27
Indicating context (*bearing in mind*)	30
Infinitive / gerund (verb + ...)	9
Intentions	11
Latin expressions (*agenda, pro rata*, etc.)	16
Likelihood (*likely / unlikely*, etc.)	13
Linking ideas	
cause (*because, as / since*, etc.)	8
time (*when, after*, etc.)	8
looks, sounds as if / as though	21
meant to, supposed to	11
Measurement (dimensions)	20
Modal verbs (*must, ought to, should*, etc.)	13
past forms (*must have*, etc.)	14
to express criticism, regret	15
Negotiating	8
Non-verbal communications (*oh, hey*, etc.)	23
Nouns	
compound nouns	12
possessive *'s*	22
Numerical information (fractions, ratios, etc.)	13
Omissions in clauses (*being the client*, etc.)	19
Opinions, views	6, 30
Passive	
Present	3, 19
Future	19
Past	4, 19
Continuous	20
Infinitive / *-ing* form	20
Past	
Simple	4, 5
Continuous	4, 5
Past Perfect	
Simple	4, 5
Continuous	5
Past tenses to express intention	11
Past time markets (*the previous year*, etc.)	4
Possessive *'s*	22
Preference (*prefer, would rather*, etc.)	23
Preposition + verb (*after / before + -ing*, etc.)	9
Present Continuous	2
special meaning of Continuous	3

	UNIT
when Simple and Continuous are interchangeable	3
as future	10
Present Perfect	
Simple	4, 5
Continuous	5
Present Simple	2
as Future	10
special use (*keep + -ing, is always + -ing*, etc.)	3
verbs not used in the Continuous	3
Presentations, terms used	29
prevent vs. *avoid*	17
Pronouns	
reflexive (*himself, herself*, etc.)	16
relative (*who, whom*, etc.)	7
Punctuation	
hyphens	14
with text layout	27
Questions	
short forms	24
tag	28
Reasons, giving	8, 20
Reference (*in respect of, with regard to*, etc.)	27
Reflexive pronouns (*himself, herself*, etc.)	16
regardless of, in spite of	24
Regret, shock	9
Relative clauses (defining + non-defining)	7
prepositions in	7
Reported speech	26
advice, commands, questions	27
verbs of reporting	25
Sequence (*first of all, then*, etc.)	28
Similarities, differences	22
Spelling	14
Structuring ideas / arguments (*in the first place, in addition to that*)	28
Suggestions / advice	11, 15, 24
Summarising	30
Tables, charts and graphs	29
Time	
future markers (*at 6.30, in five minutes, next year*, etc.)	10
past markers (*the previous year*, etc.)	4
Trends (*that represents a drop of 25%*, etc.)	29
used to, be / get used to	4
Verb + infinitive (*happen to remember*)	9
plus gerund (*keep working*)	9
+ infinitive or gerund (*like to start / starting*)	9
Warnings	2, 11
whatever, wherever, whoever, etc.	24
(the) whole / all	1
wish / if only	16